The Village Enlightenment in America

The Village Enlightenment in America

Popular Religion and Science in the Nineteenth Century

CRAIG JAMES HAZEN

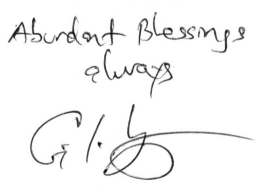

Abundant Blessings
always

UNIVERSITY OF ILLINOIS PRESS • URBANA AND CHICAGO

Library of Congress Cataloging-in-Publication Data
Hazen, Craig James.
The village enlightenment in America : popular religion and
science in the nineteenth century / Craig James Hazen.
p.   cm.
Includes bibliographical references and index.
ISBN 0-252-02512-1 (cloth : alk. paper)
ISBN 0-252-06828-9 (pbk. : alk, paper)
1. Religion and science—History—19th century.
2. Pratt, Orson, 1811–1881. 3. Hare, Robert, 1781–1858.
4. Quimby, P. P. (Phineas Parkhurst), 1802–1866. I. Title.
BL245.H36   2000
291.1'75—dc21   99-6336
CIP

1 2 3 4 5 C P 5 4 3 2 1

To Karen and to Maggie, Danika, Kent, and Garrett

Contents

Acknowledgments   ix

Introduction: Popular Religion, Science, and Authority   1

1. Mormon Cosmic Philosophy: Orson Pratt   15

2. Spiritualism and Science: Robert Hare   65

3. Science, Matter, and Mind Cure: Phineas Parkhurst Quimby   113

Conclusion: The Enlightenment Village   147

Notes   151

Bibliography   177

Index   189

Acknowledgments

Among the many people I have consulted in the writing of this book, I am particularly grateful to Catherine L. Albanese of the University of California, Santa Barbara, who went beyond the call of duty in helping guide me through some very difficult terrain. I am also thankful for the bibliographical guidance of J. Gordon Melton of the Institute for the Study of American Religion, who stimulated many of the ideas offered in this work. The late congressman and scholar Walter H. Capps and Professor Ninian Smart also provided encouragement and mentorship in many ways. Thanks also to perhaps my greatest cheerleader toward the end of this project, my colleague J. P. Moreland of Biola University, and to Jane Mohraz of the University of Illinois Press for her excellent editing work.

A word of gratitude also to those who helped fund this project through generous fellowships and research awards: the Bancroft Library of the University of California, Berkeley; the University of California General Affiliates; the Interdisciplinary Humanities Center; the Intercollegiate Studies Institute; the Humanities Research Fellowship of the University of California, Santa Barbara; the Wheeler Fellowship and Wilma Seavey Ogden Award, both from the University of California, Berkeley; the American Academy of Religion; and the American Association for the Advancement of Science.

Certainly most deserving of acknowledgment is my patient family for standing by me during the entire process. My wife, Karen, and my children, Danika, Garrett, Kent, and Maggie, provided distractions from my studies that I will always cherish.

The Village Enlightenment in America

Introduction:
Popular Religion, Science, and Authority

In 1873, John W. Draper declared in *The History of the Conflict between Religion and Science* that "the time approaches when men must make their choice between quiescent, immobile faith and ever-advancing Science—faith, with its mediæval consolations, Science, which is incessantly scattering its material blessings in the pathway of life, elevating the lot of man in this world, and unifying the human race."[1] The title of the book and Draper's rhetorical flair helped set the stage for a century of "conflict" thinking about the interaction of religion and science. Similarly, but with greater influence, Andrew Dickson White in *A History of the Warfare of Science with Theology* used a military metaphor of "warfare" to describe the history of what he saw as a long and destructive dispute. In an 1869 lecture, which inaugurated his twenty-seven-year study, White concluded, "*In all modern history, interference with science in the supposed interest of religion, no matter how conscientious such interference may have been, has resulted in the direst evils both to religion and to science—and invariably. And, on the other hand, all untrammeled scientific investigation, no matter how dangerous to religion some of its stages may have seemed, for the time, to be, has invariably resulted in the highest good of religion and of science.*"[2]

Although over a century later an affinity for the conflict and warfare approaches to the interaction of science and religion still remains on a popular level, the academic world has, since the late 1970s, taken significant steps toward discrediting these positions that set the terms of the debate for decades. Ronald L. Numbers, David C. Lindberg, and James R. Moore, historians of science, have led the attempt to disarm the military metaphor by showing that as a dogmatic interpretive scheme, it is "a gross distortion," "entirely misleading if not utterly false," and "neither useful nor tenable in describing the relationship between religion and science."[3] Lindberg and Numbers pointed out that Draper and White were correct in identifying important points of conflict, but they lamented the fact that the "battle-scarred glasses" through which they interpreted the religion and science interplay dominated in succeeding generations. Lindberg and Numbers concluded that the relationship between science and religion is much too complex to be wrapped up neatly by the simplistic conflict approach.

No one doubts that there was conflict in the history of the science-religion relationship, but the monolithic conflict approach was inadequate to make sense of the complex historical relationship between the two. The warfare interpretation probably helped foster a tendency to overlook periods of remarkable harmony that have done as much to influence our current perceptions of both religion and science as have periods of pronounced discord. Two studies from the late 1970s were refreshing because they focused on antebellum, pre-Darwinian America, where it was difficult to apply the conflict model. During this period, religion and science seemed not only content with each other but also profoundly and shamelessly symbiotic in many instances. Herbert Hovenkamp called this a "honeymoon" period, a descriptive term far removed from martial metaphors.[4] In the same vein, Theodore Dwight Bozeman concluded that "antebellum America, marked by a lively and growing interest in natural science *and* evangelical Protestantism, widely nurtured the comfortable assumption that science *and* religion . . . were harmonious enterprises cooperating toward the same ultimate ends."[5]

The attention paid to this period was welcome and fruitful. According to George M. Marsden, a historian of American religion, the resurgence of creationism in the late twentieth century and modern fundamentalist views of science in general cannot be understood without examining the interaction of religion and science during the early nineteenth century, which was the formative period for the fundamentalist attitudes toward science that are active today.[6] In addition, several modern alternative religious movements, such as New Age (including channeling), Scientology, Transcendental Meditation, and the Unification Church, have relationships with science similar to the relationships that such nineteenth-century movements and practices as spiritualism, phrenology, mesmerism, and various medical sects developed with the science of their day.[7]

There was a great deal of popular enthusiasm for religion and science in the decades preceding the Civil War. With regard to religion, the historian Jon Butler called the situation in this period a "spiritual hothouse" because of the growth, combativeness, and creativity of religious people and their movements in these years.[8] At the same time, science was coming of age in America through research, professionalization, education, technological advance, and, most important, its diffusion to the public at large.[9] In the spirit of democracy—especially the antielitism it entailed—it became much more common for ordinary people to discuss, debate, create, synthesize, modify, demonize, or embrace religious, scientific, and philosophical ideas. With the strong currents of religious and scientific enthusiasm running simultaneously through the young republic, vigorous interaction was probably inevitable. When the interaction did occur, the result was rarely a de facto conflict between religion and science. When friction did occur, it was usually over what constituted "true religion" or "true science," not whether they could be brought together in one conceptual scheme. The primary goal of those interested in the interaction was reconciliation and harmonization, not conflict and compartmentalization.

Although Hovenkamp's and Bozeman's key studies focused on mainstream Protestants of the time, the Protestants were by no means the only people at the intersection of religious and scientific ideas. The new religious movements that germinated in the "hothouse" period made the mainstream efforts at harmonization look tame in many respects. For example, at the same time the Protestant theologian Charles Hodge of Princeton was developing a scientific approach to theology that modestly sought to apply the vaunted "inductive method" to sacred scripture, leaders and thinkers in new movements as diverse as Mormonism, spiritualism, and mind cure were taking the relationship to new levels. For some in these new movements, science became the center and the circumference of their religious thinking and the authoritative foundation on which they built new views of the world. Kantian compartmentalization of scientific and religious spheres was not an option. The frame of mind for many in these movements was that if one could not reconcile or harmonize basic religious beliefs with science, then the belief system simply could not be true. New movements that did not embrace the Bible or tradition faced an uphill battle in their quest for cultural authority. That American science was revered in the popular mind and possessed prestige perhaps not yet deserved made it an impressive tool that could be used to overcome the authority vacuum and jump start or shore up new religious views. It was therefore not unusual for leaders to claim that their religious views were thoroughly scientific and often to refer to them directly as such. For instance, such expressions as "Science of the Soul," "the divine science," or "Christian Science" were often invoked for the doctrines of spiritualism, Mormonism, or the mind-cure movement, respectively.[10]

One important aspect of this study is to examine the nature of the relationship that developed between the new religious movements and science in antebellum America. This study also explores popular philosophies and attitudes toward science that made the relationship possible. Most to the point, it presents specific examples of how religious movements, both traditional and nontraditional, have, since the scientific revolution, used science as an authoritative foundation for their belief systems.[11]

Enlightened Representatives

To probe the nexus of science and new religion, I look to three representative figures in three major movements that sprang to life in the decades before the Civil War. They are Orson Pratt (a prolific and influential Mormon writer and one of the original twelve apostles of the Church of Jesus Christ Latter-day Saints), Robert Hare (a prominent American convert to spiritualism in its heyday), and Phineas Parkhurst Quimby (who is generally considered the initiator of the American mind-cure movement). I use these three as representatives because each had something important to say about the interplay of religion and science. I also use them because each engaged in scientific pursuits and is representative of some of the ways in which Americans gave their attention to science. Phineas Quimby, for instance, was an amateur scientific tinkerer. He was amazed by mechanisms and technology and had enough of a self-taught grasp on natural philosophy and natural history to consider himself a part of the emerging scientific culture. Orson Pratt, too, was an amateur, but his scientific curiosity could not be satiated by tinkering with interesting mechanisms and new technology. Pratt's interest in astronomy led him to postulate grand new theories of the operation of the cosmos, and he even fancied himself a latter-day Johannes Kepler or Isaac Newton. Although he was not part of the mainstream or a member of the nascent class of professional scientists in America, Pratt saw himself not only as part of the emerging culture of science but as an important new leader. In contrast, Robert Hare was a model of the new profession of "scientist." A knowledgeable experimenter, professor, author, and public beacon, he was regularly sought out for his opinion on matters of natural philosophy. He was a mainstream leader in his field of chemistry and was recognized by some of the scientific virtuosi in Europe for his work in electrochemistry and heat.

Although they clearly differed in their degree of scientific sophistication, all three were committed to science as the ultimate way of knowing. Contrary to the warfare thesis, this commitment did not set them against religion but directly aided each of them in their embrace of new religious ideas and worldviews. In choosing Pratt, Hare, and Quimby, I am not claiming that they are perfect representatives of the people or thinking in their movements. These three are obviously not representative insofar as they had a greater proclivity toward scientific thinking than the average person in their religious "communities." It will take another study to measure exactly how deeply their religio-scientific syntheses played out in the movements at large over time. However, my preliminary examination of primary sources in Mormonism, spiritualism, and mind cure indicates that their thinking and writing was deeply influential for at least one generation, if not more. In attempting to get at the most intense nexus of religious and scientific thinking in these movements, Pratt, Hare, and Quimby are arguably ideal subjects of inquiry.

The Village Enlightenment

At the heart of this study is the contention that these three "scientific" people developed strikingly similar conclusions about ultimate issues in spite of strikingly dissimilar backgrounds in education, location, social standing, and religious commitment. I introduce a concept useful in making sense of the obvious unity of thought that emerged from the diverse experiences of Pratt, Hare, and Quimby. Needless to say, a major interpretive structure cannot be based on the historical experiences of three individuals. In dealing with only three historical figures, the interpretive project here is obviously much more modest. Nevertheless, it may very well have utility in making sense of other similar figures, movements, and ideas at the time.

The concept I propose is one I call the *village Enlightenment.* The historian David Jaffee used the term to describe the "democratization of knowledge" that took place through changes in the "production, distribution, and consumption" of printed materials in New England from 1760 to 1820.[12] Jaffee's article provided an important look at the means by which reading material of all types proliferated and came into the hands of rural people. However, my use of the concept is related to Jaffee's only in that the "democratization of knowledge" and the "enlightenment" nature of that knowledge are crucial to my study. In the pages that follow, Jaffee's focus on the production, distribution, and consumption of reading materials is only tangentially related.

Instead, I propose the rubric of the village Enlightenment to describe the ways in which Americans on a popular level (often, but not always, in rural areas and on the frontier) used traditional Enlightenment ideas in new con-texts and in new combinations to construct or validate new religious worldviews. A wide range of Enlightenment ideas were co-opted by the new religious movements during the antebellum period—as well as by many popular medical and other sects that had religious undertones. Like the eigh-teenth-century thinkers on whose shoulders they stood, the citizens of the village Enlightenment began with the primary concepts of reason and na-ture. From these, they arrived at such other important ideas as antisuper-naturalism, deism, human freedom, anticlericalism, anticreedalism, progress, the priority of natural law, and the preeminence of Newtonian science, to name a few. The village Enlightenment was by no means a pure reflection of the elite Enlightenment, however. I use the term *village* because in the move-ments I examine traditional Enlightenment ideas were often fused with a variety of popular notions floating through antebellum society, resulting in a product that clearly warranted a distinguishing label.

The way in which the new religious movements of the antebellum pe-riod embraced and altered traditional Enlightenment concepts provides at least a partial answer to the question of what happened to the American Enlightenment embodied in the likes of Benjamin Franklin and Thomas Jefferson. Henry F. May answered that the Enlightenment was assimilated into American culture at the end of the eighteenth century primarily by first ac-commodating to Christianity "in its myriad and shifting American forms" and then by being forced into a democratic mold that sapped much of the elitist intellectual character from whence it drew its strength.[13] Although May did not mention the assimilation of many Enlightenment ideas into a vari-ety of popular movements, he did observe that "neither the Enlightenment nor any other set of ideas has much of a future unless it can find its place in mass society, among human beings as they are." Still, he added that "none of the eighteenth-century philosophers had a program with a real place in it for most people."[14] May was right on both counts. However, many of the citizens of mid-nineteenth-century America proved to be a resourceful lot in preparing a comfortable home for the Enlightenment among "human beings as they are" without the help of the eighteenth-century elites. The three religious figures and movements on which I focus are marked examples.

The idea of the general assimilation of Enlightenment ideas into the popular religious trends of the early republic is not new to this study. Nathan O. Hatch noticed this assimilation and called it a "blurring of worlds" that resulted from "preachers on the periphery of American culture" reconstruct-ing Christianity without traditional sources of authority and standard theological categories. "The crucible of popular theology," Hatch observed, "combined odd mixtures of high and popular culture, of renewed supernaturalism and Enlightenment rationalism, of mystical experiences and biblical literalism, of evangelical and Jeffersonian rhetoric."[15] Hatch's work focused primarily on the Christian experience. The "blurring of worlds" was not, however, the exclusive purview of orthodoxy or evangelical sectarians. New religious thinking—beyond the pale of organized Protestantism—was rife with similar convergences and conflations. In *Nature Religion in America: From the Algonkian Indians to the New Age,* Catherine L. Albanese maintained that in many respects the Enlightenment went to seed in American popular religion. For instance, in the context of unearthing the ethos of various religiously oriented medical sectarians, Albanese remarked, "When the Enlightenment seemed to disappear in the nineteenth century, it had in reality only shifted shapes. It had become, in truth as in rhetoric, the heritage of the people. And, now in privatized form, it had empowered them to lay claim to the erstwhile Christian kingdom of sin and grace. Being well, it turned out, was the popular, romanticized analogue to being independent."[16]

For the most part, the village Enlightenment of my study is the result of the assimilation already noticed by such scholars as Hatch and Albanese as it played out in several popular religious movements. If there is anything new in the concept I am introducing here, it is the emphasis on the way in which prominent figures in these religious movements, such as Pratt, Hare, and Quimby, embraced popular scientific ideas to gain an authoritative foothold for their new religious views. The Enlightenment village was a place where traditional religious authority held little sway but where science, as mediated through the senses, could lead an honest seeker invariably to the truth, religious or otherwise. It was also a place where the principles of democracy were held in highest esteem but where the endless stream of opinions, arguments, and confusion that democracy fostered was loathed as the source of much evil. Enlightenment villagers therefore did not harbor "opinions" on the great questions of the day. Instead, they wielded what they considered to be definitive answers, the truth of which was either self-evident or demonstrated by scientific means. Upon these answers, citizens of the village constructed what they considered to be the only "true" view of humankind and the cosmos.

American attitudes toward science were therefore at the center of the village Enlightenment. Getting at that center, then, requires at least a brief exploration of popular science and the philosophy that carried it along in the antebellum period. I thus begin with an overview of attitudes toward science before the Civil War and the popular philosophy called "Baconianism," which captured both the imagination and the senses of Pratt, Hare, Quimby, and the rest of American society.

American Baconianism and Popular Science

In 1963, Charles S. Braden published *Spirits in Rebellion: The Rise and Development of New Thought,* which had a chapter on Phineas Quimby, whom Braden considered the "founder" of New Thought. Braden listed important intellectual currents in New England in Quimby's time that may have influenced the culture from which Quimby and New Thought emerged. Braden recognized the importance of the philosophical and religious influence of the Transcendentalists, the Unitarians, and the mesmerists. But he seemed at a loss about what to do with Phineas Quimby's obvious fixation on "science" and scientific language, dismissing it (à la the warfare thesis) as a strange phase of the struggle between science and religion.[17] Braden, writing in 1963, did not have the advantage of calling on the more recent work of George H. Daniels and Theodore Dwight Bozeman, who not only challenged the warfare thesis but also helped show the relationship between the "Baconian philosophy" and the common American's infatuation with things scientific. From this perspective, Quimby's affinity for "science" was hardly unusual. His thinking was representative of a popular mind-set grounded in Baconianism, a philosophical approach that is also now known to have provided "the broad foreground of Anglo-American intellectual leadership" in the antebellum period.[18]

As Bozeman and Daniels pointed out, at a time when science was coming of age in the new republic, Baconianism, or the "inductive method," provided a tried and true foundation and framework for not only the blossoming field of natural science but all fields of inquiry where "facts" could be gathered. It was not just the scientists of the day who were "almost to a man Baconians" but "most of the intellectual community" as well.[19] The physical scientists and naturalists shared their enthusiasm for Bacon's inductive method with a variety of others, not the least of which were religious scholars. C. Leonard Allen pointed out that American Protestant theologians found Baconianism a "deft and flexible tool that could be employed in the services of numerous antebellum theologies":

> Theologians quickly and widely perceived the "Baconian philosophy" as a means of advancing theology. Their overriding concerns were for the ex-

amination of evidence, a ruthless focus on the "facts," and the systematic classification of those facts. By use of this method many Protestant theologians sought to restore and reinforce the essential harmony between natural science and Christian faith. By this means they believed that all knowledge—whether scientific, theological, or moral—could be placed on a sure foundation.[20]

Moreover, Christian theologians, most likely to their chagrin, shared the Baconian bandwagon with others who occupied themselves with more heterodox spiritual concerns. Practitioners of spiritualism, mesmerism, phrenology, psychography, and other phenomena that touched on things metaphysical also tried to hitch their claims to this powerful tool thought to be able to settle all disputes through proof by demonstration.[21]

The pervasiveness of Baconianism in antebellum thought is well documented. Daniels, who did one of the most important studies of Baconianism, attempted to illustrate the significance of this philosophy by citing the nineteenth-century bellwether Edward Everett:

> Edward Everett, editor of the *North American Review,* Unitarian minister, and Massachusetts politician, began a review in 1823 with a remark that might very well characterize the intellectual temper of the period in which he lived. "At the present day, as is well known," he observed, "the Baconian philosophy has become synonymous with the *true* philosophy." Everett's choice of the adjective "true" was not a matter of accident—it was not merely that Francis Bacon's philosophy was the most adequate or the most useful, but that it was thought to be *true,* and any other philosophy was correspondingly false. . . .
>
> The Baconian philosophy so dominated that whole generation of American scientists that it was difficult to find any writer during the early part of the nineteenth century who did not assume, with Everett, that his readers knew all about it. Dugald Stewart, in his history of philosophy, also disclaimed any need to speak of Bacon's *experimental* philosophy on the grounds that this was so well known as to be obvious.[22]

What was referred to as "Bacon's philosophy," however, had less to do with the sixteenth-century figure than the prolific application of his name might imply. It was the distinctive interpretation of Bacon by Thomas Reid, Dugald Stewart, and the school of Scottish commonsense realism, whose writings were popular among America's intellectuals in the early nineteenth century, that transformed Bacon's scientific thought into America's "true philosophy."

According to Bozeman, one of the central characteristics of this *true* philosophy that was "engrafted wholesale into the main structure of nineteenth-century American ideas" was "vagueness." Nonetheless, building on the work of Daniels, he found a pattern with four general elements: (1) a "spirited enthusiasm for natural science"; (2) a "scrupulous empiricism," with a corresponding trust in the senses and a real outer world; (3) an intense distrust of speculation and of concepts not derived directly from observed data; and (4) a celebration of "Lord Bacon" as the founder and the work of Newton as paradigmatic example of Bacon's inductive method.[23] Elaborating on the importance of the empirical nature of Baconianism and on the priority of the senses, Daniels observed:

> First, and most evidently, "Baconianism" meant "empiricism," in the sense that all science must somehow rest on observation and that it must begin with individual facts and pass gradually to broader and broader generalizations. . . . The impressions of the mind were considered direct, immediate perceptions of a real objective order. The testimony of the senses had to be admitted as true, and its validity depended upon no outside, additional evidence. The truthfulness of the testimony of the senses could not even be questioned, as one spokesperson said, "without questioning the truthfulness of our constitution, nay, the veracity of God himself—without questioning everything, through whatever channel derived."[24]

Daniels also pointed out that the Baconian method meant avoiding "hypotheses" (a term to which Baconians attached a degree of contempt) by not going beyond what could be directly observed. Going beyond observation and entering the realm of hypothesis meant moving away from indisputable fact into the world of what Pratt, Hare, and Quimby often referred to as opinion, prejudice, error, ignorance, and superstition. The average scientist of the day, assured that this philosophy was grounded in the firm foundation of common sense, believed that if one had carefully observed facts and avoided hypotheses, one could confidently deduce laws of nature. As Daniels wrote, "In other words, nineteenth-century Baconianism, as most American scientists used the term, implied a kind of naive rationalistic empiricism—a belief that the method of pure empiricism consistently pursued would lead to a rational understanding of the universe."[25]

The important studies of Daniels and Bozeman on the reign of Bacon in antebellum America tell much about the intellectual community's veneration of the "inductive method." To examine the origin of movements that began well outside of academic circles and whose leaders often had a meager education, however, we must look to the popular mind of the common farmer, smith, and shopkeeper.

For an uneducated person to have what seemed, at least in his or her own mind, a firm grasp of experimental science was not unusual in the early nineteenth century. The period from 1820 to 1860 in the United States was a time when science was moving out of the hands of aristocratic amateurs into the laboratories and studies of professional "scientific men" or "scientists," terms that were rapidly replacing "natural philosopher" by the late 1840s.[26] During the transition, what was once considered an esoteric body of knowledge was spreading to the population at large. Two fashionable mediums were most responsible: the local newspaper and the expanding lyceum lecture circuit. Although there were an average of fifty-five scientific journals in publication in a given year during this period, their circulation was still very limited, and the common person would not likely have had access to these for scientific information.

The local newspaper, however, provided such popular scientific aficionados as Pratt and Quimby with a rich source of science education. A study by Donald Zochert that surveyed more than 1,500 issues of newspapers between 1837 and 1846 found in them a wealth of material in all scientific disciplines. This indicates a vigorous and sustained interest in science among the common people and wide dissemination of the latest scientific information of all types.[27] As William Ellery Channing wrote in 1841, "Through the press, discoveries and theories, once the monopoly of philosophers, have become the property of the multitudes. . . . Science, once the greatest of distinctions, is becoming popular." Channing thought that the characteristic of the age was "not the improvement of science, rapid as this is, so much as its extension to all men."[28]

During this same period, when scientific information was regularly making it into newspapers around the country, science was also finding a particularly successful path to the public through the burgeoning lyceum system, which, at its peak in 1850, enlightened an estimated 400,000 people a week.[29] In its early stages, the lyceum movement was driven by Josiah Holbrook, who studied under Benjamin Silliman at Yale. One of Holbrook's main objectives in establishing a system of lyceums was to "apply the sciences and the various branches of education to the domestic and useful arts, and to all the common purposes of life."[30] Although after a short period the lyceum lectures encompassed all areas of learning, about a fifth of the platform time continued to be filled by scientific lectures and demonstrations, and they were commonplace in every town large enough to support a lyceum.[31] The content of the scientific information ranged from the widely respected natural history of the Swiss scientist Louis Agassiz, who packed 5,000 into Tremont Temple in Boston in 1846, to the "scientific practices" of itinerant phrenologists, spiritualists, and mesmerists (including Phineas Quimby), who, at times, found "reputable" lyceums closed to them.[32] Largely because of the successful dissemination of popular scientific information through the press and the lyceum systems, Joseph Henry, the first head of the Smithsonian Institution, could say with conviction that there were "more interested in popular science among us than in any other part of the world."[33]

In the early nineteenth century, people everywhere had learned that to invoke the name of "science" was to appeal to utility, certainty, optimism, and progress. One newspaper proclaimed in 1837 that "the world is on the threshold of discoveries in science and the arts, which must change the whole face and fabric of society. . . . Discovery after discovery, and improvement after improvement, follow each other in such rapid succession, that we are prepared to believe almost everything that may be asserted."[34] Prominent professional scientists were not immune to this unbridled homage to their own occupation, as James Dwight Dana revealed in an 1856 address to Yale alumni: "Science is an unfailing source of human good. . . . Every new development is destined to bestow some universal blessing on mankind."[35] The utility of scientific discoveries was of paramount interest to the common person. The public would probably have been shocked that most of the science generated was far removed from any direct practical use, and the scientific community helped prevent this realization by stressing the practical values of its work.[36] The utility of steam power, photography, telegraphy, and a multitude of new labor-saving machines shaped public attitudes toward science in ways that the abstract theoretical concerns of the professional scientist, such as the nature of heat, could never do.

Baconian philosophy accompanied this optimistic extension of science to the public at large, and, in turn, popular science helped defend against any, as Zochert put it, "waning vitality of Baconian observation and deduction."[37] Bozeman wrote, "Baconianism—resting on the assumption that all scientific method was a simple operation upon sense data—both presumed and reinforced the general assumption that the intelligibility sought by science did not exceed the reach of amateurs and laymen."[38]

Although the name of Bacon was less firmly attached to science on the popular level, the philosophy was still influential, especially in terms of empirical method and the disdain for speculation. Zochert pointed out that the empirical method was, on occasion, explicitly endorsed in the popular press.

One Milwaukee editor, for example, commended the author of a scientific article because he "very properly confines himself almost entirely to an examination of the facts observed, and not being influenced by any pre-conceived theory... his observations may be relied upon with perfect confidence. . . . Let us gather all the facts before we begin to deduce our theories and form conjectures."[39] Similarly, one Massachusetts educator who was promoting an "inductive science" of public education was concerned about repeating the mistakes of the "ancients," who "formed theories in their own minds, and persuaded themselves that these were true in fact. It is plain that they were in no condition to learn, for they aspired to make the laws of nature. . . . This mistake consisted in supposing that the natural powers of the human mind were adequate to declare the laws of nature, without having first learned them by actual observations and experiments."[40]

Although the rules of the game of Baconian science received a fair amount of attention and appear to have been widely understood, popular science was certainly not free of the "speculative impulse."[41] Many news writers and lyceum lecturers emphasized the exotic and curious "wonders" of science, and it appears that strict induction often lost out to the audience's desire to be entertained.[42] Even so, the spirit of Bacon still influenced the common person. Amateurs and laypeople who paid attention to the science of the day had a certain kinship with Baconian demands for observation and measurement, enough so that one might even have fancied himself a "scientific man."[43] One newspaper in 1846 parodied the "scientific man" as one who "will look at the thermometer to see when it is warm, at the barometer to see when it storms, at the clock to see when he is hungry, at the almanac to see how old he is, at the moon to see when it is high tide, at the stars to ascertain when he is in love. He is a scientific man, and does everything by rule but his devotions, which he doesn't do at all."[44] Hand in hand with the thriving democratic spirit, the "scientific man" boldly took possession of what was once in the hands of the fortunate few. "People now-a-days, when a new and startling theory is brought up, do not wait for the wise men and the doctors to analyze and investigate it, before they can venture an opinion on its merits or demerits; but they take up the subject at once for themselves; they reason it over in their own mind, and discuss it among their neighbors," the *Milwaukee Courier* pointed out.[45]

During the 1830s, the scientific enterprise was increasingly diffused to the general public in the United States. Along with the diffusion came the notion that "the common man—no less than the philosopher—could fasten upon it [science] to his advantage."[46] From 1820 to the firing on Fort Sumter in 1861, American science rapidly changed from an activity thought of as a gentlemanly leisure-time pursuit to one for the trained professional "who had a single-minded dedication to the interests of science."[47] This period of rapid change witnessed not only the professionalization of science but its democratization as well, what Channing referred to as its "extension to all men." The layperson, not just the professional scientist, was riding the wave of growth, fascination, and optimism generated by the science of the day. It was often the layperson who, in little danger of being criticized by "professional" colleagues, saw in science almost limitless possibilities for harmony, health, wealth, and entertainment.

❖ ❖ ❖

It is at this point that I turn to the three specific "scientists" who are central to this study. I begin with the amateur scientist and Mormon apostle Orson Pratt, who was able to capitalize on some of the limitless possibilities that the science of the day seemed to make available. In the midst of this period in which the population was clearly enamored of science and immersed in popular Baconian philosophy, Pratt began constructing what he thought were revolutionary solutions to age-old scientific and religious problems. In doing so, Pratt helped establish what the Mormons perceived as an authoritative scientific base on which to build a latter-day religious movement exemplifying one set of possibilities for the village Enlightenment.

1 Mormon Cosmic Philosophy: Orson Pratt

With only a few days' journey left before the Valley of the Great Salt Lake would open up before the first set of Mormon pioneers, the mantle of leadership fell to Orson Pratt. On the morning of July 21, 1847, Pratt and his fellow apostle Erastus Snow set out ahead of the wagons to climb to the summit. That afternoon, they crawled to the top and shouted "Hosanna!" three times as they became the first to behold the land of promise. "After issuing from the mountains among which we had been shut up for many days, and beholding in a moment such an extensive scenery open before us, we could not refrain from a shout of joy which almost involuntarily escaped from our lips the moment this grand and lovely scenery was within our view," Pratt reported.[1] As they descended to the valley below—Pratt on foot, Snow on horseback—Snow suddenly realized that he had dropped his coat some distance behind. He turned back to look for it, leaving Pratt to go forth on his own. Soon thereafter, wrote Pratt's biographer, Breck England, "Orson made a triumphal circle of twelve miles through the valley, a lonely figure on the plain, the first Mormon of the hundreds of thousands to follow."[2]

It is difficult to find occasions when Orson Pratt was not out in front, whether on the wagon trail or in Mormon thought. The famous apostle loomed large in the early history of the Mormon church, not only as a leader of wagons and missionaries but also as an important spiritual leader, theologian, apologist, and scientist. His love for both science and the church was revealed only a few days after his first "triumphal circle" through the valley. With Brigham Young still ill in bed, Pratt determined the coordinates of the Great Salt Lake City and its temple centerpiece with his beloved sextant, telescope, and other scientific instruments and then dedicated the site to God in the company of the Saints who had gathered with him. He had marked out the center of God's kingdom on earth with the tools of science that were as dear to him as the latter-day revelation of God that he held so tenaciously from his conversion in 1830 until his death in 1881.

The influence of Orson Pratt's leadership, life, and thought on the course of Mormon history and doctrine has not been lost on modern scholars of Mormonism. In 1982, David J. Whittaker cited a number of Mormon luminaries who had described Pratt's influence. He included Edward Tullidge, who called him the "Paul of Mormonism," as well as T. B. H. Stenhouse, who claimed Pratt made "the first logical arguments in favour of Mormonism." Wilford Woodruff said that Pratt wrote "more upon the gospel and upon science than any man in the Church."[3]

Pratt's writings on Mormon doctrine, science, and philosophy helped clarify, if not mold, many of the theological teachings of the nascent movement. His written works made up a significant body of mid-nineteenth-century Latter-day Saint literature. It was not just the sheer volume of material he wrote that moved the early church. It was also the style of writing that he used in every one of his publications. Whittaker observed that "within each work he moved carefully from one point to another, gradually developing his position with the same exactness he would have used in solving a mathematical equation."[4] Pratt's theological writings are stylistically no different from his scientific writings. He worked through his arguments proposition by proposition, always numbering them in sequence.

Pratt was an important theologian not because of the form of his arguments but because of their content. Pratt had an especially deep and uncompromising commitment to proclaiming and defending ideas that a century earlier were pillars of the Enlightenment in America, and he fought for those ideas in the context of a new and popular American religious movement. Moreover, he employed the authority of Baconian science to justify the ideas. These were the elements of what I call the village Enlightenment in America, and Pratt, by any measure, was a prime example of one who embodied the concept. He was the premier early Mormon apologist. Pratt felt called to take the prophetic utterances of Joseph Smith, divine their essences, order them, and then draw them out to their logical conclusions based on his understanding of science and philosophy. In so doing, he constructed what he thought was a logically consistent, scientifically sound, and most of all materialist cosmology, one in which universal law and the perfect mechanism of cause and effect revealed the power and glory of nature and nature's God.

Orson Pratt, the Latter-day Saint apostle and scientist, circa 1880. (Courtesy of the Manuscripts Division, J. Willard Marriott Library, University of Utah)

The Gauge of Philosophy

According to Mormon accounts, in 1820, while only a teenager, Joseph Smith, later the founder of Mormonism, "retired to the woods" to pray. His petition to God that night concerned the religious confusion he felt because of the discord he observed among the competing Christian sects around his upstate New York home. He sat quietly and earnestly petitioned God to sort out which was preaching the truth and which he should follow. In Smith's reported vision, God the Father and his son, Jesus, visibly appeared to him and answered him directly by saying that he "must join none of them, for they were all wrong."[5] Three years later, according to the Mormon account, the great restoration of true religion began with the nighttime visit of the angel Moroni to Smith's bedroom. The angel told him of a great religious history of the early Americas recorded on gold plates buried in the Hill Cumorah not far from his Palmyra, New York, home. Smith eventually unearthed the plates, translated them with the help of two seerstones—the Urim and Thummim—and published them as the Book of Mormon in March of 1830. In summary, the Book of Mormon tells the story of Lehi, an Israelite prophet of the biblical Jeremiah's time, who fled with his family to the American continent. Several centuries later, Lehi's descendants were visited by the resurrected Christ, who taught them the pure gospel. The result of Christ's visit was the establishment of a Christian utopia in America, which soon disintegrated in apostasy and wickedness. The last faithful Christian, Moroni, sealed up the record of his people for later discovery in the "times of the Gentiles." Joseph Smith testified that this same Moroni, an angelic messenger, revealed the location of the record and prepared Joseph for its miraculous translation.

Orson Pratt first encountered this story in September of 1830, only six months after the Book of Mormon first appeared in print. Pratt's conversion tale resembles that of Joseph Smith in many respects. The sectarian rivalry in upstate New York had left the teenage Pratt in a confused state about where religious truth resided. This did not, however, deter him from seeking it out. Pratt wrote that for nine years before his conversion, he "often felt a great anxiety to be prepared for a future state but never commenced in real earnest to seek after the Lord until the autumn of 1829." Pratt continued, "I then began to pray fervently, repenting of every sin. In the silent shades of night, while others were slumbering upon their pillows, I often retired to some secret place in the lonely field or solitary wilderness, and bowed before the Lord, and prayed for hours with a broken heart and contrite spirit; this was my comfort and my delight. The greatest desire of my heart was for the Lord to manifest His will concerning me."[6]

As with Smith, two "personages" appeared to Orson Pratt in response to his fervent prayers in the woods. In this case, however, it was not the Father and the Son but two missionaries. Pratt recalled that he was visited by two "Elders of the Church of Jesus Christ of Latter-day Saints . . . one of which was my brother Parley. They held several meetings which I attended. Being convinced of the divine authenticity of the doctrine they taught, I was baptized on September 19, 1830. This was my birthday, being nineteen years old. I was the only person in the country who received and obeyed the message."[7]

Orson Pratt believed he had discovered the same answer to the question Joseph Smith had asked ten years before, "Which of all the sects was right?" None of them was right. A new voice from heaven was necessary to break through the discordant religious clatter. Joseph Smith and his Book of Mormon provided the new voice and restored the gospel that had been lost hundreds of years earlier. Pratt received it with great enthusiasm and with perfect certainty of its truth. Twenty years later, he wrote that "uncertainty and ambiguity have been the principal cause of all the divisions of modern Christendom. The only way to remedy this great evil, is to obtain another revelation of the gospel. . . . Such a revelation is the Book of Mormon; the most infallible certainty characterizes every ordinance and every doctrinal point revealed in that book. In it there is no ambiguity—no room for controversy."[8]

Orson Pratt (1811–81) was born in Hartford, New York, the fifth of Jared and Charity Pratt's six children. Pratt wrote that his parents "were numbered among the poor of this world" and that "a succession of misfortunes kept them down in the low vales of poverty."[9] Except for some home instruction in which he learned to read the Bible while very young, Pratt's schooling took place in the winter months when there were not so many farm chores. Because of his family's poverty, Orson was sent at age eleven to work in the fields of other farmers in return for room, board, and a few months of winter schooling.

He and his brother traveled a great deal from 1822 to 1830, hiring on at different farms in places as far removed as Long Island, New York, and Lorain County, Ohio. These early travels may have instilled in him and his brother Parley a certain degree of contentment with continual uprootedness. Both went on to become the most traveled evangelists in the early church. Orson Pratt himself crossed the Atlantic no less than sixteen times on missionary journeys. He recounted, however, that this constant relocation as a youth did not affect him negatively because he had the abiding influence of his parents:

"From the age of ten to nineteen I saw much of the world, and was tossed about without any permanent abiding place; but through the grace of God, I was kept from many of the evils to which young people are exposed; the early impressions of morality and religion, instilled into my mind by my parents, always remained with me."[10]

Orson Pratt remembered that he "seldom attended any religious meetings, as my parents had not much faith in them, and were never so unfortunate as to unite themselves with any of the religious sects."[11] The family sampled much of the religious fare that was offered in the region that historian Whitney R. Cross called the "burned-over district" of upstate New York, but, according to Pratt, the family put no "faith in the modern sectarian principles of Christianity."[12] Although his parents taught him to "venerate [their] Father in Heaven," the "Pratt tradition of independence in religious matters was carefully maintained."[13] He had no religious instruction other than what he received at home in response to his questions about what he read in the Bible.

The rest of Pratt's education was likewise sporadic and sometimes informal. He recalled when he became quite familiar with the rules of Daball's arithmetic after he first moved away from home, and for the next eight years of intermittent work and school, he studied bookkeeping, geography, grammar, surveying, and more arithmetic. Parley Pratt commended the education they received in that "excellent system of common school education," which afforded them the "opportunity to learn, and even become familiar with the four great branches, which are the foundation of literature and the sciences."[14] Although Orson Pratt's school education ended in 1830, he continued to study on his own obsessively for the rest of his life, especially in mathematics and the sciences. David J. Whittaker emphasized that Pratt held even more tightly to his study of mathematics and science "during great crises, for the 'finality' of empirical evidence provided a shelter from the storms of his life."[15] Pratt's fascination with science and mathematics took on a whole new dimension after his baptism in September 1830. Henceforth, his spare time would be dominated by the attempt to build a grand scheme unifying the new revelations of the prophet Joseph Smith and the scientific workings of the cosmos.

Pratt met Smith at Fayette, New York, only a month or two after his conversion. He was ordained an elder and in December was sent on the first of many missionary journeys. After several years of faithful missionary service, Pratt was admitted to the newly formed Quorum of the Twelve Apostles in 1835. Four years later, he was commissioned to carry the gospel to the British Isles. In Edinburgh, Scotland, Orson Pratt published his first apologetic pamphlet, which included, in Whittaker's words, the first "*public* recording of Joseph Smith's First Vision and a list of fifteen 'Articles of Faith.'"[16]

During his mission and for several years after his return in 1841, Pratt spent what little leisure time he had studying mathematics and science. He wrote, "[I] made myself thoroughly acquainted with algebra, geometry, trigonometry, conic sections, differential and integral calculus, astronomy, and most of the physical sciences. These studies I pursued without the assistance of a teacher."[17] In September 1841, Orson Pratt was given the degree of master of arts by the chancellor of the new University of the City of Nauvoo and was elected professor of mathematics.

Pratt found a way to express in print his fascination with mathematics and science with his second publishing venture in 1845 and 1846. In each of those years, he published an issue of the *Prophetic Almanac*. Although almost no attention has been paid to these little publications, few of Pratt's writings could be pointed to as better encapsulations of his worldview. Against the backdrop of the precise, orderly, and certain universe displayed in the astronomical computations—the backbone of the American almanac—Pratt set forth what he saw as the equally precise, orderly, and certain doctrines of the restored church. In the 1845 edition, he included a section called "The Mormon Creed," which, as Breck England observed, was "one of the earliest summary statements of Mormon belief."[18] In a terse question and answer format, Pratt presented the fundamentals of Mormon theology and cosmology with simplicity and finality:

> What is man? The offspring of God. . . .
> What is his final destiny? To be like God.
> What has God been? Like man. . . .
> How many gods are there? There are Lords many, and gods many. . . .
> How many heavens are there? They are innumerable.
> What is Mormonism? It is all truth. . . .
> What is the kingdom of God? A theocracy.[19]

While other American almanacs of the period became famous for their wit, humor, and proverbs, the *Prophetic Almanac* took on the character of its "philomath," Orson Pratt.[20] His almanacs were tools of evangelism and had no room for frivolity. In place of the wit and wisdom of "Poor Richard," Pratt printed extracts from the discourses of Joseph Smith. For Pratt, a better marriage could not have been arranged than the one between the prophet's words and astronomical science. In Pratt's mind, Smith's role as prophet gave him a timeless perspective. He was one who could bring the light of the past to the present and who could predict the future from the present with perfect precision. Smith's prophetic words were also able to reveal the power and glory of God. Pratt saw astronomical science in much the same way:

> [Astronomy] is that science which lifts the veil of obscurity, and exhibits the grand scenery of the universe as it existed in ages past, as it now exists, and, if not interfered with by causes unknown, as it will exist in ages to come. It is that science which above all others, is calculated to give us the most profound, sublime and exalted views, of the power, wisdom and goodness of that Being who formed those magnificent systems from eternal elements, and devised laws, calculated to maintain their stability through all their complicated and infinite variety of movements, for indefinite ages to come.[21]

The almanacs provide the first concrete indication that there was to be no "warfare" between theology and science in Mormon thought. Orson Pratt—the Latter-day Saints' most able theologian and scientist—saw nothing but harmony between religion and science when both were properly understood. As Pratt himself said in 1860, "The study of science is the study of something eternal. If we study astronomy, we study the works of God."[22]

The same year that his second almanac was published, Pratt helped organize and lead the first wave of Mormons to Utah. He had little time to become acquainted with the new land of promise because he was soon asked to cross the Atlantic and take over the presidency of the British Mission. He arrived at Liverpool in July of 1848 and found many English people hungry for and responsive to the restored gospel. In addition to overseeing church operations, Pratt lectured to the Saints and preached regularly in the streets.

Pratt's itinerant teaching and preaching did not have as much influence as his published writings, though. Upon his arrival, he took over the editorship of the *Millennial Star,* a Mormon periodical started by his brother Parley Pratt on his mission to Britain in 1838, and he announced that the *Star* would be printing a series of pamphlets on first principles and definitive theological statements of Mormonism. The sixteen pamphlets that resulted from this promise endeared Pratt to the British Saints for their impeccable logic and clear prose. Edward Tullidge recalled that the British "almost worshipped Orson" because through his work he had become their "theological father" and because his writing became the catalyst for some very successful mission work. In addition to their evangelistic and apologetic value in Britain, Pratt's pamphlets would become the main instrument through which he would help mold Mormon theology and cosmology everywhere the Latter-day Saints could be found for years to come. In 1851, the pamphlets were bound together and published as a book eventually known as *Orson Pratt's Works,* a book that the Mormon bibliographers Peter Crawley and Chad J. Flake considered "extremely influential" for several generations because it "simply outnumbered all other [Mormon publications] by many thousands."[23]

In August 1852, Brigham Young decided that it was time to proclaim the doctrine of plural marriage publicly. Orson Pratt was the natural choice for the job because it needed to be done with great force of reason to overcome the emotional objections that were anticipated across the country. Pratt was sent to Washington, D.C., where he wrote in the pages of a new periodical called the *Seer* what is still considered, in Whittaker's words, the "most detailed analysis of the doctrine [of plural marriage] in Mormon literature."[24]

In 1856, Pratt took command of the church in Europe and once again used the time to write another series of theological pamphlets, which were collected and published together, this time under the title *Tracts by Orson Pratt.* One of the tracts, *The Holy Spirit,* caused a controversy in the apostolic ranks over the nature of God. In this tract, Pratt reiterated what he had already stated in the *Seer,* maintaining that gods do not "progress in knowledge and wisdom, because they already know all things past, present, and to come."[25] Brigham Young vehemently opposed the idea and strongly defended the doctrine that gods continue to increase in knowledge and wisdom throughout eternity. Four years of conflict over doctrine and authority ensued that resulted in Young's formal denunciation of Pratt's "heretical" speculations and Pratt's halfhearted capitulation to the president's position in 1860.

As a good example of Enlightenment village thinking, Pratt was obstinate when he thought reason and scientific thinking were being challenged. He was not always an apologist for the pronouncements of Mormon leaders; he was a defender of what he saw as the truth. He tried to make his case before Young that "without these arguments . . . it would be entirely vain for me to try & enlighten the world upon this subject by reason."[26] It was a monumental personal struggle for Pratt to concede points that he found logically compelling, but he did so begrudgingly in a confessional discourse published in 1860.[27]

After his painful doctrinal conflicts with President Young and his fellow apostles in the Quorum of the Twelve, Pratt appears to have avoided public theological construction by turning his creativity to scientific pursuits. He continued to work hard for the church, however, and for the Utah Territorial Legislature, where he served until 1881. His health then began to go down

THE SEER.

All ye inhabitants of the world, and dwellers on the earth, See Ye, when He lifteth up an Ensign on the Mountains.—*Isaiah* xviii, 3.

Vol. I.   JANUARY, 1853.   No. 1.

PROSPECTUS OF "THE SEER."

THE SEER is a title assumed for this Periodical in commemoration of JOSEPH SMITH, the great SEER of the last days, who, as an instrument in the hands of the Lord, laid the foundation of the Kingdom of God, preparatory to the second coming of the Messiah to reign with universal dominion over all the Earth.

The pages of the SEER will be mostly occupied with original matter, illucidating the doctrines of the Church of Jesus Christ of Latter Day Saints, as revealed in both ancient and modern Revelations. The Prophecies, relating to the grand and remarkable events of the last days, will be carefully examined and unfolded. The doctrine of *Celestial Marriage, or Marriage for all eternity,* as believed and practised by the Saints in Utah Territory, will be clearly explained. The views of the Saints in regard to the *ancient Patriarchal Order of Matrimony, or Plurality of Wives,* as developed in a Revelation, given through JOSEPH, the SEER, will be fully published. The Celestial origin and pre-existence of the spirits of men—their first estate or probation in a previous world—the great benefits, derived by descending from Heaven, and entering fleshly tabernacles, and keeping the laws of their second estate, and their final redemption and exaltation, as Gods, in their future state—are subjects which will, more or less, occupy the pages of the SEER.

It is hoped that the President elect, the Hon. Members of Congress, the Heads of the various Departments of the National Government, the high-minded Governors and Legislative Assemblies of the several States and Territories, the Ministers of every Religious denomination, and all the inhabitants of this great Republic, will patronize this Periodical, that through the medium of our own writings they may be more correctly and fully informed in regard to the peculiar doctrines, views, practices, and expectations of the Saints who now flourish in the Mountain Territory, and who will eventually flourish over the whole Earth. And we say to all nations, subscribe for the SEER, and we promise you a True and Faithful description of all the principal features, characterizing this great and last "dispensation of the fulness of times."

The SEER will be published Monthly, at $1 per annum, in advance.

ORSON PRATT, *Editor,*
        Washington City, D. C
DECEMBER 21, 1852.

The front cover of the first issue of Pratt's monthly periodical, the *Seer,* which he published and distributed in Washington, D.C., in 1853–54.

hill and plummeted when diabetes began to ravage his body. He died on October 3, 1881, leaving behind eight wives and thirty living children.

Mormon Baconian and Scientist

Orson Pratt left behind more than a substantial legacy of children, wives, and doctrinal theology. He also left behind a creative body of amateur scientific work. Even though he was able to pursue his scientific interests only when his church work allowed, Pratt probably thought he had an advantage over most of the non-Mormon and "professional" scientists of his day. After all, he was in possession of an incontrovertible answer to a fundamental question for which the others could offer only conjecture: what is really real? The answer that Pratt held was one based on the certainty of truth from God as revealed through the prophet Joseph Smith: *matter* was eternal and really real, and anything that was not material simply did not exist. Therefore, even spirit was matter.[28]

Whether Smith knew it or not, his utterances on the nature of matter opened the door for believing Mormons to investigate, especially through scientific means, the elusive world of spirit that was conceptually closed for the more orthodox Christian sects of his day. If, as Mormons still believe, the spiritual universe is made up of nearly the same substance as the physical one, science certainly had the potential to probe the spirit world as thoroughly as it had probed the physical. Smith made possible a grand unified theory of the cosmos that could include gods, angels, demons, and other unseen spiritual entities, in addition to the visible physical world with which antebellum American scientists had been preoccupied. The Mormon seer offered no arguments for these propositions but felt no need to. Since Smith's followers regarded them as divinely inspired, the propositions became inerrant theological and scientific "First Principles." This is the conceptual world in which Orson Pratt began and pursued his scientific interests.

By his own account, Pratt's fascination with science and mathematics was sparked early, and it does not appear that his energetic quest after such knowledge was ever set aside for any significant length of time during the course of his life. He corresponded with the editors of such journals as *Mathematics Monthly* (Cambridge, Massachusetts) and the *Analyst* (Des Moines, Iowa), and his published scientific lectures were accurate renderings of current astronomical thought, which indicates that at least during his mission assignments in cities where mathematical and scientific publications were readily available, he attempted to keep abreast of new findings. However, determining the extent of Pratt's day-to-day scientific thinking and activities is problematic since he rarely recorded these in the early journal entries that survive today. He may have kept a separate journal in which to catalog his scientific ideas, but, because most of his journals, diaries, and notebooks were deliberately destroyed in a bonfire ignited by his first wife, Sarah, we may never know. Fortunately, even without most of his day-to-day jottings, plenty of evidence indicates that scientific and mathematical concerns were constantly in the forefront of Pratt's thinking. A few of the journal entries that survived Sarah's inferno suggest the high level of Orson's scientific interests.[29] Especially pertinent are the surviving travel logs that Pratt kept during the first journey to the Utah territory. From these entries, one can see that he was devoted to scientific measurement and observation. He recorded detailed data on everything, including flora and fauna, geography, minerals, weather, and stars, all of which, he wrote, "constantly excited the analyzing and cause-seeking powers of our chemists and natural philosophers."[30] Enamored of mathematics, Pratt made many calculations from his collected data. The science historian Donald Skabelund remarked that these calculations showed Pratt's obsession with precision: "Today one seldom finds planetary densities expressed to better than three-place accuracy; Pratt, however, employed five-place numbers for these densities, and on one occasion he multiplied a five-place density by the earth's volume given to twelve significant figures, and obtained the earth's weight in pounds expressed to 26 places!"[31]

According to his own account, Pratt had no formal scientific training or even any amateur tutelage. One may rightly ask, then, where he developed such a passionate scientific and philosophical mind-set. Although Pratt had always had scientific and philosophical interests, his biographer, Breck England, suggested that Pratt was "profoundly influenced by the ideas current in Edinburgh" during his nine-month missionary assignment there in 1840 and 1841. England observed that the city during those years "resounded with philosophical and scientific discussion," but more important for Pratt, it was the center of the "Scottish 'Enlightenment' and the 'common sense' school of philosophy . . . empiricists who sought a science of knowledge, not speculative metaphysicians."[32]

During Pratt's tenure in Edinburgh, he was inspired to write his first tract for publication, *A Interesting Account of Several Remarkable Visions, and the Late Discovery of Ancient American Records Giving an Account of the Commencement of the Work of the Lord in This Generation.* He argued, with solid Baconian methods, that the new Mormon church was based not on the "decisions of fallible men" and complicated theories derived from speculation but on certain knowledge from God, supported by incontestable eyewitness testimony that "was revealed in great plainness, so that no one who reads [the Book of Mormon] can misunderstand its principles."[33] Pratt's Edinburgh experience certainly moved him forward in his appreciation of the Baconian approach to knowledge. It likely gave him a sort of international confirmation of what he had already encountered in North America, where, according to contemporary observers, Baconianism had already become the *true* philosophy.[34]

Pratt's Baconianism was by no means limited to the written work he produced in Scotland—the philosophy's conceptual cradle. This epistemological approach pervaded all of his formal publications. Generally, it would be difficult to trace how a particular American of the early nineteenth century "became" a Baconian because Baconianism, as we have already seen, was more a frame of mind that was absorbed than a method that was explicitly taught.[35] Anyone with investigative, scholarly interests would have encountered it in the course of such pursuits. Pratt no doubt acquired this frame of mind from a wide variety of sources, but he certainly encountered it by example as he read the scientific work published in his day. More important, we know that he read, mentioned by name, and used the arguments of some of the most significant proponents of the philosophy, such men as Dugald Stewart, Thomas Brown, and Sir John Herschel.[36]

Simply because Pratt never mentioned Francis Bacon's name or directly referred to Baconianism or the Scottish philosophy in any of his writings does not indicate a less than vigorous devotion to the method. Only rarely did an American scientist of the period mention the method by name or discuss it because, as George Daniels demonstrated, "the Baconian philosophy so dominated that whole generation of American scientists that it is difficult to find any writer during the early part of the nineteenth century who did not assume . . . that his readers knew all about it."[37] Daniels also pointed out that on the rare occasion when a scientist did discuss method, sometimes the name of Isaac Newton was used instead of Bacon to refer to the same set of epistemological principles because Newton was considered an almost perfect embodiment of Baconian ideals.[38] Pratt periodically employed the name of Newton in just this sense, referring to the immortal, profound, and illustrious Newton and his method of discovering "infallible standards" by means of "reason and observation" by which "thousands of truths in modern times have been discovered."[39]

As it was for many of his more religiously orthodox contemporaries, the Baconianism that Orson Pratt employed was a method that could be applied to theological issues as well as to the investigation of the natural world. The raw data obtained from revelation, whether from the Bible or the words of Joseph Smith, were epistemologically equivalent to, if not better than, the raw data of nature obtained through observation. Pratt, like his counterparts in Protestantism, used both types of data to build a comprehensive worldview. Pratt's theological tracts read very much like his scientific work because they inductively argued toward general theological law from the specific "facts" of revelation, just as his scientific works argued for natural law inductively from the "facts" of nature.[40] Although he never addressed the potential weaknesses of the argument, Pratt seemed thoroughly convinced that once the revelation was established as true by eyewitness testimony, fulfillment of prophecy, and internal consistency, it was on an equal footing with the observable facts of nature and could be used with equal certainty in building the Mormon intellectual world.[41] Not surprisingly, establishing Mormon revelation claims as authoritative and true was the purpose of his very first published tracts, *A Interesting Account of Several Remarkable Visions* and *Divine Authority, or the Question, Was Joseph Smith Sent of God?* From then on, for Pratt, it was simply a matter of a careful combination of inductive and deductive inference from the data of revelation and nature to logically certain laws and conclusions on all subjects, ranging from the ideal form of government to grand new theories of the cosmos.

Orson Pratt was by no means the only Baconian influence among the early Mormons. Pratt and Joseph Smith were likely influenced by two other Mormon elders who embraced this philosophy: Parley Pratt, Orson's brother, and Sidney Rigdon, one of the most renowned early Mormon converts. The Baconian mind-set among the Latter-day Saints was carried into the late nineteenth century by none other than Brigham Young, who maintained that most of the world's woes are attributable to "ideas and notions for truth which are in opposition to and contradict facts demonstrated by science." On other occasions, Young declared that "our religion will not clash with or contradict the facts of science in any particular" and that "the Lord" was "one of the most scientific men that ever lived; you have no idea of the knowledge he has with regard to the sciences."[42]

It is Orson Pratt, however, who at least comes across today as the most obvious Baconian of the early intellectual core because of his frequent publishing and the rigor of his writing style. There is also little question that he was the only early Mormon leader who pursued natural science as a serious amateur with an eye toward discovery and publication. Although among the

Mormons Pratt was best known as a teacher of mathematics and astronomy, he was also, by all accounts, the foremost practitioner and theorist.

Pratt produced more along scientific lines than one would expect for a man with his enormous church work load and constant traveling. Although some of his work could best be described as amateur "tinkering" in mathematics and science, at least two of his discoveries, if widely accepted, had the potential to be taken quite seriously. His very first published "discovery" was of this character. In 1854, he publicly claimed to have discovered the "Law of Planetary Rotation," a summary of which he published in the pages of the *Deseret News* eight months later.

The "Law of Planetary Rotation" was Pratt's attempt to find mathematical order in the seemingly anomalous rotational periods of the earth and other planets. The German astronomer and mathematician Johannes Kepler had been successful two hundred years earlier in uncovering a mathematical law that could describe and predict the revolutions (or orbits) of the planets of our solar system as satellites around the sun. In the same way that Kepler was able to describe and predict the planets' revolutions, a few astronomers since his day had been attempting to discover a law that would do the same for the planets' rotations (or axial spins). Orson Pratt thought he had come up with the answer: a mathematical relationship between the density of a planet and its period of rotation. He described it as a "beautiful law," which stated that "THE CUBE ROOTS OF THE DENSITIES OF THE PLANETS ARE AS THE SQUARE ROOTS OF THEIR PERIODS OF ROTATION."[43] Although this law has since proven to be imprecise and does not appear to have made any impact beyond Mormon circles, it did give, as Donald Skabelund argued, "better than order-of-magnitude agreement with modern observations for the superior planets then known."[44]

More than that, Pratt's announcement of his discovery of this "beautiful" and "remarkable" law in some respects sounded as if he received a personal revelation about the workings of nature:

> Permit me to announce to the world . . . an astronomical discovery made by me on the eleventh day of November, 1854.
> . . . Many eminent and distinguished astronomers have eagerly sought after some law, connecting the rotative periods of the planets with some known data of the solar system . . . but all of their laborious researches to develop such a law have not been crowned with success—the law of planetary rotation has eluded their grasp.
> Firmly believing, from my early youth, that the diurnal periods of the plan-

ets were the results of some hidden law, I have endeavored, at different times, to discover the same, so as to determine the periods of rotation by calculation. . . . After many fruitless researches in regard to the original causes of planetary motion, I was led by the indications of certain hypothesis to seek for the law of rotation connected with the masses and diameters of the planets, or, in other words, with their densities.

According to standard church accounts, Joseph Smith's first revelation was a reward for the sincere and lonely search after hidden religious truth by a very young man who persevered despite the failings of other seekers for hundreds of years. Orson Pratt saw his discovery of this "hidden law" of nature in much the same way. Since his youth, he had sought the answer, and, finally, he believed he had grasped it in 1854 after generations of astronomers had failed. This announcement was one indication that Pratt did not make great distinctions between occultic, religious, and scientific revelation. Hidden laws and truths could come to the surface in many ways. Pratt himself observed the occultic methods of Joseph Smith when on several occasions he saw Smith put his face in a hat that held a white "seer stone" in order to prophesy.[45] Pratt also knew better than most the story of Smith's first vision—a more traditional religious revelation—and was certainly familiar with the ways in which science could reveal grand "hidden" truths.

Because of its inherent malleability, Baconian philosophy was not necessarily at odds with any of these three ways of knowing. We already know that Baconianism was an accepted way in which to approach religious and scientific scholarship, but the occultic practices of folk magic could easily be considered Baconian if those practicing them thought them to be empirical, practical, results producing, and free from conjecture, opinion, or mere human impression. Orson Pratt may not have been as deeply impressed by the folk practices of what D. Michael Quinn has called the "magic world view" as some of the other early Mormons were, but he was still a part of it. Pratt not only was on the lookout for long hidden laws in the planets and pyramids but also, as I show in detail later, embraced a theory of animate, intelligent matter that ushered him into a historical line of hermetic, occultic philosophers.[46]

The coming forth of Orson Pratt's "Law of Planetary Rotation," however, appears to have been far less mysterious, isolated, and original than Pratt was willing to admit. More than five years before Pratt's published announcement, Daniel Kirkwood, a young mathematics teacher from the backwoods of Pennsylvania, produced a law quite similar to Pratt's that generated excitement and controversy within scientific circles in the United States and abroad. Kirkwood wrote a paper entitled "On the Law of the Planet's Rotations" that was presented at a meeting of the American Association for the Advancement of Science in July of 1849 and subsequently reported in a number of professional publications.[47] His "Law," known as "Kirkwood's Analogy," posited that there was an invariable mathematical relationship between the number of rotations a given planet makes in a year and what he called the planet's "sphere of attraction based in the nebular hypothesis."[48] Pratt's "Law" was strikingly similar to Kirkwood's, and Pratt's mathematical formulations could have easily been derived from Kirkwood's. Pratt's formula simply replaced Kirkwood's "sphere of attraction" with planetary density and then inverted the equation. Because "sphere of attraction" and planetary density were proportionally related to the mass of a planet, Pratt's reformulation gave almost identical results.

Kirkwood's discovery not only was published in several professional journals but also was picked up and discussed by several newspapers in 1849 and 1850.[49] Because Kirkwood's Analogy was seen as an important new confirmation of the controversial theory of planetary origins called the "nebular hypothesis," it was widely disseminated and vigorously debated on both sides of the Atlantic. It would be highly unlikely that someone with Pratt's astronomical interests could have missed it. Pratt's own law of planetary rotation had some innovative aspects but was not original enough to justify the absence of Kirkwood's name in his article. He made no mention of Kirkwood or any other contemporary astronomer in his announcement except Sir John Herschel, F. G. W. Struve, and Urbain Leverrier, from whose work he obtained the most current data on planetary density and rotational periods with which to test his law.

It can be argued that part of Pratt's motivation in reissuing Kirkwood's Analogy in new terms was to break the link between the discovery and the nebular hypothesis. The nebular hypothesis of the French scientist Pierre Simon de Laplace posited that the planets of the solar system were formed by natural chemical and physical processes. Laplace argued that when the original nebular atmosphere of the sun—which reached the edge of the solar system—began to condense into the star we now know, it left behind spinning rings of matter that eventually condensed into planets. This hypothesis—which contained some naturalistic-materialistic assumptions—was viewed by many in the early nineteenth century as removing God from the creative enterprise and was opposed by many who had problems with this. Although Orson Pratt was a materialist, he took great pains to distinguish

Mormon materialism (which was teleological) from the materialism of Erasmus Darwin and Joseph Priestley (which was naturalistic). The naturalistic character of the nebular hypothesis was contrary to Pratt's contention that the Holy Spirit was an active participant in the formation of the heavenly bodies.

Kirkwood's law of planetary rotation would have been anathema to Pratt because it was derived directly from the nebular hypothesis in that the "sphere of attraction" was a way of measuring the original nebular ring or rings that condensed to form particular planets. The "Keplerian" magnitude of Kirkwood's discovery based on Laplace's idea had actually breathed new life into the nebular hypothesis in America, where it had been falling into disfavor because of mounting contrary evidence. Pratt's reformulation was therefore timely and practical. He removed the nebular hypothesis from the law by eliminating the "sphere of attraction" related to the original nebular ring and replaced it with an argument about density. He seemingly kept the "beautiful law," removed the naturalistic dross, and presented it as his own discovery within Mormon circles—and for Mormon theological reasons.

Pratt likely took not only the idea for the law from Kirkwood but the accompanying appellation as well. After Kirkwood published his analogy, he was christened the "new Kepler" by some of the foremost scientists in America. Orson Pratt was also called a latter-day Kepler, but in his case the appellation was self-proclaimed. He considered his own discovery of the "Law of Planetary Rotation" to be as important as Kepler's, and, just as Kepler's laws were foundational to the formulation of Newton's "great" law of universal gravitation, so Pratt saw his discovery as the likely foundation for another great law of a higher order. As Pratt himself wrote in 1855:

> This remarkable law, connecting the periods of rotation with the masses and diameters of the planets, appears to point to some more original law of a higher order of generalization. Such was the case in regard to Kepler's law connecting the orbital periods of the heavenly bodies with their distances from their respective centers of motion. Newton demonstrated Kepler's law to be a necessary result of the more general law of universal gravitation.
>
> Providence may raise up a Newton in our day who shall disclose to us the reason why the cube roots of the densities of the planets are as the square roots of their periods of rotation.

These remarks suggest that Pratt had someone in mind to wear the mantle of the latter-day Newton—himself. He left no doubt about this as he concluded, "I intend, in some future communication, to present an hypothesis which will, if I am not mistaken, account for this curious law obtaining in the solar system."[50]

Pratt fulfilled his intentions but probably much later than he had planned. It was not until 1879, twenty-four years after the announcement of his "Law of Planetary Rotation," that he finally published his second "great discovery," the *Key to the Universe, or a New Theory of Its Mechanism*. Although this work was published after the pre–Civil War period on which I am focusing, it embodied the same philosophical, theological, and scientific arguments that Pratt used in his early days and showed that Pratt changed very little in these respects in the intervening years.

The title of this publication was only slightly more grandiose than the content of the work. The hundred-page treatise was a presentation of a new and, in some respects, creative theory concerning the mechanism by which the heavenly bodies moved. It was an honest attempt to solve some of the most difficult conceptual problems facing astronomical theorists in Pratt's day. In the preface, Pratt set forth a set of nine questions that needed to be addressed by astronomical science, and he lamented that current theories, especially Laplace's nebular hypothesis, had been unable to answer some of them satisfactorily. Pratt thus saw a need for a new theoretical model of celestial mechanics and announced that "as none have recently volunteered their services in this great enterprise, the author, unaided and alone, has launched his humble barque upon this great unexplored ocean, with a compass of his own invention."[51]

The theory that Orson Pratt set forth to solve the problems that bedeviled the astronomers of the period was developed from two initial postulates. The first postulate, as summarized by Donald Skabelund, was that "the universe is pervaded by an ether which exhibits the properties of gross matter, including gravitation and resistance; this ether is not a plenum, but is atomistic; being ponderous it collects with increased density about massive bodies."[52] This idea was not very different from cosmological constructions of the day. Although soon after Pratt published his work leading theorists were beginning to see the ether as, in the words of Sir Edmund Whittaker, "an immaterial medium, *sui generis,* not composed of identifiable elements having definite locations in absolute space," the nature of the ether was still far from settled in 1879.[53] Meanwhile, the second postulate stated, again in the words of Skabelund, that "gravity is not propagated instantaneously, but with the velocity of light, and, as with light, motion relative to its source gives rise to an aberration of the gravitational force, which results in a component of force in the direction of motion."[54]

KEY TO THE UNIVERSE,

OR A

NEW THEORY OF ITS MECHANISM.

FOUNDED UPON A

I. CONTINUOUS ORBITAL PROPULSION, ARISING FROM THE VELO-CITY OF GRAVITY AND ITS CONSEQUENT ABERRATIONS;

II. RESISTING ETHEREAL MEDIUM OF VARIABLE DENSITY.

WITH

MATHEMATICAL DEMONSTRATIONS AND TABLES.

BY

ORSON PRATT, SEN.

SECOND EDITION,
FROM THE FIRST EUROPEAN EDITION.

PUBLISHED BY THE AUTHOR, AND FOR SALE AT THE HISTORIAN'S OFFICE, SALT LAKE CITY, UTAH TERRITORY.

Title page of Orson Pratt's "scientific" magnum opus, which offered a modification of Newton's celestial mechanics and a defense of the materiality of "ethereal substance."

This second postulate contained what may be Orson Pratt's most original scientific idea—that "gravity is not propagated instantaneously, but with the velocity of light." Skabelund wrote in 1965, "I can find no indications of this idea being anyone's but his own."[55] No historians of science have thus far dredged up a theorist in the latter half of the nineteenth century who considered gravitational force anything other than an instantaneous phenomenon or at least a force that was propagated at a speed many times greater than light. Although there was certainly no contact or influence involved, the first scientist other than Pratt to employ this idea was none other than Albert Einstein, who set it up as one of the pillars of his special theory of relativity in 1905. In *Key to the Universe,* Pratt attempted to demonstrate mathematically that because gravity was propagated at a finite speed, there must be an accelerating force generated by the sun that pulled the planets along their orbital paths.

Given these two postulates, the theory was simple. Pratt argued that the regular and predictable motion of the planets in our solar system, or in any solar system, was due to the perfect balance between the resisting force of the ether through which a planet must travel and the propelling force generated by the geometry of the gravitational effect of the sun on the planets. This was Pratt's key to the universe. In his view, simple extrapolations from this model offered satisfactory answers to the astronomical mysteries that challenged him. Probably more important for Pratt was the notion that this propulsion-resistance equilibrium ensured perfect and invariable planetary orbits *forever* in accordance with eternal and invariable laws of force.

It is true that the apostle's grand attempt to settle once and for all the questions of celestial mechanics did fall short. If Pratt's *Key to the Universe* had been disseminated widely, it would have been ignored by his contemporaries mainly because it was not "theoretically current," as Skabelund put it.[56] His work showed that he was not familiar with the ether drag experiments of Hippolyte Fizeau and Martin Hoek, did not take energy conservation into account, did not employ calculus, had an "insufficient grasp of fundamental dynamical principles," and, as William J. Christensen observed, made some "unwarranted simplifying assumptions."[57]

Although his scientific arguments lacked the technical substance to be taken seriously in contemporary scientific circles, it is clear that the apostle wanted his work to stand on scientific merit alone and not to be dismissed by the gentiles as a Mormon apologetic tract. Nowhere in *Key to the Universe* did he state that one of his objectives was to show that modern cosmological thought, if properly construed, was in perfect harmony with the Mormon worldview. Nor did he ever mention Joseph Smith or quote his writings—except for a single benign phrase from the Doctrine and Covenants on the frontispiece, the source of which he does not cite. The only religious reference—a brief paean to the "Great Supreme Architect" and the "Great Creator" in the last few pages—carries no Mormon distinctives and could have been written by any theist or deist in North America. Pratt thus succeeded in setting forth his work in an unobtrusive scientific manner, even though, ironically, few gentiles ever saw it.

Although Pratt wrote *Key to the Universe* as a testable theory in strictly scientific terms, the work actually meant much more for its author. Pratt prevailed in setting forth a celestial mechanics that was remarkably consistent with what he and other Mormons considered to be the revealed truth of God. He wrote in his preface that one of his main objectives was to save Newton's "grand discovery" by vindicating the universality of Newton's law of gravity. He wanted to "rescue it from the environed limits sought to be thrown around it: and to give it that unlimited freedom of action, which the distinguished name 'UNIVERSAL,' so appropriately and definitely imports."[58] Pratt tried to do this by extending the law of gravity to the "immense ocean of ethereal substance."[59] In the process, Pratt accomplished two things that were of tremendous value to the Mormon worldview. First, he made the ether unmistakably material by endowing it with inertial properties, thus bringing ether theory in line with the proclamation of Joseph Smith that there was no such thing as immaterial matter. Second, he made Newton's law unmistakably universal, applying it to both gross matter and the more rarefied ethereal matter and thus vindicating Joseph Smith's insistence on the universal applicability of natural law.[60] Pratt did not argue in *Key to the Universe* for a Mormon position, but the presuppositions from which he launched his argument were based on vintage early Mormon ideas. Moreover, the conclusions he reached were, in his mind, no less than scientific confirmations of the prophet's words.

As he did with the "Law of Planetary Rotation," Pratt wrote the *Key to the Universe* as though his new model was born in conceptual isolation, as if he alone sought the truth about the workings of the universe. And as he did with his "Law of Planetary Rotation," he described the revolutionary character of his scientific discovery in terms that could just as easily describe the coming forth of Joseph Smith and the Latter-day Gospel:

> Advanced research, oftentimes, calls for an alteration of theories, and sometimes for an entire renunciation of them. A theory shown to be

insufficient or untrue in may respects, should not be cherished and upheld, because of its antiquity, or its general popularity, or because there is no other known theory more in accordance with existing phenomena. First, free the mind from error, and it will be better prepared for new fields of research, and to decide as to the truth or falsity of any new theories which may be propounded.[61]

In this respect, Pratt's *Key to the Universe* fits firmly into the Mormon restorationist theme. In the same way that Joseph Smith had restored the true religion of Christ that had been lost since the first century, so Pratt was restoring a proper view of the workings of the cosmos. Although *Key to the Universe* contained, for the most part, concepts that were being discussed in the scientific circles of the period, it did set forth some new ideas and at least one that might be considered startlingly ahead of its time. What is most important was that Orson Pratt and the Mormons themselves considered it a revolutionary work, *the* key to the universe, hidden, like the gold plates of Cumorah, until the fullness of time.

Orson Pratt's *Key to the Universe* and his "Law of Planetary Rotation" were just two of the works that earned him a legendary status as a scientist and mathematician among the Utah Mormons. The years between these two publications, from 1855 to 1879, were by no means unproductive. In 1866, he wrote a mathematics textbook entitled *New and Easy Method of Solution of the Cubic and Biquadratic Equations*. Although—as in the case of "Law of Planetary Rotation" and *Key to the Universe*—there were some legends floating about in Mormon communities concerning the international impact of his scientific and mathematical work, there was no evidence that Pratt's *New and Easy Method* was known outside of Mormon circles.[62] During these years, Pratt also finished a textbook manuscript on differential calculus that was never published, started one on determinants, and had plans for writing one on integral calculus.

The last thesis that Pratt published was issued on May 6, 1879, just two months after *Key to the Universe*. Unlike *Key to the Universe*, however, this little treatise, printed in the Mormon periodical the *Latter-day Saints' Millennial Star* was, for Pratt, an unabashed "scientific" apologetic for the truth of Mormonism. While on his last missionary sojourn in Great Britain, Pratt became caught up in a wave of fascination with Egyptian pyramids. A Scottish astronomer named Charles Piazzi Smyth helped generate Pratt's interest in 1864 with his book *Our Inheritance in the Great Pyramid*, in which he argued that the spatial dimensions of the Great Pyramid of Cheops, when properly measured, provided a time-line of divine history.[63] Pratt likely read

Smyth's "much enlarged" third edition, published in London in 1877, with enthusiasm. Given Pratt's love of geometry and the prominent role that Egyptian language and artifacts played in Mormon revelation, Piazzi's work must have been a natural fit. Pratt wrote that he immediately brought the "penetrating and remarkably clear and concentrative power of his mind to bear upon the subject."[64] After digesting Smyth's book, Pratt focused on one of the as yet unresolved structural components inside the "Great Pyramid," a "Great Step" that ran the length of the "Grand Gallery." About his discovery, Pratt recounted:

> While in London, some time last March, only a few weeks since, in the night time, he [Pratt] was suddenly struck, as if by inspiration, with the idea that he had found the solution to the problem. . . . Elder Pratt was tempted, then and there, to arise in the night, make the necessary calculations and satisfy his mind; but he concluded to delay till morning. Judge of his surprise and pleasure, when, on making the line from the upper frontal edge of the Step perpendicular with the inclined floor of the Gallery, and continuing the measurement of the Gallery to that point, he found it demonstrated, by plain figures, that it reached the Pyramid date of April 6th, 1830, the exact day on which the Church and Kingdom of God was organized, by the revelation and commandment of the Most High, at Fayette, Seneca County, New York, U.S.A.[65]

By similar computations, Pratt also discovered another important date, this one still to come. He thought the year 1891 corresponded to a prophecy from Joseph Smith and was convinced that it would be a time of "momentous occurrences" or "some remarkable phase of history," perhaps even the Lord's return.[66] Piazzi Smyth, who believed that God had directed the construction of the Great Pyramid as a testimony to later generations, had already determined the dates of some of the great biblical events based on his own measurements of the Great Pyramid. Pratt accepted Smyth's time-line but found that Smyth's system, like salvation history, was incomplete without the latter-day religious events ushered in by Joseph Smith. With Pratt's addition, the time-line was complete.

Pratt viewed the Great Pyramid in exactly the same way that he viewed the universe at large. Both were constructed under the direction of God, and both not only showed God's general handiwork but also testified to the truth of the Mormon worldview. In a passage that stands as a good example of the apostle's perception of both the Great Pyramid and the relationship between religion and science, Pratt concluded:

[The Great Pyramid] is like a book in stone, on which is written the great events of the history of this earth and its people. The historical epochs of the past are indicated with scientific clearness, and now it is demonstrated, by the researches and mathematical deductions of Prof. Pratt, aided by the inspiration of the Mighty God, that it also stands as an incontestable evidence of the divine authenticity of the Church of Jesus Christ of Latter-day Saints.

It stands as a marvelous proof of the existing harmony between the exact sciences and true religion, for in that wonderful structure there is a beautiful blending of the two. It is one of the wonders of the age, and the great truths it embodies should call forth praise and thanksgiving from the righteous to Him by whose wisdom and power the construction of the Great Pyramid was evidently directed.[67]

The evidence from the Great Pyramid was just one more piece of evidence in what Orson Pratt considered the "endless train of circumstances—all harmonizing—all combining—all concentrating as it were into one focus." That focus was the irresistible truth that it was impossible for the careful scientific investigator "to reject the divinity of Joseph Smith's mission."[68]

Early Mormon Cosmology

What I am calling the village Enlightenment may have had a stronger grip on the first generation of Mormons than on other sects of that period by necessity. Joseph Smith and the Mormons had thrown down the gauntlet with their claim that true Christianity had been lost for nearly all of its eighteen hundred years. Joseph Smith claimed a revelation from Jesus Christ himself that "all their creeds were an abomination in his sight; that those professors were all corrupt. . . . They teach for doctrine the commandments of men."[69] With those kinds of challenges being offered to the religious mainstream, the Mormons were in no position to be unsure or uncertain that they had a new word from God. The seeking out of certainty and assurance is central to the village Enlightenment scheme.

The most prominent village figure, Orson Pratt, led the charge in almost all of his writings. To him, a stronger message from a more authoritative source seemed inconceivable. Pratt carried the attack forward in all of his written work but most directly in his tract *Divine Authority,* in which he wrote that "a message of simple truth, when sent from God—when published by divine authority, through divinely inspired men, penetrates the mind like a sharp two-edged sword, and cuts asunder the deeply-rooted prejudices, the iron-bound sinews of ancient error and tradition, made sacred by age and rendered popular by human wisdom. . . . Opinions, creeds invented by uninspired men, and doctrines originated in schools of divinity, all vanish like the morning dew—all sink into insignificance when compared with a message direct from heaven."[70] With little regard for the self-refuting nature of the argument—after all, the Mormon prophet and his apostles were also "humans" who held "opinions"—Pratt's tract provided several generations of Mormons an apologetic against any religious thought preceding Joseph Smith. So important was Pratt's apologetic material that Edward Tullidge interrupted his biography of Joseph Smith by inserting an entire chapter devoted to Pratt and his brother because "much of the integrity of Mormonism rests with the Pratts."[71]

To defend Joseph Smith's revelations, Pratt thought it best to show how they made better sense of the cosmos than any other system did. Smith's inspired words concerning the materialistic nature of the cosmos were especially important to Pratt. Although he may have believed it, Pratt never made the case that revelation in and of itself could settle any question simply because it was a message from an omniscient being. The truth of the revealed message had to match other obvious truths. For instance, regarding the revealed truths of the Book of Mormon, he wrote that "if we compare the historical, prophetical, and doctrinal parts of the Book of Mormon, with the great truths of science and nature, we find no contradictions—no absurdities—nothing unreasonable. The most perfect harmony, therefore exists between the great truths revealed in the Book of Mormon, and all other known truths, whether religious, historical, or scientific."[72] In the specific case of the doctrine of materialism, he stated, "Our belief . . . in this doctrine, is founded, not on any modern supernatural revelation . . . but on reason and common sense. The doctrine of immaterialism, in our estimation, is false, and in the highest degree absurd, and unworthy the belief of any true Christian philosopher."[73] In context, this passage is not a denial of revelation but an argument that one need not appeal to revelation for the truth of something considered commonsensical or self-evident. Something just does not come from nothing. Thinking otherwise opposed sound reasoning and human experience. Pratt was also convinced that the concept of immaterial substance was a logical absurdity. Immateriality, for the Mormons, equaled nonexistence. To hold to the position that God was an immaterial or disembodied being was atheistic because such a god could not exist:

> There are two classes of Atheists in the world. One class denies the existence of God in the most positive language: the other denies his existence in dura-

tion or space. One says, "There is no God;" the other says, "God is not *here* or *there,* any more than he exists *now* and *then.*" The infidel says, There is no such substance as God. The Immaterialist says, There is such a substance as God, but it is "*without Parts.*" . . . Therefore, the immaterialist is a religious Atheist; he only differs from the other classes of Atheists, by clothing an indivisible unextended NOTHING with the powers of god.[74]

That said, the materialism that Pratt articulated first appeared tangentially. In a four-part tract series entitled *The Kingdom of God,* Pratt explicated a Mormon theory of government, arguing for the theocratic rule of God through the agency of the Holy Spirit working through world leaders. To set the stage for his theocratic arguments, Pratt made the case for God's materiality. He maintained that "God the Great King" had to exist and to be able to communicate in order to rule. A disembodied god neither existed nor communicated and, therefore, certainly could not rule.[75]

First published and circulated in the British Isles, Pratt's main thesis concerning theocratic governance apparently received no response, but his supporting thesis concerning materialist theology drew significant negative attention. Soon after *The Kingdom of God* was issued, a British theologian from Liverpool, T. W. P. Taylder, responded with a well-researched, forty-page critique. Taylder quoted the Bible, classical philosophers, and the best thinkers in the commonsense school of philosophy to demonstrate that Pratt and the Mormons were "Irrational, opposed to True Philosophy," "Unscriptural and Anti-scriptural," and "Of no Utility to Man, and Derogatory to God."[76] Taylder's rejoinder is all but forgotten, but Orson Pratt's subsequent response, *Absurdities of Immaterialism,* was his finest essay and perhaps the most sophisticated philosophical defense of Mormon materialism in the nineteenth century. It was, however, not the first. Eight years before Pratt's *Kingdom of God* was published, his brother explained the distinctive Mormon doctrine of materialism to the public. Parley Pratt's essay "A Treatise on the Regeneration and Eternal Duration of Matter" sketched some of the radical themes that his brother later argued more systematically and in greater detail.[77] Peter Crawley maintained that "'The Regeneration and Eternal Duration of Matter' . . . was the first writing to deal with the truly distinguishing doctrines of Mormonism." He added that articles written by Sidney Rigdon and other Mormons up to that point "could just as well have been published in the magazine of any Christian denomination."[78]

Orson Pratt was therefore not creating something out of nothing when he wrote his response to Taylder's attacks. He had received a certain amount of grist for his philosophical mill directly from his brother, but the response to Taylder was Pratt's own work. Parley's published responses to Mormon critics were much more rhetorical, literary, and emotional.[79] *Absurdities of Immaterialism,* in a style characteristic of Orson, plodded systematically, responding point by point to Taylder's attack and carefully citing technical scientific and philosophical works, which Parley Pratt's writings rarely did.

In responding to Taylder, Orson Pratt was forced to refine and sharpen the arguments for Mormon doctrine in much the same way that the early Christians were forced to refine and sharpen their ideas when responding to "heretics." For instance, by offering his own definition of material and immaterial substances, Taylder forced Pratt to do the same. Taylder wrote that "an *immaterial substance* is merely this, that something exists which is *not matter* and is evidently distinct from matter, which is *not dependent* on matter for its existence, and which possesses properties and qualities *entirely different* from those possessed by matter." Pratt found this definition to be ambiguous and problematic and responded with his own: "The term *matter* should be given to all substances which possess *any* properties in common, however wide they may differ in other respects. A substance to be *immaterial* must possess NO properties or qualities in common with matter. All its qualities must be entirely *distinct* and *different.*"[80] Pratt's definition was much tighter than Taylder's and left the "immaterialists" with a case impossible to prove. Taylder argued that the properties or qualities should be different; Pratt argued that they all must be absolutely distinct.

The centerpiece of Taylder's argument against "mormo-materialism" was that "mind thinks, matter cannot think. It is the *existence* of this *thinking principle* which clearly *proves* the *immateriality* of the *mind* or *spirit.*" Pratt dismissed Taylder's best argument by accusing him of "*petitio principii.*" Taylder had demonstrated nothing, Pratt maintained; he had only assumed what he wanted to prove.[81] Unfortunately, Pratt was not able to offer much of a demonstration for his "self-evident" position either.

Part of the problem in this exchange of "pamphlets" was that the two writers were using philosophical terms in different ways. Taylder, for example, used the term *substance* to refer to that which was material or immaterial. In so doing, he was not in the least out of line with its usage in the history of philosophy. Pratt, however, thought that using the term *substance* in anything other than a materialistic sense was a logical absurdity. He reasoned that only material things existed; if a substance was immaterial, it simply did not exist. Pratt therefore found Taylder's "immaterial substance" to be an oxymoron.[82]

At one remarkable point in his response to Taylder, Pratt, without warning, shifted gears and admitted that the argument was really not a matter of "demonstration" after all but a battle over definitions and first principles:

> There are many truths which may be called FIRST TRUTHS, or self-evident truths, which cannot be demonstrated, because there are no truths of a simpler nature that can be adduced to establish them. Such truths are the foundation of all reasoning. They must be admitted without demonstration, because they are self-evident. That space and duration are essential conditions to the existence of all substance, may be denominated a self-evident truth; if so, it is useless to undertake to prove it. And in this case, the foregoing need not be considered a demonstration, but merely different forms of expression representing the same self-evident truth.[83]

Curiously, this paragraph appears almost halfway through the text. Its import is startling, though, for it effectively negates much of the first half of Pratt's treatise. Everything he had written up to that point was couched in the terminology of proof and demonstration. It was as if he had gotten to the middle of his manifesto before he realized he might be engaged in a fallacy: offering reasons for that which was foundational to all reason.

Nevertheless, Pratt's work had an impact on the development and defense of Mormon doctrine, not because it offered any evidence for a "self-evident" first principle—which Pratt finally realized was an irrational notion—but because it accomplished two things. First, it distinguished between Mormon materialism and the mechanical materialism of Joseph Priestley and Erasmus Darwin—both of whom were to orthodox Christians symbols of rebellion against God and true religion. Second, it was the first Mormon attempt to show not just that the concept of "spiritual matter" was true because it was revealed but also that its truth better explained the working of the cosmos.

That Taylder did not fully understand the Mormon concept of materialism was obvious when he attempted to lump Orson Pratt with Joseph Priestley and Erasmus Darwin. Taylder should not be faulted for this, however, because Pratt's tract *The Kingdom of God,* to which Taylder was responding, did not explicate the finer points. Taylder's critique was a common counterargument orthodox theologians used against mechanical materialism.[84] To taint Pratt by comparing him with the likes of Priestley and Darwin, Taylder argued that materialism ultimately "*destroys man's accountability to God*" because it reduces ideas to things, thinking to mechanism, and human actions to "irresistible necessity."[85] Taylder's critique was powerful, but he unwittingly missed the mark. The Mormon materialism that Pratt was articulating and defending was likely unfamiliar to Taylder. Pratt attempted to enlighten Taylder and to set the record straight about the distinctions. Matter, according to Mormon revelation, was "intelligent thinking substance: it can originate its own motions, and act according to its own will, independently of the laws of mechanism: hence, a perfect freedom characterizes all its movements. Before Priestley or any other man can logically assert that 'mechanism is the undoubted consequence of materialism,' he must first prove that matter cannot think, and will, and move, or, in other words, he must prove that mind is not matter."[86]

For Pratt, conceiving of matter as an "intelligent thinking" substance solved problems that were perennial to radical materialism. He answered Taylder's most pointed charge that materialism "destroys man's accountability to God" by asserting that mind or spirit was an intelligent substance and was not dependent—as Erasmus Darwin argued—on such mechanical actions as "contractions, motions, or configurations" of organic fibers.[87] The material substance called spirit or mind had the same qualities that the immaterialist attributed to spirit or mind. It was not mechanical in the sense of mindlessness, but rather it "feels, thinks, reasons, and remembers" and therefore did not remove any accountability to God.[88]

In addition to distinguishing between Mormon and other brands of materialism, Pratt offered several arguments to demonstrate that there was nothing unreasonable about the idea of spiritual matter. He argued that the cosmos made far more sense when spiritual matter was recognized as a component of the material stuff of the universe. Taylder himself raised an important issue that had to be explained by Pratt: "How can *spiritual* matter occupy the same space with the matter of which the body consists?"[89] This was not a trifling question since both men appealed to Newton's laws of motion and to his concept of matter as "solid, massy, hard, impenetrable, moveable particles" to validate certain points in their arguments. Pratt stated categorically "that [spiritual matter] cannot occupy the same identical space with other matter for this is in all cases an absolute impossibility." He successfully answered the question without violating Newton's laws, however, by maintaining that "all substances are porous" and that "there is room for the material spirit to exist in close connexion with its component parts, and this too without infringing upon the impenetrability of substances."[90] He insisted that "like heat or electricity . . . each refined particle of the spirit can . . . pass between the fleshly particles; and thus the whole body of spiritual particles can liberate themselves; and by their own self-moving powers and free will, can still preserve and maintain their own organization."[91]

Pratt argued that mind or spirit behaved like matter in that it could accompany the body and thus move from place to place. He thought, too, that spirit was capable of condensation, which he said was "evident from the fact of their occupying the small bodies of infants." The ability of spirits to condense also explained how a legion of devils could inhabit one man.[92]

Material spirit solved still another perennial problem that the immaterialist could not resolve. Pratt seemed to delight in the fact that the Mormons had the answer to an enduring philosophical quandary. "Philosophers have endeavored to invent numberless hypotheses to account for the action of matter on mind, which they have assumed to be immaterial." The problem was solved because, for the Mormons, it disappeared. There was no conceptual snag in the idea that gross matter could interact with spiritual matter because they both resided in the universe of extension and duration. Mind and matter could interact freely because there was no ultimate distinction between the two. Both were equal players in Newton's universe. For Pratt, traditional solutions to the problem of the interaction of mind (or spirit) and matter were simply nonsensical: "For extended substances with parts to act upon unextended substances is without a parallel, and inconceivably absurd. Indeed, there could be no action at all. . . . To talk about matter affecting that which is inextended and without parts, is to talk about matter affecting nothing."[93]

In the midst of this thoroughgoing commitment to materialism, the Mormons—and, as we shall see, such spiritualists as Robert Hare and the mental healer Phineas Parkhurst Quimby—were able to keep the explanatory benefits of Cartesian mind-body dualism.[94] Although gross matter and spiritual matter were both material substances, they were different enough— gross matter being less refined and less intelligent than the more exalted spiritual matter—to exhibit a functional dualism. Spirits could therefore leave the body at death. Sensation, emotion, intelligence, and will, although not absent from gross matter, were greater in spiritual matter, thus explaining the marked difference between a stone, which contained little spiritual matter, and a human being, who embodied much more.[95]

Pratt probably had discerned that the notion of intelligent, self-moving, willful matter might lead one to believe that materiality was in some sense not really the most fundamental philosophical notion for the Mormons. In the "Essence of Substances," a section of *Absurdities of Immaterialism* that seems to be a late insertion or a digression from his primary line of thought, he addressed the issue. "Instead of being entirely ignorant on the subject, as modern philosophers assert," wrote Pratt, "it is directly the opposite; we know the essence of all substances." He argued that this essence was "solidity":

> We are as certain that the ultimate atoms of all substances are solid, as we are that they exist. What we mean by solidity is, that all substances completely fill a certain amount of space, and it is impossible for them ever to fill a greater or less amount of space. . . . Solidity is universally supposed to be a property of atoms, but this is an error. Solidity is not a property, but only another name for the essence. A property must be a property of something; but solidity is not a property of *anything*—it is the essence itself—the thing that exists, aside from all properties and powers.

Concerning the powers of intelligence, emotions, and sensation associated with these primary particles, he reasoned that "every feeling or thought is the feeling or thought of solids. . . . Solidity, then, is the essence to which all qualities belong—taste, smell, colour, weight, &c., are the affections of solids."[96] Pratt clearly thought that Mormon ideas had forever solved another one of the perennial philosophical conundrums, the essence of substance. His argument, however, was again based on the "commonsense" notion that the concept of "immaterial substance" was an absurdity. Solidity was therefore the essence, not a property, of everything that existed. Pratt did not really provide an argument to solve the problem; he simply expounded the position that he considered self-evident fact.

Pratt answered the important "what" question about the essence of matter by proclaiming it to be "solidity." But the "how" questions still loomed large. For instance, how could the seemingly inert, lifeless matter of the body think, emote, will, and sense? Pratt's answer was that the solid particles have these "qualities" innately. When these particles gather to form the material body, or material spirit, the mental qualities gather as well. Instead of solving the mind-body problem by postulating "intelligent particles," Pratt only succeeded in removing the problem to another, more fundamental level. The issue for Pratt then became the mind-*particle* problem. He never addressed the question of how these particulate solids could exhibit mental qualities.[97] Common sense, self-evidence, and revelation appear to have provided him with enough justification.

Regardless of whether the idea was philosophically sound, living, solid, self-moving, particulate matter was the other "key" to Orson Pratt's universe and his Mormon cosmology. He was one of the few Mormons who ever attempted to articulate a metaphysics for Mormon theology. Although he was influential in this regard, few Saints followed his lead in any formal sense.[98]

More than that, Pratt's attempt to construct a set of foundational ideas was not just an intellectual exercise but also a missionary endeavor, as Pratt's biographer, Breck England, has argued.[99] It is likely that from Pratt's point of view nothing could be superior to a system that brought together Joseph Smith and Isaac Newton in one harmonious conceptual package. By any measure, the main task in his writings that followed *Absurdities of Immaterialism*—such as *Great First Cause, The Holy Spirit,* and portions of his periodical, the *Seer*—was to do just that.[100] The need for a consistent natural and revelational theology was great. Not only did the Mormons have a bevy of questions that cried for answers, but some of the basic conceptual problems of the Newtonian system had not been solved satisfactorily even though great minds had worked on them for well over a hundred years. For Pratt, addressing unanswered problems within Newtonianism was as important as addressing theological problems. To Pratt, they were one and the same. Newton may have set Pratt's research agenda in "Query 28" of *Opticks*—a passage familiar to Pratt—in which Newton raised a full range of problematic issues that faced his system. Pratt may have thought Newton was offering a challenge directly to him.[101]

Pratt was certain that the answers to Newtonian questions were contained in the first principles Joseph Smith reintroduced to the world. Newton was simply looking at the universe through the wrong glasses. His mathematical formulations were correct, but his interpretation was wrong. Pratt felt that he was called to right it because he was in possession of the lenses of a new philosophy.

Orson Pratt's adjustments to Newton were first presented in 1851 with the publication of the *Great First Cause.* Newton had seen his own work in natural philosophy as drawing humanity ever closer to a knowledge of the First Cause—that intelligent, powerful creator who remained independent from his creation. Pratt, however, viewed the First Cause as indistinguishable from the universe. The "Great First Cause" was identical with the "pre-existent, intelligent, powerful, and eternal particles of substance," which provided the self-moving force of the universe.[102] With this basic ontological construction, Pratt was prepared to address all the unanswered issues that Newton raised, ranging from the motion of comets and the beauty of animals to the design of the eye and the connection between will and bodily motion. Pratt considered intelligent, self-moving, willful, solid, material particles the key to producing the long-sought grand unified scheme of religious, scientific, and philosophical thought.

In his sixteen-page pamphlet on the Cause, Pratt argued that although Newton's laws were mathematically correct and worthy of great admiration, his philosophy led him down the wrong path. Newton conceived of matter as a passive particulate substance acting and acted upon by abstract forces.

Pratt viewed force as an inherent quality of matter by which individual particles *willed* to maintain or alter their *own* state of motion. Newton's true mathematical description of the law of universal gravitation was thus reconceptualized as the "Self-moving Theory," in which particles intelligently willed to "approach" one another instead of being passively "attracted" together:

> Those particles of this self-moving substance which constitute the worlds and which are generally known under the name of *ponderable* substances, do not act at random, but act systematically and intelligently according to the following law:—*Every particle of this kind has a tendency to approach every other particle of the same kind with a force which varies inversely as the square of the distance.* All the phenomena of universal gravitation can be far more simply explained by this law of *self-moving* particles, than by assuming the absurd hypothesis of *attracting* particles.[103]

If one accepted Pratt's basic premise about the nature of matter—which was no small *if,* since it required a fundamental paradigm shift on the order of religious conversion—it actually closed some troubling conceptual loopholes in Newtonianism. For instance, Pratt asked if it would not "be infinitely more simple for a particle to move itself . . . than to move a universe of substance towards itself" and how "can a substance which cannot move itself, move other substances which exist at a distance?"[104]

Pratt thought his theory not only better fit the principle of parsimony in explanation but also forthrightly answered the perennial difficulty with Newton's theory: action at a distance. Few hobgoblins were more frightening to such a thoroughgoing materialist as Pratt than the prospect that matter acted on matter without direct physical contact, for such action implied some immaterial intermediary. Unfortunately for him, virtually inexplicable actions at a distance were at the heart of Newtonianism. A plausible explanation of the mechanism of the force by which material bodies attracted one another was one of the single greatest scientific prizes of Pratt's era. Some of the greatest scientific minds of the day were working on solutions. The professional scientists, however, were seeking answers in a totally different direction. As the science historian Erich Robert Paul pointed out, because they did not have any religious commitment to a materialist philosophy, such scientists as Thomas Young (wave theory of light), Hans Oersted (electric-magnetic connections), and Michael Faraday (electromagnetic induction) began to use a less-than-materialist "field theory" to achieve impressive scientific results. By the 1860s and 1870s, James Clerke Maxwell was using mathematical constructions of field theory to unify phenomena of electricity, magnetism, and light. His radical field theory, in Paul's words, "posited the existence of nonmaterial fields of force that exist in space even where there is no matter and through and by which natural phenomena were thought to be manifested."[105] There is no evidence that Pratt kept up with developments in field theory, but it probably would have made little difference.[106] His answer to the problem of action at a distance cut out all competitors. The argument that matter moved of its own volition, he contended, was simpler, more beautiful, and therefore more reasonable than the others. Just as in his approach to the mind-body problem, he solved the problem of action at a distance by defining it out of existence. Particles of matter did not attract other particles of matter across empty space by mysterious invisible forces for the simple reason that "no substance can act where it is not present."[107] Rather, quantifiable gravitational phenomena were the result of intelligent particles choosing to follow basic behavioral laws.

From the age of Newton to the time of Einstein, the problem of action at a distance was most often approached utilizing one or another theories of universal ether that could bridge the gap between material bodies, thereby providing a conduit for interaction. Ironically, although Orson Pratt had solved to his own satisfaction the action-at-a-distance problem without reference to ether, he still held tenaciously to ether theory because it was useful in solving a variety of other scientific, philosophical, and theological problems. A "resisting ethereal medium" was not only central to his scientific conclusions in *Key to the Universe* but also a "key" to his theological work. Although he rarely used the term *ether* outside his scientific work, he considered the idea divine. For Pratt, the microscopic intelligent particles could combine in etherlike aggregates to make up something macrocosmically grand and decidedly theological: "All the organizations of worlds, of minerals, of vegetables, of animals, of men, of angels, of spirits, and of the spiritual personages of the Father, of the Son, and of the Holy Ghost, must if organized at all, have been the result of the self combination and unions of the pre-existent, intelligent, powerful, and eternal particles of substance. These eternal Forces and Powers are the Great First Causes of all things and events that have had a beginning." Identifying and describing the individual particles that made up the universe was just one side of the story. Collectively the particles became for Pratt a holy "fluid," a divine ether that had the potential to be not just the explanatory god of the gaps but the literal life force for all things in existence.[108]

Although everything was material in the Mormon universe, not all materials were equal. To understand Pratt's theological cosmology, one must understand his distinctions between materials. Pratt's system posited three basic types of matter. The first and least exalted of these was gross matter—the matter that made up the tangible cosmos. Like all matter, it existed from eternity, never having been created and incapable of being destroyed. Although material particles were not able to change their individual physical form, collectively they could reorganize to bring about physical changes of cosmic proportion. Small-scale chemical reactions, too, were the result of a breakdown and rearrangement of gross material particles. Since no matter was ever created or destroyed, the creation of anything—including the universe—was never ex nihilo. Rather, it was a large-scale reorganization of existing particles.

In its mental abilities, gross matter existed on the lowest level. It could "receive intelligence" or learn, but it was always in a remedial class "in the grand school of the universe."[109] Pratt maintained that the gross matter that made up the physical worlds, such as the earth, was capable of learning and following specified laws.[110]

The second and third types of matter in Pratt's universe were both in the category of spiritual matter, but their qualities were sufficiently different to treat them as separate substances. He called them "spirit" and "Holy Spirit." Spirit was, for Mormons, a substantial step above gross matter, and Pratt was emphatic about the distinction. For instance, when describing the difference between a human's "fleshly body" and "spiritual body," he argued that they were "entirely different things. One is a body of material flesh; the other is a body of material spirit—they are entirely different kinds of matter, as much as iron and oxygen."[111] Although there were obvious similarities—like gross matter, spirit was eternal, teachable, and solid—the differences were repeatedly punctuated. Some of these differences were differences of degree. Gross matter could learn, but spirit was far superior in "receiving intelligence" and had a full range of developed mental qualities. Pratt wrote, "It is the spiritual substance, and not the body, that sees, hears, tastes, smells, feels, thinks, enjoys, suffers, and manifests every other affection or passion characteristic of the animal creation."[112] In this respect, spirit was equivalent to mind, a term Pratt used interchangeably with it on several occasions.[113]

Every living thing also had a spirit, whether it was sentient or not. According to Pratt, there was a one-to-one correspondence between any object and its spirit in terms of shape, size, and intelligence: "Vegetable and animal life is nothing more nor less than vegetable and animal spirit. The spirit of a vegetable is in the same image and likeness of its tabernacle, and of the same magnitude, for it fills every part thereof. . . . If the spirit of an apple tree were rendered visible when separated from its natural tabernacle, it would appear in the form, likeness, and magnitude of the natural apple tree; and so it is with the spirit of every other tree, or herb, or blade of grass, its shape, its magnitude, and its appearance, resemble the natural tabernacle intended for its residence."[114]

Orson Pratt was clearly supportive of the idea that living plants had spirits, but he was hesitant in attributing spirits to material that was neither animal nor vegetable. His brother and Brigham Young were much more inclined to do so because they both strongly emphasized infinite levels of organization in the realms of both spiritual and gross matter and a direct correspondence between the two.[115] They followed the lead of Joseph Smith himself, who revealed in the Book of Moses that all things existed spiritually before they were created.[116]

Orson Pratt's penchant for logical analysis probably made him less comfortable with the idea that spirits took up residence in mineral matter in the same way that they inhabited living things. The idea was inconsistent with two of the characteristics that Mormon leaders agreed most distinguished spiritual matter from gross matter: self-motion and preexistence. Pratt was insistent about self-motion. "Here is manifested the great superiority of spiritual matter to all other matter," he wrote, "each particle has the power of self-motion."[117] However, Pratt never seems to have taken a firm stand on whether such inanimate objects as rocks had the capacity for self-motion, perhaps because of the apparent observational paradox of never seeing an individual rock move on its own yet seeing the planets—which were literally aggregates of rocks—"move themselves" according to exacting mathematical laws.

The Gods of the Gaps

The third type of matter in Pratt's universe—also a form of spiritual matter but even further refined—was called the Holy Spirit. In some respects it is not fair to lump the Holy Spirit with other types of matter, although Pratt himself did so. The Holy Spirit was "super-matter," with abilities far beyond those of ordinary matter. The Holy Spirit was a literal and figurative god of the gaps. In Pratt's world, it literally filled the gaps between other material bodies and figuratively filled the gaps in his cosmological theories.

Discussion of the concept of the third person in the Godhead was rare in the history of Mormon thought, but when the Holy Spirit did come up for discussion, it was clear that it was a doctrine in flux. One Mormon historian has commented that "the subject of the Holy Ghost has been one of the most taboo and hence least studied. Church writers have published prolifically on the operations and gifts of the Holy Ghost, but they have had little to say regarding his origin, identity, and destiny."[118] Apostle Joseph Fielding Smith encouraged the Saints to leave the subject alone. "We should have no time to enter into speculation in relation to the Holy Ghost," he wrote. "Why not leave a matter which in no way concerns us alone."[119] Ideas about the Holy Spirit or the Holy Ghost evolved over the first hundred years of Latter-day Saint (LDS) thinking.[120] In 1830, the Holy Ghost was discussed in a manner not unlike discussion in the more orthodox sectarian faiths. According to the canonical Doctrine and Covenants, "Father, Son, and Holy Ghost are one God, infinite and eternal, without end."[121] By 1835, the Holy Spirit was identified as the single mind of the Father and the Son. This was the doctrine contained in the "Lectures on Faith," a document that was printed along with the Doctrine and Covenants.

Early in 1841, however, the slow, subtle evolution that had been taking place began to advance quickly. In February of that year, Joseph Smith explicitly stated that the "Holy Ghost is a personage of spirit" who, unlike the Father and the Son, did not have a body of flesh and bones. In the same month in which he was killed in 1844, Smith announced that the Godhead was made up of three distinct personages who were three separate gods.[122] Unfortunately, this revelation was not printed publicly until 1856 and was not included in the canon until 1876. Even after the doctrine was officially included in the Doctrine and Covenants, it was still in flux because Smith's statement still had to be reconciled with other passages of LDS holy writ. The church leader George Q. Cannon was instrumental in keeping the older view contained in the "Lectures on Faith" as the primary view. But upon Cannon's death at the turn of the century, the notion that the Holy Ghost was a personage and a separate part of the Godhead was championed by such Mormon leaders as John A. Widtsoe, B. H. Roberts, and James E. Talmadge, and it became the official interpretation of the church in 1916.[123] That declaration, however, only answered one specific question: was the Holy Ghost a person and therefore a separate god? Or was it an impersonal force, the common mind of the Father and the Son? The church's decision to call the Holy Ghost a personage and a separate god raised more questions than it answered. What was the exact relationship between the Holy Ghost and the other members of the Godhead? And how did a personage of spirit, finite in size, affect the course of the heavenly bodies and the course of human events?

It was especially the problematic "how and what" questions—the questions of mechanism and metaphysics—that Joseph Fielding Smith wanted the Saints to avoid. But it was exactly those questions that most appealed to Orson Pratt, who—over a hundred years before J. F. Smith's admonition to think about something else—thought and wrote more on the topic than anyone else had or would. Pratt's work on the subject was done while the doctrine of the Holy Ghost was still ambiguous. He was aware of Joseph Smith Jr.'s non-canonical statements that the Holy Ghost was a personage of spirit, but he was also familiar with the scriptural passages that could be interpreted as countering the idea.[124] He took the middle road, as signaled in his discourse in 1855, in which he stated that there was honest room for discussion and that, although he was inclined to believe in a personal Holy Ghost, there was no "positive fact" or "revelation" to finally decide the issue.[125]

By "person" or "personage," Pratt, Smith, and the others meant a being of spirit in the form of a man, not with flesh and bones as the Father and Son had, but with holy, spiritual matter arranged in the shape and size of a human. Although Pratt made it clear that he was not sure that this man-sized personage of spirit existed, he was not opposed to the idea. One thing about which he was absolutely certain, however, was that there was "an inexhaustible quantity of that Spirit that is *not* a person."[126] For Pratt, the issue of the Holy Spirit's existing as a personage was an afterthought, a secondary issue. His primary concern was maintaining the notion of the Holy Spirit as an infinite, universally diffused substance. Once that was established, the issue of a personage was not a burning one. If an infinite and omnipotent Holy Spirit chose to take the form of a man in one distinct area of space, that was well within the realms of reason and probability. "It is just as probable to my mind," Pratt wrote, "that there should be a portion of [the Holy Spirit] organized into a person, as that it should exist universally diffused among all the materials in space."[127]

All of Pratt's writings on the subject of the Holy Spirit indicated that he was more concerned about a useful concept than about the exact makeup of the Godhead. It would not be an overstatement to say that the Holy Spirit that was described in his writings was the glue that held Pratt's system of thought together. Without this concept, he would have been just another religious figure attempting to make sense of a universe full of abiding mysteries. With the concept of the Holy Spirit, however, he was able to reconcile science and religion in his mind once and for all, setting the Mormon worldview apart from all others in its ability to replace mystery with knowledge.

The Holy Spirit was awe-inspiring to Pratt. In the opening paragraphs to his primary essay on the topic, the stoical Orson sounded more like his more romantic brother Parley: "Man beholds himself surrounded by a universe of materials, filled with power. . . . Nothing is dormant; nothing acts at random without law." Behind all this was a "subtle, living, powerful agent," one "perceived, by its operations, to be widely and copiously diffused through all the materials of nature." Nothing, for Pratt, varied "from the path ordained by the wisdom and power of the living fluid agent which envelops it." Pratt asked rhetorically:

> What is this living, self-moving, powerful, and most wonderful fluid? What is it which so copiously pervades universal nature?
> . . . Is it heat? Is it magnetism? Is it electricity? Is it galvanism? Is it light? We answer; all these are its effects—the manifestations of its power, as it operates upon, in, and through the visible and invisible elements. These are some of the outward and more common exhibitions of its glory; while its invisible workings, its secret springs of power, and the fulness of its eternal glory, are withheld from the gaze of mortals. Heat, light, electricity, and all the varied and grand displays of nature, are but the tremblings, the vibrations, the energetic powers of a living, all-pervading, and most wonderful fluid, full of wisdom and knowledge, called the HOLY SPIRIT.[128]

Pratt's writings on the Holy Spirit demonstrated, more than any of his other works, his presumptuousness that so rankled Brigham Young and some in the Quorum of the Twelve. Pratt—with his ability to reason and his insistence on constructing a worldview that was consistent regarding revelation, philosophy, and science—occasionally confounded the other church leaders. He was also quick to point out when a new doctrine or revelation was not in line with a previous "word from God." During one of Pratt's quarrels with Brigham Young in 1860, Young declared that he did not "know of a man who has a mathematical turn of mind but what goes to[o] Far. The trouble between Orson Pratt & me is I do not know enough & he knows too much."[129] Later that same year, Young expressed further exasperation with the senior apostle: "No man can understand the things of Eternity   And Brother Pratt and all men should let the matter of the gods alone   I do not understand these things   Neither does any man in the flesh and we should let them alone."[130]

Pratt felt that his mission in life was to solve the mysteries of eternity, not to learn to live with them. The Godhead was not in the least mysterious to him. It was composed of two gods of flesh and bone, the Father and the Son, who were omniscient and omnipotent; and a third god, the Holy Spirit, who was omniscient, omnipotent, and omnipresent. The Holy Spirit was an agent of the Father and Son that had the ability to carry out their wishes through the farthest reaches of infinite space.

Pratt had already gone further on theological construction than most of his fellow Saints had. But that was not enough. He felt there was still work to be done in reconciling the idea of the Holy Spirit with other revelations and self-evident truths to produce a consistent, harmonious worldview. He reasoned that the Holy Spirit had to be material because, according to Joseph Smith, all spirit was matter, just in a more refined state. It had to be a solid because the essence of all substances was solidity. The Holy Spirit had to be made up of particles diffused throughout space, because if it were a vast solid covering all space, there would be no room for any other material object. These deductions from bits and pieces of revelational "fact" prepared Pratt's notion of the Holy Spirit to reach its full potential. But logic compelled Pratt to add more pieces to the theological puzzle, and there was no direct revelation to confirm his radical idea that *each particle* of the Holy Spirit had to have an infinite capacity for knowledge and wisdom and had to be one with the Father and Son in mind, will, and purpose. It was this creative part of his system that was later censured by his fellow church officials.

The fledgling Mormon theology was hardly prepared to deal with such ideas, regardless of whether they accurately reflected revealed truths. Brigham Young probably did not understand much of Pratt's thinking or its implications.[131] If he did, Young likely would have rejected a great deal more of it. Pratt's emphasis on bringing systematic coherence to the basics of Mormon revelation and reconciling them with self-evident facts did not rank as a high priority for that generation of Mormon leaders. Young was not even interested in the apologetic value of Pratt's thinking. In one meeting with President Young, Pratt maintained that "many of his doctrinal arguments had been advanced while in England in answer to the numerous inquiries that were made of him by reasoning men." Young was not impressed and responded that "when questions have been put to me, by opposers, who did not want to hear the simple Gospel message [I] would not answer them."[132]

Orson Pratt's pamphlets that addressed the Holy Spirit were all written in England and seemed to have had apologetic value in demonstrating the truth of Mormon beliefs to "reasoning men." For them, the explanatory power of the Holy Spirit was great. Few questions—theological, philosophical, or scientific—seemed left unanswered. One of the most important problems that Pratt considered answered by the Holy Spirit was that of "divine" action at a distance. As mentioned earlier, in his pamphlet *Great First Cause,* Pratt solved the problem from a scientific and philosophical standpoint, demonstrating that Newton's law of gravity was based on two mistakes: (1) inert mindless matter cannot follow a law of nature, and (2) no action is possible at a distance. For Pratt, avoiding these two mistakes was essential in understanding divine activity. The finite, flesh and bone bodies of the Father and the Son who resided in time and at particular coordinates in infinite space could not cause action beyond the reach of their physical appendages. For their will to be carried out elsewhere, an intermediary with at least three attributes was required. First, it must be present in vast quantities everywhere in infinite space. Second, it must be intelligent in order to understand its orders; in fact, it must be able to match thought for thought the all-knowing, all-wise minds of the Father and the Son because it must be able to comprehend their most complex instructions. Furthermore, it must contain the same will so it would not deviate from the divine plan. Third, it must be all-powerful to execute the grandest of commands on a cosmic scale.

In the scientific world, various ether theories were being utilized in hopes of coming to terms with the notion of action at a distance and a variety of natural phenomena that remained fairly mysterious, such as the propagation of light, electricity, and magnetism. For Pratt, the connection was obvious. The invisible, undetectable ether that filled all space was the Holy Spirit or, as Pratt often referred to it, the Holy Fluid. That Pratt had what might be considered a sophisticated view of ether was demonstrated by his ability to discuss the topic in his scientific work *Key to the Universe*. But he transformed the cold ether of nineteenth-century science into a "boundless ocean of Spirit [that] possesses in every part, however minute, a will, a self-moving power, knowledge, wisdom, love, goodness, holiness, justice, mercy, and every intellectual and moral attribute possessed by the Father and Son."[133]

Parley Pratt also characterized the Holy Spirit as an ethereal fluid. He even saw spiritual fluid as the basis for spiritual communication between minds. Like his brother, Orson Pratt characterized this type of communication as a "spiritual telegraph," a popular phrase among spiritualists and mesmerists. Just "as the electric fluid passes through bodies opaque to the natural light, and conveys its message thousands of miles almost instantaneously, so does the still more powerful spiritual fluid convey its message," he declared. According to him, what was necessary to enjoy this spiritual telegraphy was "a proper condition to receive the impression," a condition that included the possession of a special spiritual "sense more powerful, more extended, and more glorious, than all the other senses combined."[134]

In his discourse on spiritual gifts, Pratt sounded much like some of the spiritualists of the day, who held beliefs about special spiritual senses in the next life. "Spiritual seeing," Pratt asserted, "will no doubt be the method of seeing in a future state. The eyes of the Celestial body, being quickened and enlightened by the power and light of the Holy Ghost, will, at all times, be prepared to behold the wonderful works of God, and gaze upon the glories of the Universe. The eyes of mortality behold objects on this side of the vail [sic], according to the laws of natural light; the eyes of immortality will behold objects on both sides of the vail, according to the laws of both natural and spiritual light."[135] Because of the apostle's speculative tendencies, at least one historian has expressed doubts about some aspects of Pratt's Baconian commitment, especially his Baconian reliance on the senses and facts.[136] In the context, however, Pratt was demonstrating a superior commitment to Baconian principles. Like many mesmerists and spiritualists in his day, Pratt did not limit the senses and the facts to which they testified to the realm of gross matter alone. There were superior spiritual senses that were much more sensitive, that could sniff out facts from beyond the veil, and that were much more certain.

Again, sounding as if he could be writing for a spiritualist periodical, Pratt echoed spiritualist doctrines concerning increased capacities for the mind in the next life: "In a future state, the capacities of the mind will be developed and enlarged, in proportion to the increased facilities for acquiring knowledge. . . . If the immortal eye, at one glance, can behold all the elements and particles of a world, with their infinitely varied operations, the immortal mind will be able to comprehend the scenery, and to remember the world of new ideas thus poured in upon it."[137] The concept of the Holy Spirit as set forth by Orson Pratt—and by his brother—actually helped temper Mormon attitudes toward such nineteenth-century movements as spiritualism, mesmerism, and phrenology, even to the point that some Saints embraced some of their main ideas.[138] Brigham Young, for instance, went so far as to admit that "the very principle the philosophers call animal magnetism was taught and practiced by Jesus and his Apostles," and he attributed such spiritualist phenomena as rapping and table moving to this "true principle."[139]

Most important for Pratt, though, was the ability of the Holy Spirit to explain scientific phenomena. The grandest of all scientific laws at the time was that of universal gravitation. In the *Great First Cause,* Pratt introduced the "Self-moving Theory" of all matter to replace the long-held Newtonian idea of the "attracting hypothesis" and delineated the role of the Holy Spirit in this cosmic law: "All theologists who adopt the attracting hypothesis, require a Great First Cause, who not only gives laws to blind, unconscious, unintelligent matter, but also forces it to act according to those laws. All theologists who shall adopt the self-moving theory will require the Great First Cause itself to consist of conscious, intelligent, self-moving, particles, called the Holy Spirit, which prescribe laws for their own action, as well as laws for the action of all other intelligent materials."[140] Pratt reasoned that some particles in the universe had to be eternal and all-knowing to teach the other particles the nature of the universal laws and how to obey them. This infinite fluid substance enveloped all other matter and was in constant contact. Each particle of the Holy Spirit had to be infinite in knowledge; how else could it help the less intelligent particles know "how to vary the gravitating tendency . . . every moment, precisely in the inverse ratio of the square of its distance from every other particle in the universe"? Explaining gravitation seemed to capture his imagination in a special way. Pratt did not offer a detailed explanation for other mysterious natural phenomena, such as electricity, magnetism, galvanism, light, and heat. Mainstream scientists were diligently searching for clues to the laws governing these, but Pratt simply called them the effects of the Holy Spirit, "the manifestations of its power, as it operates upon, in and through the visible and invisible elements."[141]

For Pratt, the Holy Spirit seemed the only god worthy of worship. The Holy Spirit had more divine attributes than the Father and the Son, since it was omnipresent as well as omnipotent and omniscient. Indeed, each *particle* of the Holy Spirit was omniscient. It was a primordial substance, matter in its most glorious and fundamental form. It was purer and more refined than any other substance in the universe, and it filled infinite space. In a universe where even the gods were material and dynamic in nature, the Holy Spirit was the unchanging eternal absolute. In several passages dealing with the Holy Spirit, Pratt strongly implied, if not directly asserted, that the spiritual natures of the Father, Son, and Holy Ghost were contingent on the Holy Spirit.[142] In the *Great First Cause,* Pratt wrote that "all the organizations of worlds, of minerals, of vegetables, of animals, of men, of spirits, and *spiritual personages of the Father, of the Son, and the Holy Ghost,* must if organized at all, have been the result of the self combinations and unions of the preexistent, intelligent, powerful, and eternal particles of substance. These eternal Forces and Powers are the Great First Cause of all things and events that have had a beginning."[143] Of course, in LDS theology, gods had a beginning. Pratt therefore found nothing illogical in using the arguments of the English philosopher William Paley to demonstrate that the perfect spiritual personages of the Father, Son, and Holy Ghost implied an even more perfect, eternal designer. Paley maintained that the more complex the being, the more that being displayed evidence of design. From this, Pratt reasoned the designer of the most "superior of all personages . . . must have been a self-moving intelligent substance capable of organizing itself into one or more most glorious personages."[144]

As noted earlier, one of Pratt's ideas that bedeviled his relationship with Brigham Young and the Quorum of the Twelve was his attempt to reconcile passages of the Bible and the Book of Mormon that clearly taught that there was *one* god with Joseph Smith's revelation that there were many gods.[145] Pratt solved the problem by positing that "God is one, being a unity, when represented by light, truth, wisdom, or knowledge; but when reference is made to the temples in which this knowledge dwells, the number of Gods is infinite. . . . there are more Gods than there are particles of matter . . . but the attributes of Deity are one; and they constitute the one God that the Prophets speak of, and that the children of men in all worlds worship."[146]

It was this line of reasoning that disturbed other church leaders. Pratt thought worship should be directed at the unified, preeminent power in the universe, "the principles of light and truth, or knowledge" that he called "the attributes of God." However, the attributes of God were all but indistinguishable from the Holy Spirit in Pratt's writing.[147] In his open-air sermon on the topic in the Temple Block in Salt Lake City, Orson Pratt made the connection between the two unequivocal: "How was it that Joseph Smith was enabled to make [our] doctrines as plain as the alphabet? It was because God was with him; God was in the work; and we would just as soon *worship that Holy Spirit or intelligence* in Joseph Smith or in any person else, not the person, but the God that is in him, as to worship the same attributes somewhere else."[148] The infinite, intelligent, holy fluid was Orson Pratt's God and the light that shone both day and night for him in the Enlightenment village.

Conclusion

Attempting to explain the origin of Mormonism in a more naturalistic fashion than the LDS faithful explain it has been a popular undertaking by observers and historians of religion in America since the earliest days of the movement. Even a year after the first printing of the Book of Mormon, the journalist James Gordon Bennett pointed to Sidney Rigdon (or Henry Rangdon) as the author of the Book of Mormon, while the restorationist preacher Alexander Campbell pointed to Joseph Smith as the sole human author. Theories of this sort continued with the publication of one of the most famous books purporting to explain Mormon origins, Eber D. Howe's

Mormonism Unvailed, which maintained that the Book of Mormon was a reworking of a manuscript originally written by Solomon Spaulding. Early in the twentieth century, explanations of Mormon origins took on a psychological flavor. Again focusing on Smith as the human author, such studies as *The Founder of Mormonism: A Psychological Study of Joseph Smith, Jr.,* by I. W. Riley asserted that Smith was an epileptic, a paranoid, and a dissociated personality and argued that his visions, revelations, and the Book of Mormon were products of his subconscious mind.[149] In 1945, Fawn M. Brodie offered a less polemical look at LDS beginnings with her biography of Smith, *No Man Knows My History,* in which she focused on the early nineteenth-century environment of the region and on Smith's personal charisma. Others, such as Marvin S. Hill and Jan Shipps, maintained that personal charisma was not enough and that authentic religious motivation had to be considered. Studies investigating the environment from which the early Mormons sprang predominate today. Some have looked into the "magic world view" or the lingering occultic and hermetic traditions in the young republic; others see Mormonism as a reaction to skepticism or to deism.[150] Environmental studies may even have reached their first peak with Klaus J. Hansen's *Mormonism and the American Experience,* in which he commented that given the state of affairs at that time, "if Mormonism had not already existed, it would have had to be invented."[151]

With all the well-attested environmental factors that have been cited in recent years, though, it is clear that many streams fed into Mormonism. Among them was the felt need of Americans for a secure source of authority during that era. In a perceptive essay on this theme, Mario S. De Pillis pinpointed *authority* as perhaps *the* central theme in any explanation of Mormon origins: "This principle [of authority] was a response to the 'social sources' of rural Jacksonian society in western New York, a society which burned with religious fervor but was torn by sectarianism. At the time and place there were many other responses to the religious yearnings and sectarianism, but Smith alone clearly saw the need for authority and this might have made Mormonism a unique solution even if his new, heterodox scriptures had not been published."[152]

What De Pillis acknowledged was important. But he had conceptualized the source of authority too narrowly by focusing solely on the authority the Mormons generated by reestablishing the Melchizedek and Aaronic priesthoods. The sacerdotal foundation of authority was only one aspect. A solid case can be made from early LDS preaching and writing that the ability to minister through the dual priesthood was not the exclusive, most attractive, or most useful source of authority for the new religious movement. Rather, the ability of the Saints to overcome diversity of *opinion* generated an authority more persuasive still. The early LDS movement offered much more than priestly titles and functions; it also offered new answers to popular questions that believers felt set them apart from the orthodox sects and other religious competitors.[153] One of the first written responses to Mormonism, that of Alexander Campbell, recognized immediately that one of the distinguishing marks of the new sect was its attempt to give final answers to every theological problem found in the burned-over district: "infant baptism, ordination, the trinity, regeneration, repentance, justification, the fall of man, the atonement, transsubstantiation, fasting, penance, church government, religious experience, the call to the ministry, the general resurrection, eternal punishment, who may baptize, and even the question of freemasonary, republican government and the rights of man."[154] As revelation continued to come, they addressed other questions: Were there beings on other planets? What was the nature of life before and after death? How did the mind affect the body? What was spirit? How was action possible at a distance? What happened to infants who experienced a premature demise? What was the nature of electricity? Why were there different races of humans?

Most of the answers that the Mormons had to such questions—not to mention most of the themes of Mormon doctrine and practice—were available in popular form from one source or another during the period. Whether Joseph Smith acquired the ideas from his environment or from God or created them himself is not the point here. Rather, it is that the basic doctrines and answers the early Mormons offered met many of the intellectual needs of people on the frontier. Popular American movements and teachings had paved the way for what was to come. The prophecies and doctrines Smith announced had strong cultural precursors in rural society. Smith's greatest contribution might be characterized as recognizing, capturing, and sacralizing these disparate currents and then building a church structure to support them and ordaining missionaries to preach them.

The success of this linkage of heads and hearts in the early years of this new religious tradition would likely not have been realized, however, had it not been for Orson Pratt. He was the premier Mormon apologist. As such, he confronted almost all of the popular currents of thought and then either co-opted them or refuted them. Previous studies that viewed Mormonism as an attempt to counter deism made two basic mistakes. First, they looked too much to the formal deism of the previous century rather than to the popular forms represented in Smith's day by Thomas Paine, Ethan Allen, and

Elihu Palmer. Second, they did not give enough recognition to the popular deistic ideas and practices co-opted by Pratt and the early Saints, such as beliefs in a distant deity, materialism, rationalism, justification through good deeds, the inadequacies of the Bible, and the centrality of natural theology. Pratt was instrumental in helping assimilate these ideas in Mormon circles. He was also able to assemble the various revelations and doctrines of the prophet, which embodied much of the thinking of popular culture, into a coherent whole that had intellectual appeal to the new converts and the missionaries who used his ideas.

For Pratt, the authority of Mormonism lay in its unique ability to rise above opinion and deliver absolute certainty with absolute certainty. "Opinions, creeds invented by uninspired men, and doctrines originated in schools of divinity, all vanish like the morning dew—all sink into insignificance when compared with a message direct from heaven," he declared, later adding, "Joseph Smith's doctrine is reasonable, scriptural, perfect, and infallible in all its precepts, commands, ordinances, promises, blessings, and gifts."[155] Orson Pratt was among those Mormon leaders who imparted this vision to the fledgling church. His attempt to convince people outside of the church through his published tracts and articles did not have much success, however, and the legends that he had greatly simplified the field of mathematics and revolutionized astronomical thinking circulated only among the faithful. Although Pratt made a valiant effort to compete with scholars and thinkers in such places as Washington, D.C., and Edinburgh, Scotland, he was highly regarded only in frontier settlements.[156]

In this respect, Pratt was a key exemplar of the village Enlightenment, a professor of scientific, religious, and philosophical knowledge "suitable to the requirements of rural folk in the rising republic," as David Jaffee put it.[157] In the spotlight of the learned urban elite, Pratt's ideas were found wanting. But on the Mormon frontier, he was the foremost scientist, theologian, and philosopher; few questioned him. For a self-educated person, his intellectual contributions were quite remarkable. He constructed, proposition by proposition, a theory of the structure of reality by means of revelation, scientific investigation, and unwitting philosophical speculation. The resulting cosmology was probably about as consistent and coherent as any system could be that attempted to be completely true to a wide range of sometimes conflicting revelational data.

The system of thought that Pratt developed was, in his mind, infallible. Without formal education in his fields of study and without time or resources to remain theoretically current, he was likely unaware of the holes in his system. Meanwhile, the Baconian methodology to which he was committed in much of his work was commonly thought to lead *invariably* to the truth, and he was absolutely convinced that the revelational data with which he started were infallible. Any hole that he did recognize in his system was quickly and easily patched by the Holy Spirit, the all-knowing fluid that filled infinite space. Finally, Pratt was convinced that the omniscient Holy Spirit was infallibly enlightening him about his system (which, of course, included the Holy Spirit), in spite of the question-begging nature of the notion.

Pratt's penchant for logic and certainty was probably the primary reason he came into conflict with Brigham Young. Even his untutored studies led him to believe that there had to be an anchor somewhere in the cosmos. At least one being had to have all knowledge. There had to be an absolute source somewhere. Young, however, admitted that he did not see the need; even the gods progressed in knowledge. As Gary Bergera recognized, the conflict was really "between Young's dynamic revelation, which provided for the possibility of superseding past revelation, and Pratt's fundamentalist adherence to the written word of divine canon and past revelation."[158] Pratt could not ultimately subscribe to Young's dynamic view because he recognized the need for a transcendent arbiter to choose between conflicting "infallible" revelations. Ironically, the dynamic nature of Mormon theology has allowed church general authorities in the twentieth century to return to Pratt's absolutism. Bergera recently acknowledged that "several of Pratt's unpopular ideas have now found acceptance among such influential twentieth century church exegetes as Joseph Fielding Smith," who declared, "I believe that *God knows all things* and that *his understanding is perfect, not 'relative.'*" In addition, wrote Bergera, the influential Mormon theologian Bruce R. McConkie's *Mormon Doctrine* "shows a kindred debt to Pratt's theories in his sections on 'God,' the 'Godhead,' and 'Eternal Progression.' Reliance on Pratt is strong and surprising."[159] Still more, some of Pratt's other theories, including those on the attributes of godliness and the omnipresence of the Holy Spirit, were adapted by such later influential church writers as Charles W. Penrose, B. H. Roberts, and Hyrum Andrus.[160]

It is important to underscore here that it was a Baconian predilection for common sense that moved Pratt to contend for absolutes and to construct a unified worldview. No argument was necessary to persuade him of the idea that if Joseph Smith was "truly sent of God," then every fact in the universe should line up with his utterances. The twin pillars of science and religion were entirely reconcilable. In fact, given the role of the infinite ether—the Holy Spirit—in both teaching gross matter how to behave and inspiring prophets what to say, any type of compartmentalization of science and religion was ultimately unjustifiable.[161]

Orson Pratt was a key figure of the village Enlightenment and, if he had his way, would have brought all Latter-day Saints with him. In one of the few discourses he gave late in life, he made a plea for the next generation of Mormons to institutionalize this way of thinking through education: "Our educational system must be revolutionized—must be re-constructed upon a new and more perfect basis, adapted to a new age—a new era—far in advance of this old. The great temple of science must be erected upon the solid foundations of everlasting truth; its towering spires must mount upward, reaching higher and still higher, until crowned with the glory and presence of Him, who is Eternal."[162] The influence Pratt had on the success of the early church and the legacy he left for those who followed reflected his inextricable yoking of religion and science and his invariable commitment to the ideals that constitute the village Enlightenment.

2 Spiritualism and Science: Robert Hare

In his Pulitzer Prize winning book, *The Launching of Modern American Science*, Robert V. Bruce located the launching of modern American science in the year 1846, primarily because that was the year some important institutionalizing steps were made, such as the founding of the Smithsonian and the Yale Scientific School. Bruce himself admitted, however, that such a complex story as this cannot be lopped off cleanly at the edges. Before 1846, infrastructures were built, relationships were formed, enthusiasm was nurtured, and steps were clearly taken without which no "launching" of the scientific enterprise would have been realized.[1]

One of the relationships formed during the earliest decades of the nineteenth century was particularly beneficial for the "pre-launch" stages of American science. In a Philadelphia boardinghouse in 1802, the paths of two emerging luminaries of antebellum science crossed, which resulted in a firm and intimate lifelong friendship. Benjamin Silliman, twenty-three years old, had just been appointed professor of chemistry and natural history at Yale College. Before assuming his duties, he was commissioned to go out and gather the latest scientific ideas and techniques from the top practitioners and teachers of the day. Philadelphia was the home of the University of Pennsylvania's Professor James Woodhouse, president of the Chemical Society of Philadelphia, and Silliman's first stop on his educational tour. Friends had recommended Silliman stay at a certain Mrs. Smith's boardinghouse, which often accommodated "a very select class of gentlemen." One of his fellow boarders at the Smith house was Robert Hare, a twenty-two-year-old native of Philadelphia who was auditing the Woodhouse lectures in chemistry.[2] Hare and Silliman, who already had much in common, got to know each other while at Woodhouse's lectures during the day and at meals in the evening. Silliman would later remember Hare and the other guests for their "courteous manners," "brilliant intelligence, sparkling sallies of wit and pleasantry, and cordial greeting."[3]

According to Silliman's diary, Woodhouse's chemistry lectures were largely disappointing. To supplement the course, he teamed up with Hare, whom he already discovered to be "a genial, kind-hearted person, one year younger than myself, and already a proficient in chemistry upon the scale of that period." He persuaded Mrs. Smith to allow them to set up a makeshift laboratory in the cellar.[4] At that point, Silliman became a student of Hare as well as a collaborator because of Hare's proficiency as an experimenter. Although the laboratory was not up to professional standards, the project on which they worked was. With the assistance of Silliman, Hare set out to perfect an apparatus he had already invented that could efficiently burn oxygen and hydrogen gases to produce very intense heat. The invention had already put Hare's name among the luminaries of American chemistry. In January 1803, Hare exhibited his apparatus to the famous discoverer of oxygen, Joseph Priestley, one of the leaders of chemical thought in the world. That same month, Hare was elected to the prestigious American Philosophical Society.

After his winter studies, Silliman left Philadelphia to continue his educational travels and in 1808 settled in at Yale. During his fifty-year career at the college, he became one of the great scientific educators of his era. While he is not known today for original research, his name is strongly associated with the best in early American science. This because he was the founder and for twenty years the sole editor of the *American Journal of Science and Arts*—often called *Silliman's Journal*—one of the country's foremost scientific journals.[5] Hare also earned a place in American scientific history in his long career as a professor of chemistry at the Medical School of the University of Pennsylvania in Philadelphia and as an original thinker, researcher, inventor, and author of more than a hundred articles. He became known as a brilliant experimenter and carried on active debates with some of the most important scientists of the nineteenth century.

Silliman and Hare were fast friends who lived nearly parallel lives. They corresponded regularly on more than scientific matters—seeking each other out for personal and professional advice and mutual encouragement.[6] They also made it a point to visit each other whenever it was convenient for the 150 miles separating them to be traversed.

Both men had at least one other commonality—each eventually thought it important to use his scientific expertise to advance the cause of religious truth. Ironically, this shared interest also became the primary cause of their greatest divergence. Silliman found scientific facts and methods to be in per-

Robert Hare, the professor of chemistry at the University of Pennsylvania who became a spiritualist late in life. (From an oil painting begun by John Neagle in 1858 and finished by J. L. Williams in 1877. Courtesy of the University of Pennsylvania Archives)

fect accord with holy scripture and preeminent apologetic tools for demonstrating the truth of traditional Christian beliefs. Hare, however, rejected unscientific "biblical superstition" and late in his life found science pointing toward religious truth in the circles of the spiritualists.

On a mutual visit to Albany in 1856, Hare gave Silliman his recently published book, *Experimental Investigation of the Spirit Manifestations,* which presented the results of his research into spirit communication. Although he was an extremely unlikely convert, Silliman courteously read the volume with respectful attention. Early in 1857, one year before Hare's death, Silliman responded in kind by sending Hare a recently published book by John Young that provided a "scientific vindication" of Christian faith.[7] Accompanying the book was a letter that reflected continuing affection for his friend but also directly challenged him on methods and evidence:

> I ask that you will in turn read this little book, which presents a view of the Saviour, to my mind both original and convincing.
> . . . The little volume which I now send you comprises, as you are aware, but a small portion of the copious evidence which supports the divine origin of the Scriptures. . . . Had your course of research been fully devoted to these subjects as it has been to physical science, I trust you would not have been an unbeliever; and it is even now not too late to ascertain whether the Bible is really, as you intimate, a cunningly, or even a clumsily devised fable.[8]

Neither man was convinced by the arguments or literature of the other, but both were convinced that *true science* pointed exclusively to his own resolute religious convictions. The relationship between religion and science in the thought of Benjamin Silliman has been examined in several studies that accurately depict him as a classic Protestant Baconian reconciler of God's revelation and the natural world.[9] Almost no attention has been paid to his colleague and counterpart, however. In what follows, I look at the relationship between religion and science in the thinking of Robert Hare.

The question that arises about Hare is how did he arrive at such strikingly different conclusions about religious questions when he employed scientific methods nearly identical with—if not more rigorous than—those of his more orthodox colleagues, such as Silliman? What I demonstrate in this chapter is that the answer probably lies in the fact that, like his contemporaries Orson Pratt and Phineas Quimby, Hare was able to forge "natural" pathways into "supernatural" realms because he, too, came to believe that there was no ultimate distinction between matter, mind, and spirit. All, he thought, were material substances differing only in their relative densities or properties. In coming to many of the same conclusions that the less professional, less polished Pratt and, as we shall see, Quimby did, Hare showed that the village Enlightenment had a great deal more to do with frame of mind than with population density or formal education. As we shall see, the village Enlightenment was available not only to cultivated metropolitans but to less-refined provincials as well. Hare is an example of the elite joining the popular ranks. The only requirement was to be willing—in good Baconian fashion—to break the lingering ties to "medieval superstition" and not only investigate but also proclaim, demonstrate, and defend a commitment to a materialism and a universe where no fact of nature or supernature could hide from a scientist—professional or otherwise—in search of the truth. Some in the elite ranks flirted with these ideas, but these notions were embraced with popular religious fervor in the village Enlightenment. I also show that the ethos of the eighteenth-century Enlightenment—which included such pillars as reason, progress, moral certainty, antisupernaturalism, and universalism—was alive and well in yet another popular religious movement, spiritualism. Finally, I hope to establish that once again American science in the Baconian mode provided means, motive, and opportunity for the growth of an "enlightened" alternative movement in what Jon Butler called "the antebellum spiritual hothouse."[10]

American Scientific Virtuoso

One of the greatest scientific advantages of Robert Hare (1781–1858) was his birth in Philadelphia.[11] Being born and reared in Philadelphia put him at the hub of American scientific activity. Benjamin Franklin was omnipresent and personally embodied the intellectual currents of the new republic's leading city, where scientific thought flourished and revolutionary ideas about government were generated, debated, and implemented.

Hare grew up in the highest social ranks of the city. His father, Robert Hare Sr., was an educated man of "good family" from England who arrived in Philadelphia in 1773. The father entered the social world of old Philadelphia through his marriage to Margaret Willing, whose family had enduring roots there. "The elder Hare was not without honor in the country of his adoption," wrote Edgar Fahs Smith, the former provost of the University of Pennsylvania, "as evidenced by his membership in the Convention which framed the first Constitution of Pennsylvania; by his becoming speaker of the Senate of the State; and by his occupancy of a seat in the Board of Trustees of the University of Pennsylvania."[12] As a businessman, Robert Hare Sr. became known in Philadelphia as the brewer of "Hare's American Porter," a drink his son Robert Jr. supplied in plenty to the residents of Mrs. Smith's boardinghouse, including Silliman, some years later.[13]

Little is known about the younger Hare's childhood and education except that one Hare family observer noted that Robert and his five siblings had "the rudiments of a good classical education." Their father also "planted in their hearts the stern sense of individual responsibility, love of truth, and high principles which marked their whole intercourse with the world."[14] Robert Hare Jr. went to work with his father in the brewing business until he entered the University of Pennsylvania. There, with no formal school of chemistry at that time, he sought out the few courses in the discipline that were offered. Students who wanted to concentrate on chemistry rather than medicine were taught by James Woodhouse. Hare soon did what anyone truly serious about chemistry in the region did: he joined the Chemical Society of Philadelphia as a junior member.

His first presentation of original research to the Chemical Society in 1801 was remarkable. Hare was searching for a way to provide a steadier flow of air to a flame-producing device called a blowpipe than could be generated using a bellows or human lung power. In the midst of his investigations, he created a dual-compartment barrel and only as an afterthought decided to store oxygen in one and hydrogen in the other. He had originally set out simply to improve on the ordinary blowpipe, but by releasing both gases simultaneously and allowing them to mix and exit a nozzle, he ended up, when igniting the mixture, producing a flame with a heat intensity far beyond anything previously generated. As with many scientific discoveries, it was noticed not purely because it was a solid step in the advancement of knowledge but also because it was an innovation of great utility. The intense flame of the "oxyhydrogen blowpipe," as it came to be known, allowed scientists and artisans to fuse metals that could not be joined with flames of lesser heat. Hare's invention led to the development of the Drummond light (later known as the "limelight") used as a spotlight in lighthouses and theaters. The invention also spawned whole industries involved in working with new metals.[15] This invention did more than anything else to establish Hare in scientific circles, according to Edgar Fahs Smith.[16] His findings were subsequently published by the society in 1802 and later in Alexander Tilloch's *Philosophical Magazine* (London) and in the *Annales de chimie* (Paris).[17] The discovery of the oxyhydrogen blowpipe was a catalyst to Hare's scientific legitimacy and honor. Already a member of the American Philosophical Society, in 1839 Hare became the first recipient of the Rumford Medal from the Boston-based American Academy of Arts and Sciences.

When Hare met Silliman—a less skilled chemist than his new friend—in 1802, Silliman had already been appointed to a scientific professorship at Yale. Hare's dream was to dedicate his life to scientific pursuits in the same fashion, but the opportunity had not yet arrived. While Silliman went off to Europe to study full-time with scientific virtuosos, Hare continued working with his father for a living and engaging in scientific activity in his spare time. When Silliman returned to New Haven in 1806, he helped persuade Yale to offer Hare an honorary M.D. degree, which was Hare's first academic recognition. Harvard conferred the same degree on Hare ten years later.

In 1809, Philadelphia's premier chemistry educator, James Woodhouse, suffered a fatal stroke. Candidates for his position barely waited long enough to be respectful before communicating their or a colleague's interest in his prized academic chair. Letters poured in to the trustees of the University of Pennsylvania in support of Hare, citing him as the most qualified young chemist in the region. Impressed as the trustees were by the support, they were reluctant to fill a position in the medical school with someone who did not have formal training in medicine. The job went to John Redman Coxe. Hare continued patiently in business and in his part-time chemical pursuits for nine more years. At that time, Coxe resigned as the chair of chemistry to take a professorship in materia medica, the branch of medical science dealing with drugs. Letters again arrived on behalf of Hare, and again opposition arose for the same reason. This time, however, Hare prevailed and settled in for a long and distinguished career.

Professor Hare was never known as a stirring lecturer, but his classroom demonstrations and experiments apparently more than made up for the deficiency.[18] Meanwhile, he became a valued commodity in American science and a source of pride among the national scientific community. On at least one occasion, the American scientific community fought to protect Hare as the inventor of the oxyhydrogen blowpipe.[19] Hare himself responded vigorously and combatively in his own defense, which he continued to do in the future.

Hare became known for his combative nature not only when academic integrity was at stake but also in matters of fact and scientific interpretation. The writers of the entry on Hare in the *Dictionary of American Biography* felt compelled to mention that Hare "invariably display[ed] a tendency to turn a discussion into a controversy."[20] Likewise, George Daniels observed that Hare was not intimidated by even the highest-ranking European scientists and carried on "active controversies with the most important scientists of the nineteenth century."[21] Hare also clashed with the Swedish chemist Jöns Jacob Berzelius over the organizing principles of chemical nomenclature, with the British chemist and physicist Michael Faraday over electricity and the nature of matter, with the English scientist William Whewell over the necessary properties of matter, with the American meteorologist W. C. Redfield over the forces behind storms, and, as Daniels pointed out, "with all comers over the materiality of heat."[22] Hare seemed to relish public debate, whether in print or in public meetings, and he never gave up engaging his opponents by answering them publicly before making any attempt at dialogue with them in private.[23]

Hare was not wrong on a regular basis about any scientific issue, but his strengths lay in the practical, experimental, and mechanical, not in the theoretical. None of his accomplishments ever surpassed the invention of the oxyhydrogen blowpipe, but there were several that came close. Hare's primary research interest was always the dynamics of heat and electricity in chemistry, and most of the highlights of his career involved these subjects. In 1819, he invented the "calorimotor," a device designed to generate intense heat through electro-chemical reaction. Hare and others employed the device to produce enough heat to fuse large rods of iron or platinum. In 1822, he published a report on another new device, called the "deflagrator," which also produced intense heat electrochemically but had the added advantage that it could be turned on and off by lowering or raising the coils by a lever. Hare's technological successes did not mean he eschewed the theoretical side of science. He is simply not remembered for theorizing because he argued the losing side in several early nineteenth-century scientific debates. Two of the theoretical notions that he strongly maintained—which today, of course, are dismissed—played an important part in his conceptual acceptance of the spiritualist cosmology: (1) the notion that heat and electricity were unique material substances, not the result of particles in motion, and (2) the notion that a type of weightless or "imponderable" matter existed. Because these theories relate to his spiritualism, they are detailed in a later section. The point here is that although he was following the wrong path by today's standards, these ideas were at least arguable in legitimate scientific circles during his day. There was a wide range of thinking on the nature of matter. At one end of the spectrum was Isaac Newton, with his concept that matter was ultimately composed of infinitesimally small, hard, massy, and impenetrable particles that had location, extension, and the property of inertia. At the other end were scientists, such as Roger Boscovich, who postulated that matter was not "particulate" but was really made up of mathematical points in space from which fields of force emanated.[24] Those at Newton's end of the spectrum, however, ruled the day, and the burden of proof was on anyone who wished to challenge them. Hare's twist on the subject—that particulate matter could exist that did not exhibit the property of weight—was not on the fringe but was certainly more speculative than most.[25]

The theoretical concerns that Hare articulated in his career did not all relate to the physical sciences. He published several works on government policy and economics, with a focus on banking issues.[26] Late in his life, Hare wrote three lengthy works that had nothing to do with the physical sciences, public policy, or economics. In 1850, under the pen name of Eldred Grayson, Esq., he produced a three-hundred-page historical novel entitled *Standish the Puritan: A Tale of the American Revolution,* an adventure story about three college classmates in New York during the War of Independence. Two years later, under the same pen name, he published a second novel, a historical romance of four hundred pages entitled *Overing, or, the Heir of Wycherly.*[27]

The third book he published in 1855, three years before his death. All the biographical sketches of Hare mention this book with a detectable degree of embarrassment. Hare's written contribution to the spiritualist movement, *Experimental Investigation of the Spirit Manifestations*—a 460-page treatise published by the successful spiritualist publishing partnership of Partridge and Brittan—is treated as an anomalous eccentricity by those who have studied Hare in the context of early American science. It is a work often attributed to Hare's old age and possible senility. Most scientific historians who revere Hare's scientific contributions tend to agree with Joseph McCabe, who remarked that "it is kinder to leave Professor Hare's spiritualist work in oblivion and remember him only as a distinguished and devoted student of chemistry."[28] This is a shortsighted view of Hare's approach to spiritualism, which Hare contended was as rigorous as any of his other scientific investigations. Other critics of Hare suggested that the old man had been hoodwinked. Hare caught wind of this before the publication of his book and added a "supplemental preface" in which he stated:

> The most precise and laborious experiments which I have made in my investigation of Spiritualism, have been assailed by the most disparaging suggestions, as respects my capacity to avoid being the dupe of any medium employed. Had my conclusions been of the opposite kind, how much fulsome exaggeration had there been, founded on my experience as an investigator of science for more than half a century! And now, in a case when my

own direct evidence is adduced, the most ridiculous surmises as to my probable oversight or indiscretion are suggested, as the means of escape from the only fair conclusion.[29]

Upon the publication of his book, Hare became the darling of the spiritualist movement because he was far and away the most respected and recognized scientist to put his stamp of approval on the spirit manifestations as real, demonstrable phenomena. The "testimony" of his late-in-life conversion to belief in spirit communication was particularly powerful because, according to Hare, it was a dramatic turn from skepticism to belief based on what he considered the weight of objective evidence obtained through scientific means.

In the last few years of his life, Hare continued to be productive scientifically but lost some of his prestige among his colleagues because of his fervent, evangelistic commitment to spiritualism. In 1854, he attempted to introduce his spiritualist research into the mainstream of American science. At the annual meeting of the American Association for the Advancement of Science (AAAS) held in Albany, New York, that year, Hare struggled to get on the program to read a paper on spiritualism. He was reluctantly permitted, according to Edgar Fahs Smith, "in deference solely to his age and to his reputation as a scientist." His article did not, however, appear in the published transactions of the association.[30] On another occasion, he was rejected outright by the AAAS program committee because "the subject did not fall sufficiently within the objects of the Association."[31] A more embarrassing incident took place in April of 1855 at yet another scientific meeting. A journalist for the spiritualist periodical *Spiritual Telegraph* reported:

> Before the close of the session Professor Hare of Philadelphia, read to the convention an invitation made on the part of the Spiritualists of Washington by a Committee, to attend the lecture of Reverend T. L. Harris, on Spiritualism, on Saturday evening, April 29th. In the midst of the reading of his paper, Professor [Joseph] Henry entered the hall, and upon hearing the subject of "Spiritualism" mentioned, he turned red in the face and interrupted Professor Hare by his inquiry, "I would be glad to know, Mr. President, whether the subject is in order?" Professor Hare remarked, that, whether the subject were in order or not, it was hardly in order to interrupt a member of the Convention in that manner before he had finished reading his communication. Professor Henry replied that this was "a dangerous subject to be introduced into this Convention," that it had better be let alone; and he moved that it be laid upon the table.

EXPERIMENTAL INVESTIGATION

OF THE

SPIRIT MANIFESTATIONS,

DEMONSTRATING

THE EXISTENCE OF SPIRITS AND THEIR COMMUNION
WITH MORTALS.

DOCTRINE OF THE SPIRIT WORLD RESPECTING HEAVEN, HELL,
MORALITY, AND GOD.

ALSO,

The Influence of Scripture on the Morals of Christians

BY

ROBERT HARE, M.D.

EMERITUS PROFESSOR OF CHEMISTRY IN THE UNIVERSITY OF PENNSYLVANIA, GRADUATE OF YALE COLLEGE
AND HARVARD UNIVERSITY, ASSOCIATE OF THE SMITHSONIAN INSTITUTE, AND
MEMBER OF VARIOUS LEARNED SOCIETIES.

FOURTH EDITION

Verba animi proferre, vitam impendere vero.

Denounce dark Error and bright Truth proclaim,
Though ghastly Death oppose, with threat'ning aim.

NEW YORK:
PARTRIDGE & BRITTAN, 342 BROADWAY.
1856.

Title page of Robert Hare's influential spiritualist work, *Experimental Investigation of the Spirit Manifestations,* originally published in 1855.

The convention followed Joseph Henry's motion and tabled the announcement. The *Spiritual Telegraph* reported that it was ironic how scientific savants rejected the scientific pursuit of spiritual communication but "held a very learned, extended, grave, and profound discussion at the same meeting in which they voted to put the above invitation on the table, upon the cause why roosters crow between twelve and one o'clock at night."[32]

Just a few years after that professional snub, Robert Hare died suddenly, leaving behind his wife of forty-seven years, Harriett Clark Hare, and four children (two others had died quite young). Upon his death in May of 1858, the scientific community overlooked what they considered his late dalliance with fringe science and deeply mourned a significant loss. The regents of the Smithsonian Institution issued an official resolution acknowledging his life and the work that "placed him among the first in his country of the great contributors to knowledge."[33]

Hare had certainly built a reputation and was well known in the scientific community. However, it was his spiritualist conversion and testimony that made him a household name for four years, from Washington, D.C., to Boston and beyond. More than three thousand turned out to hear his lecture on spiritualism in New York City. With the public relations efforts of Charles Partridge and Samuel B. Brittan, Hare was catapulted to the front lines of this new religious movement that in a few short years had captured America's popular fascination.

Spirits of the Times

Early chroniclers of spiritualism saw their movement as a new dispensation of spirit communication that began when the spirits rent the veil between their world and ours in the small home of the Fox family in Hydesville, New York, on the evening of March 31, 1848. Strange rapping sounds that seemed to be coming from the floor of the Fox home had first been heard two weeks earlier, but on March 31 the family came to believe that there was intelligence behind the sounds and that this intelligence would knock in response to questions. Upon questioning, claimed Fox family members, they had discovered that the rapping sounds were being made by the spirit of a peddler who had been murdered in the house by a former resident. That very night the family brought in neighbors to experience the phenomenon and to ask questions of the spirit. By mid-April, hundreds supposedly had visited the house, making it impossible, as the father, John Fox, remarked, "to attend to our daily occupations."[34] The rappings seemed to occur most often in the presence of two daughters, Margaret and Kate Fox, who, because of this, began to be referred to as "mediums." Even when the two girls separately visited relatives in two different cities, the rappings followed them and became more vigorous. Soon, Margaret and Kate moved to Rochester, New York, to live with their older widowed sister, Leah Fish. Throngs visited the Fox sisters at their new residence, and less than a year later, hundreds in western New York had become believers in spirit communication. Local committees were appointed to investigate the popular but mysterious occurrences, and even the spirits themselves, it was claimed, were in favor of this type of study. In fact, they were said to communicate through mediums a threat to leave for good if serious examinations did not take place. The newspaper editor E. W. Capron was so satisfied with his own investigations that he began taking what he believed to be the advice of the spirits. Capron was obedient when the spirits recommended that he set up public demonstrations at the largest hall in Rochester and charge twenty-five cents for admission. More than four hundred people attended each of three performances, and the committees that investigated could find no fraud.

The local phenomenon went national when Horace Greeley's widely circulating *New York Weekly Tribune* published a report that Capron wrote concerning the events in Rochester. People around the country began to relate all types of inexplicable phenomena in spiritualistic terms, and many (mostly women) found that they, too, had mediumistic abilities. By June of 1850, newspapers throughout the country regularly printed articles and letters concerning spiritualistic phenomena. Popular pamphlets and books appeared, such as Dellon Dewey's *History of the Strange Sounds or Rappings* and Capron's *Singular Revelations*.[35] These contained much in the way of eyewitness testimony and positive reports from investigators. Probably the greatest impetus for the popular spread of the movement was the lengthy visit that Mrs. Fox and her three daughters paid to New York City in the summer of 1850. Horace Greeley, after investigating for himself, became enchanted with the phenomenon, as did Charles Partridge, a wealthy businessperson who became an important financier of spiritualist investigations. The séances of the Fox sisters must have been compelling. People tended to come away less skeptical than they had been. One prominent New York lawyer wrote, "I went away convinced that what before appeared to me much like a nice plump humbug, deserved investigation by the best minds among us."[36]

The influence of the Fox sisters should not be underestimated. However, to maintain, as some early spiritualists did, that modern American spiritualism began in Hydesville is to ignore historical precursors. The groundwork for the movement was laid by the overt spiritualist practices in Shaker communities and by the ideas and practices of the itinerant mesmerists of the 1840s, who, if nothing else, introduced the idea that invisible substances can cause visible and knowable effects. In many respects, the spirit-rapping phenomena in western New York helped stoke the fire of a movement that was already underway but was going slowly. Much of the theology and cosmology that would later be promulgated by the spirits was already codified by 1847 in an eight-hundred-page work entitled *The Principles of Nature, Her Divine Revelations, and a Voice to Mankind.*[37] This volume contained transcribed "public" lectures by Andrew Jackson Davis, who delivered them while in a trance state. At the heart of the often rambling tome was Jackson's "Harmonial Philosophy," which announced the coming of an era when the advanced societies of other "spheres" would produce a transformation of this world.

Much of what Jackson taught concerning the spirit worlds and the reform needed in this world—ideas Jackson himself may have gleaned from the Swedish seer Emanuel Swedenborg and the French socialist Charles Fourier—was a few years later being taught by the spirits in séances around the country. With this in mind, Catherine L. Albanese identified Jackson as "the leading light of philosophical spiritualism, by all counts *the* spiritualist theologian if the movement had one."[38] Jackson's emphasis on the spiritualist philosophical message sometimes put him at odds with those who were more interested in spiritualist experience. However, it was the empirical phenomena that gave Jackson's message the greater audience as spiritualism reached its peak. Objective public demonstrations and investigations lent Jackson's subjective revelations more credibility.

Investigation and public demonstration were dominant themes in the success of spiritualism. Unlike occultic movements that attempted to stay true to the etymology of the word *occult* and keep their ideas and activities secret, esoteric, or hidden from the uninitiated, spiritualists, more often than not, invited the skeptical inquirers or critics to test the spirits for themselves. The historian Ernest Isaacs noted that spiritualists welcomed investigations, "whether by individual customers or by committees that the customers appointed." He also noted that "the results of the investigations brought more customers and more investigations, for the skeptical had to admit that they 'were unable to detect any motion on the part of the ladies, which could have originated the sounds.'"[39] Other historians of the spiritualist movement, such as Bret E. Carroll, Mary Farrell Bednarowski, and R. Laurence Moore, agreed with Isaacs's assessment. They argued that this was a movement that would not have had the impact it did if it had not been able to claim empirical pre-eminence over other types of religious experience and offer open demonstrations. Isaacs wrote that these "spiritualist philosophers were children of the Enlightenment, drawing on and extending its traditions of scientific experimentation and speculation, and the use of reason as the way of understanding nature."[40] Moore argued persuasively that approaches to the movement that postulated wholesale fraud or charlatanism did not adequately make sense of the historical data. True, he thought, many people going to spiritualist events were in a position to be easily fooled—the elderly, the grief-stricken, or wonder-seekers—but that did not deal adequately with women and men of good health and reputation who were not so easily fooled.[41] Capron reported that investigators even had the Fox sisters communicate with the spirits while standing naked before a committee of women, who still detected no visible physical action that could have produced the sounds.[42]

The spiritualists had plenty of detractors, however. The movement took nearly as many "knocks" as it dished out. Although many Christians from mainstream churches were involved because they saw spiritualism as an empirical demonstration of what the Bible taught about the reality of life after death, the more theologically rigid attributed much of the phenomenon to demonic activity. Others pursued nonreligious lines of explanation. Professor James Stanley Grimes of Castleton Medical College attributed spiritualist phenomena to a combination of mesmerism (for knowing the thoughts of those attending a séance) and trickery (the source of such noises as raps). Charles Chauncey Burr and his brother Herman published a book in 1850 in which they claimed they had closely examined the best mediums in five states and found no cause for the mysterious sounds other than "*fraud* and *delusion*."[43] Some faculty members of the University of Buffalo Medical School examined the Fox sisters in 1851, and by employing the same reasoning processes they used in diagnosing disease, they came to the conclusion that the raps were produced by "moveable articulations of the skeleton," or the voluntary snapping of joints.[44] No matter how much the detractors of spiritualism desired it, however, no "natural" explanation ever provided a "death-blow" to the movement. Spiritualist enthusiasts published reasoned responses to printed exposés and countered the reports of debunking squads. The spiritualists could do this because they were confident that true science was on the side of the spirits.

As spiritualism spread far beyond the Fox sisters and western New York, so did the types of manifestations and the entertainment value of the experiences. The phenomenon of "table turning"—in which the spirits were said to cause tables to move, shake, or jump—became nearly as famous as "rapping." The Davenport brothers (Ira and William), a pair of mediums who traveled widely, provided demonstrations that boasted a variety of inexplicable noises, including bells and music. The medium Henry Gordon introduced levitation of the human body. D. D. Home became known for manifesting phantom hands that would materialize and dematerialize in the presence of the sitters.

As the movement spread, techniques for purported spirit communication became much improved. Early on, a believer needed to read through the entire alphabet waiting for a spirit to rap out the letter it wanted next, thus laboriously producing a message. Later, through "trance writing" and "automatic writing," a spirit was said to take indirect charge over the writing instrument either by completely taking over the medium or by manipulating the medium's hand and arm.[45] This method was also used to produce putative drawings and paintings of the spirit world. Held even more efficient was "trance speaking," in which a spirit reportedly used the body of the medium to communicate verbally.[46] There were also reports of direct, independent writing, in which a spirit would take up the instrument itself. Charles Partridge claimed to have left a blank piece of paper with a pen on a table overnight and in the morning to have found the paper containing a spiritual manifesto signed by John Hancock, Benjamin Franklin, Samuel Adams, and over forty others.[47] It appeared that the spirits also became adept at entertaining the full range of human senses. There were accounts of sounds, smells, visions, and even spirits touching and physically harassing the sitters.

According to an estimate in the spiritualist periodical *Spirit World,* in 1851 there were a hundred mediums in New York and fifty to sixty in Philadelphia. In April 1855, the venerable *North American Review* claimed that it was probably not an overstatement when the New England Spiritualist Association placed the number of spiritualists in America at nearly 2 million. The *Home Journal,* edited by Nathaniel Parker Willis, estimated that there were 40,000 believers in New York alone, while the author and medium Emma Hardinge Britten announced optimistically that at least a fourth of the U.S. population had joined the ranks.[48] Arriving at accurate numbers is, of course, problematic. But the fact that there were hundreds of thousands of believers is not in doubt, nor is the fact that spiritualism captured the attention of the country in a dramatic way. "What would I have said six years ago to anybody who predicted," wrote the careful observer of things American George Templeton Strong, "that before the enlightened nineteenth century was

ended hundreds of thousands of people in this country would believe themselves able to communicate with the ghosts of their grandfathers?"[49]

Another reason for the wide acceptance of the movement was that notable people were drawn in varying degrees to spirit communication. Reports
of the spiritualist meetings involving such people as Horace Greeley, James
Fenimore Cooper, George Bancroft, William Cullen Bryant, Harriet Beecher
Stowe, Theodore Parker, and Jenny Lind were featured prominently in newspapers and other periodicals. Most of the celebrity "sitters" considered the
séances credible and successful. Capron later wrote, "Such candid statements,
made on the authority of men eminent for their literary attainments and
sense of honor, attracted very general attention, and it was hard to conceive
how a whole company of them could be deceived by a couple of girls."[50]

Other prominent people readily lent their names to endorse spiritualism
because of their deep commitment. Nathaniel P. Tallmadge, former U.S. sena-
tor from New York and governor of the Wisconsin Territory, was an outspo-
ken proponent who was accepted summa cum laude into the spiritualist fold
because of the courage he displayed when he publicly embraced spiritualism.[51] Joining Tallmadge on the front lines was John Worth Edmonds, a New
York supreme court judge, who probably attracted more ridicule than anyone save the Fox sisters. Edmonds became the movement's first martyr when
he lost his place on the court because his enemies charged that he consulted
the spirits about his decisions.

Probably the most well-known names claimed by the spiritualists were
those of Abraham Lincoln and Mary Todd Lincoln. The Lincolns did attend
several séances, but attempts by later spiritualists to demonstrate that the
president was a firm believer were not credible. Besides, in 1863 and 1864, the
years the Lincolns participated, the movement was already well past its peak
of the mid-1850s.[52]

The names of the supporters of the movement are eclipsed only by the
names of the spirits with whom they communicated. Although the most
sought-after spirits at séances were those of recently departed loved ones, a
pantheon of visitors from the top ranks of human history also, believers
claimed, paid regular visits to spirit circles, even in the smallest of towns.
Benjamin Franklin and George Washington were enormously popular.[53] But
séance reports also related messages from Isaac Newton, William Ellery
Channing, Francis Bacon (who assured the sitters that proper scientific
method would at last vindicate them), and Thomas Paine. Shakespeare and
poets introduced new verse, the Swedish seer Emanuel Swedenborg contin-

ued his description of the spirit realms, while Jesus, St. John, and St. Paul occasionally communicated from the highest levels of the spirit world.

Mainstream newspapers were not the only source of reports of such note-worthy conversations and other spiritualist activity. A number of spiritual-ist periodicals also chronicled the movement.[54] Andrew Jackson Davis began the publishing trend even before the rappings were first heard in Hydesville by promoting his harmonial philosophy in the *Univercoelum* and later in the *Spirit Messenger.* Other periodicals followed, such as *Spiritual Philosopher, Spirit World, Spiritual Telegraph, Herald of Progress,* and *Banner of Light.*

Spiritualist publications did not live on phenomena alone. Once the re-ports and empirical data succeeded in winning a person over, the next step for the convert was to listen carefully to the spirits, who almost always claimed to have advanced knowledge and greater understanding of the human situ-ation in the mundane world. The spirits—and those who were paying atten-tion to their teachings—were adamant about the direction American soci-ety should go: toward reform. That the spiritualist movement was at the forefront of mid-nineteenth-century reform movements is well docu-mented.[55] The spirits, it was thought, had rapped their approval of women's rights, abolition, labor reform, communitarianism, health reform, marriage law reform, and occasionally "free love"—an issue that was more divisive than unifying in spiritualist circles. Not only did spiritualists claim the spirits had spoken out on progress for women, but because mediums were predomi-nantly female, they indirectly created the first large group of female religious leaders and the first sizable group of American women to speak from the public platform.[56]

Although the dominant spiritualist social message was reform, its method was scientific. Modern scholarly treatments are singular in their insistence that the only place to put popular scientific attitudes and practices was squarely in the center of the movement.[57] With this in mind, the importance of the conversion of one of America's most distinguished scientists, Robert Hare, takes on increased historical and symbolic meaning. Not only did Hare become, for a time, the preeminent celebrity in the movement, eclipsing both Edmonds and Tallmadge, but he immediately became the premier apologist as well. Excluding fraud and delusion, most of the naturalistic explanations that the opponents of the spiritualists proposed involved theories of electric-ity, magnetism, and matter. Hare was North America's foremost expert in each of these areas. It was no wonder the spiritualist promoter Samuel B. Brittan was almost beside himself upon hearing of Hare's dramatic change of heart and mind regarding spirit communication.

Séance, Science, and Truth

In recounting his conversion, Robert Hare left little room for "will" or "passions" in the process. As he tells it, his conversion was a change of mind based on the weight of the scientific evidence and sound reasoning. He dispassionately followed through to what he believed was the only logical conclusion that could be derived from the raw data and brute facts concerning spirit communication. Other sections of his lengthy book on spiritualism, however, revealed another side of the story. At one point, Hare admitted that he longed for it all to be true, and he made no attempt to hide the sentiment he felt when communicating with departed family and friends. It is important to note at this point that for Hare and other Baconians, there was not necessarily a contradiction here. The Baconian approach did not deny will and passions; in fact, it affirmed their existence by regularly pointing out the danger of following them exclusively. Allowing volition and emotion alone to set the course could lead only to the evils of superstition and opinion. Letting science and reason lead the way had the natural effect of keeping will and passions in check and leaving the path clear for an unimpeded march toward truth. Despite the passion and sentimentality that crept in on occasion, Hare was convinced that his conclusions about spirit communication were eminently scientific and not in the least tainted. The story of Hare's conversion to spiritualism—along with the multitude of similar conversion stories from other spiritualists—indicates that the purported Baconian ability to keep will and passions in check was an essential part of the movement's success.

Baconianism had still other strengths that were well suited to the spiritualist experience. Although Baconianism was embraced by conservative American Protestants as a means of drawing correct theological conclusions from the "raw data" of scripture, a tension remained between traditional Christian belief and the new philosophy of science because an immediate appeal to the senses was not part of the Protestant methodology. Protestants could surely appeal to the "facts" that pointed to the truth of Christian religious claims, but these were historical facts and relied on the testimony of those who had "seen, heard, and touched" the "Word of life" over a millennium and a half earlier.[58] Such demonstration of truth from the facts of ancient history was certainly not the Baconian ideal. Instead, anyone who could muster a repeatable immediate demonstration before the eyes and ears of skeptics would, by definition, be more scientific and, hence, closer to the truth. Empirical Baconian ideals were never perfectly suited to such a religion as Christianity, which rested heavily on a long tradition of inner illumination and subjectivity in the salvation experience. Spiritualism, more than any other religious movement in antebellum America, had the Baconian approach to indisputable knowledge on its side. Of the spiritualists, none embodied the Baconian approach better than Robert Hare.

According to Hare, his conversion was neither sudden nor easy. He was a legitimate skeptic with an open mind ready to follow the evidence of his senses. He recalled, "I did not yield the ground undisputed, and was vanquished only by the facts and reasons which, when understood or admitted, must produce in others the conviction which they created in me. If I was the victim of an intellectual epidemic, my mental constitution did not yield at once to the miasma. It took some three months to include me among its victims."[59] This, of course, made his testimony all the more valuable to the spiritualist cause. One who was at first a skeptic and was won over only after a lengthy struggle with the facts was of much greater value for public relations than someone who became emotionally enthralled after a single séance.

Hare's attention was first given to spiritualist phenomena in July of 1853. He received several letters asking him for his opinion on possible "electrical" explanations for the phenomenon of "table turning." Rather than answer each letter privately, he used the same method that he used with scientific issues; that is, he immediately published his conclusions. To answer them all publicly, he sent a letter to the *Philadelphia Inquirer* in which he— North America's foremost expert on electricity—inadvertently gave a boost to the spiritualist movement. He did so by attempting to slam the door shut on what had become a common but ill-informed natural explanation of the occurrences—that they were the result of electricity. Although he did not spare the technical terms in the body of his letter, Hare concluded with a statement everyone could understand: "I am of the opinion that it is utterly impossible for six or eight, or any number of persons, seated around a table, to produce an electric current. Moreover, I am confident that if by an adequate means an electrical current were created, however forcible, it could not be productive of table turning. . . . If the power of all the galvanic apparatus ever made was to be collected in one current, there would be no power to *move* or otherwise affect such a table." Unfortunately for the spiritualists, that was the only part of Hare's letter that they could use for their purposes. Hare went on to remind the inquirers that "if there is any law which is pre-eminent for its invariability, it is, that *inanimate* matter cannot, *per se,* change its state as respects motion or rest."[60] Hare brought the point home by suggesting that if the earth did not follow this law perfectly, we would all be drowned when, because of a change in motion, the oceans spilled over their shores and overflowed the land. He closed by calling table turning a hallucination and recommended that those interested in spiritualism read the work of the British physicist Michael Faraday. Hare agreed with Faraday's conclusion, published in several American newspapers, that spiritualist phenomena resulted from involuntary muscular actions on the part of those involved.

At that point, Hare himself had never attended a "circle." Now, however, an "observant and sagacious" letter from the spiritualist Amasa Holcombe on the scientific nature of the manifestations and a personal invitation from a certain Dr. Comstock convinced Hare that he should do so. The experiences he reported were not unlike those of others who attended séances in those days. Seated with five others around a table, Hare heard tappings that sounded as if they were coming from beneath the table but "from the perfect stillness of every one of the party, could not be attributed to any one among them." The medium asked questions of the spirits, and they responded "no," "I don't know," or "yes" by rapping one, two, or three times, respectively. She then moved to another, smaller table—one that Hare had examined carefully beforehand—"yet the taps were heard as before, seemingly against the table," Hare reported.[61] Even more remarkable for Hare was that the table moved with nothing more than the medium's hands on top of it. Even with his "utmost exertions," Hare could not keep it from moving to and fro. Adding still more weight to the strange occurrences for Hare was that he was surrounded by people he held to be honorable and not easily fooled. "Even assuming the people by whom I was surrounded, to be capable of deception, and the feat to be jugglery, it was still inexplicable," he declared. "But manifestly I was in a company of worthy people, who were themselves under a deception if these sounds did not procced [sic] from spiritual agency." Hare was impressed enough that he began serious investigation "immediately afterward."[62]

He began regularly visiting spirit circles and experiencing a variety of manifestations. On one occasion, the medium placed an "alphabetic pasteboard" on the table and passed her finger over the letters while looking at the ceiling. Each time the medium's finger came upon a letter that the spirit purportedly selected the table would tilt, and the letter was recorded by someone in attendance. The message addressed all those in the circle, but the subject was Robert Hare: "*Light is dawning on the mind of your friend; soon he will speak trumpet-tongued to the scientific world, and add a new link to that chain of evidence on which our hope of man's salvation is founded.*"[63]

The step that Hare took next set him apart from other people who investigated the spirit manifestations of the mid-nineteenth century. Most of the investigations focused on determining a natural source for the sounds and unmasking frauds. The critics of the Fox sisters, for instance, who suspected the women were producing the rapping sounds by cracking their knee or toe joints, invented ways to prevent the leverage necessary for the Foxes to manipulate their joints by asking them to stand on pillows or sit with their legs in the air. Nonetheless, conclusive proof or disproof was not forthcoming. Hare's starting point for investigation was different. After repeatedly witnessing inexplicable physical occurrences, he was willing to give the spiritualists the benefit of the doubt that the source of the rapping and table tipping was outside the medium. Setting the physical phenomena aside, he focused on testing spiritualist claims that the *messages* that were coming forth were also independent of the medium. He had already witnessed some corroboratory evidence under uncontrolled circumstances, such as when the medium looked at the ceiling rather than the alphabet on the table and was still able to produce a coherent message. The task before him, then, was to bring the prowess of laboratory science to bear on the phenomenon of spirit communication to eliminate what might be manipulation by the medium. He wanted to set up controlled experimental conditions to test the reality and responsiveness of spirits.

Since Hare's fame in American science derived primarily from his creativity in developing new scientific apparatus and his clever experimental design, it is no surprise that the mark he made in the history of spiritualism was based on similar achievements. Hare invented a device called a "spiritoscope," which allowed spirits to spell out their communications on disks. In the course of his investigations, Hare developed several types of spiritoscopes, but the basic design had two elements important to his investigations: (1) direct contact between the medium and the device, which most mediums claimed was necessary for manifestations to occur; and (2) placement of the alphabet disk so that the medium could not view the letters or pointers. His first spiritoscope was designed to harness the "table tipping" phenomenon and allow it to be used for communication. A disk with the alphabet randomly printed around the perimeter was attached to a small table (see figure 1). The disk was able to spin, and a stationary pointer (or "index") was attached that could indicate the chosen letter. A rope was wound around the axle of the disk and anchored to the ground so that when the table tilted the disk would spin in proportion to the degree of movement. The most important aspect of the design for Hare was that the disk was not visible to the medium.

Hare was anxious to unveil and test his prototype, confident that it would provide the means to an *experimentum crucis* about the hypothesis of spirit agency. He made arrangements for the first test with an experienced medium:

> An accomplished lady, capable of serving in the required capacity, was so kind as to assist me by taking her seat behind the screen, while I took my seat in front of the disk.
>
> I then said, "If there be any spirit present, please to indicate the affirmative by causing the letter Y to come under the index." Forthwith this letter was brought under the index.
>
> "Will the spirit do us the favour to give the initials of his name?" The letters R H were successively brought under the index. "My honoured father?" said I. The letter Y was again brought under the index.
>
> "Will my father do me the favour to bring the letters under the index successively in alphabetical order?" Immediately the disk began to revolve so as to produce the desired result. After it had proceeded as far as the middle of the alphabet, I requested that "the name of Washington should be spelt out by the same process." This feat was accordingly performed, as well as others of a like nature.
>
> The company consisted of but few persons besides the medium, who now urged that I could no longer refuse to come over to their belief. Under these

Figure 1. One of Robert Hare's early spiritoscopes designed to ensure that the medium would not influence the message since the alphabet disk could not be seen and a screen cut off the medium's view of the spinning. (All figures are from Hare's *Experimental Investigation of the Spirit Manifestations,* v)

circumstances the following communication was made by the revolving disk:
"*Oh, my son, listen to reason!*"

I urged that the experiment was of immense importance, if considered as
proving a spirit to be present, and to have actuated the apparatus; affording
thus precise experimental proof of the immortality of the soul: that a matter of such moment should not be considered as conclusively decided until
every possible additional means of verification should be employed.[64]

Hare's companions that night accused him of "extreme incredulity."
Another person in attendance declared Hare to be "insusceptible of conviction" and gave up on him.[65] Hare was much closer to conviction than his
companions realized, though. It is clear from his total immersion in the research that Hare himself was anxious to remove any lingering doubts he was
having. Perhaps improvements in his apparatus would help, and as quickly
as he made improvements, he tested them. In one experiment, he put castors and wheels on the legs of the table so horizontal motion could be used
in addition to vertical tippings (see figure 2).

Figure 2. One of Hare's improved spiritoscopes, which had castors and wheels on the
legs of the table to facilitate the tippings and allowed the medium to make contact
with the table through large brass spheres, making it impossible for the medium to
influence the rolling motion of the table that was responsible for turning the disk.

On one occasion, after Hare had made what he thought were significant improvements, no words came from the apparatus, but he thought the spirits were there because they were manifesting themselves in other ways. Hare moved the medium to an ordinary table and used alphabetic cards to ask the spirits themselves what improvements in the device would help their communication. The reply was "let the medium see the letters."[66] (Later, after his conversion, the spirit of his father purportedly informed him that the spirits usually used the eyes of the medium to see but that because of the screen blocking her view, the spirits were attempting to use the eyes of others in the room, with much less success.)

In principle, Hare thought, a visible alphabet would nullify the experiment because he could no longer be certain that the medium was not producing the result. "However," Hare said, "it soon occurred to me that by means of a metal plate, made quite true, and some brass balls, like billiard balls, with which I was provided, I could neutralize the power of the medium to move the table, so that she could not influence the selection of the letters, though permitted to see them." The medium placed her hands on top of the plate resting on the balls, thus making the physical contact that spiritualists deemed "necessary." She could move the balls and plate on top of the table but not the table itself (see figure 2), and communications came forth as the table moved apparently unaided by the medium.

In another design, Hare let the medium see the letters but removed his ability to manipulate them because he used water as the "conducting substance" (see figure 3). He took a board and set one end on a sawhorse and hooked the other end to a spring scale that held it aloft. Then he set a large bowl of water near the middle of the board and instructed the medium to put his hands in the water without touching the bottom or sides of the bowl. The board was able to move up and down as, it seemed, the spirits saw fit. As the board moved, it caused the needle on the spring scale to rotate. Hare replaced the numbers indicating pounds with letters of the alphabet (similar to the device in figure 3) and seemed quite pleased with how well it worked. Since the medium had contact with only the water, there was no way he could move the plank attached to the disk. Hare believed this feature effectively removed the agency of the medium so that any message coming through had to be from the spirits. During one séance, however, the device would not operate until the water was warmed, and then it began producing intelligible spirit messages. Hare became increasingly intrigued with the physical "conduction" of spirit messages because of the parallels with his electrical studies. He tried other designs of his spiritoscope and a variety of experiments.

Although he does not record at what point the evidence finally convinced him, Hare seemed to be especially intrigued by what he considered the spirits' ability to respond accurately to questions for which only he knew the answer. If he was not already a believer, he probably took the plunge in the spring of 1854, when he witnessed something he considered more astonishing than any of the other manifestations—a table moving without any human contact at all.[67] After that, Hare's investigations seemed to take on a different tone. His experiments shifted from attempting to answer the question "Is there intelligence behind these phenomena?" to addressing a differ-

Figure 3. A spiritoscope Hare designed so that the medium had contact with only the water and thus could not possibly manipulate the plank attached to the disk.

ent question, "How is it possible for these disembodied spirits to perform these feats?" Somewhere along the line, he had become a believer.

The scientific studies in which he engaged certainly cleared the path for Hare to march into the spiritualist camp. But the fact that he initially used scientific methods to investigate spiritualism does not answer the question of why, once converted, Hare was eventually so willing—almost eager—to accept, often uncritically, even the most speculative spirit messages. There are at least three factors that help explain this.

First, Hare already had an inclination toward the underlying ethos of the spirit world. The comments of the spirits on most subjects relied on ideas that Hare considered to be obvious, commonsense notions, positions that resonated with his own beliefs about human nature, values, history, the cosmos, and the afterlife. Even if the content of spirit communications bordered on what the culture deemed bizarre, such noble underlying themes as moral progress, love of learning, and egalitarianism succeeded in making the strange more familiar and hence more palatable. In other words, some of the spirit messages were particularly odd-shaped pieces that nonetheless fit into a larger picture that Hare recognized and valued.

Second, at some point in his scientific investigations and conversion process, he felt he had enough proof of the genuineness of the spirits, at least enough to let down his guard about the truth of the communications he was receiving. Like his contemporaries Orson Pratt and, as we will see, Phineas Quimby, Hare eventually crossed a sort of "Baconian threshold," beyond which he was ready to stop critical analysis of every minor datum and start embracing the new world to which his trusted scientific compass had led him. This action was a leap, but it probably did not seem like a leap of *faith* to these men. It seemed more like an enlightened action that was sanctioned by a scientific imprimatur. For Hare, it was also a leap not without its logic. After all, if the reality of spirit communication had been convincingly demonstrated and the spirits themselves were found to be advanced in wisdom and knowledge far beyond the mortal sphere, it would only be prudent to pay close attention to their teachings and to receive them with a fair degree of humility.[68]

Third, and no doubt most important for Hare, who had labored for years to make minor advances in scientific knowledge, these alleged spirit beings knew science and were therefore living repositories of advanced knowledge in the disciplines. They could thus give clues to new discoveries or—of great importance to the contentious Hare—make judgments about whose theory on a particular matter was correct. What better reward could a scientist receive for his lifelong devotion, and what better tribute could there be to the Baconian spirit of the antebellum period? Science not only had helped discover such technological marvels as the telegraph and steam engine but now had verified life beyond death as well. As if that were not enough, the spirits that Hare believed science had discovered were about to effect a quantum leap in science itself through their superior understanding of nature and its laws.

The Physical World of the Spirits

The descriptions that séance participants said spirits gave of the afterlife were not monolithic. In fact, many of the earthbound who regularly sat in spirit circles found the divergence of spirit opinion not unlike that among humans, and some found it very difficult to reconcile the conflicting messages from different spirit sources. Despite the discrepancies in the descriptive details, a rather well-recognized body of underlying themes was promulgated with surprising harmony. Some have called these themes collectively spiritualist doctrine, theology, or theory. These teachings regularly came from séances and were elaborated on in spiritualist periodicals. Such prominent spiritualists as Adin Ballou maintained that the principal doctrines of spiritualism were reliably "put forth by ninety-nine one hundredths of the communications of reliable spirits throughout the country."[69]

This unity of theme amidst the diversity in the movement was not lost on Robert Hare and is clearly reflected in his *Experimental Investigation of the Spirit Manifestations.* Fortunately for historians, Hare made no attempt to hide his enthusiasm for his spiritualist discoveries. In fact, I included Hare in this study primarily because of the wealth of personal information and beliefs that he openly espoused and codified. In addition to his own observations, Hare included in his book some of the written accounts from other spiritualists that he had read and found compelling. His work thus embodies a full range of spiritualist theory and praxis in the antebellum period. More important, it contains the testimonies and ideas in the movement that Hare deemed worthy and with which he most likely agreed. In revealing the spiritualist world, I rely primarily on his descriptions and the accounts of other spiritualists he thought important enough to include in his work. Although Hare's book does not provide an exhaustive view of the spirit world, there is enough cross-fertilization involved in his experience and his writing to consider his book an admirable representation of the spiritualist experience of the period.

According to the messages said to have come from the spirits, Robert Hare's conversion was one of their crowning achievements in the new era of communication with mortals. One medium, J. F. Lanning of Philadelphia, sent Hare a message he claimed he had received from an unnamed spirit anxious to tell the scientist that "brilliant minds with brilliant thoughts are burning to give utterance to earth through you. You are a selected instrument of our own choosing, and we are watching and guiding in the path and to the goal you seek. You may not only 'speak trumpet-tongued to the scientific world,' but in *thunder-tones* to those savans [*sic*] who think they are the masters of the keys of knowledge."[70] Directly after his conversion, however, Hare felt he was not yet equipped with enough information to act as spokesperson for the spirit world. He had plenty to say about his own detailed investigations of the reality of spirit communication but relatively little of substance to say about the nature of the life beyond. He wrote that "as soon as [I was] convinced that the phenomena were due to the shades of the dead, I looked with eagerness for some consistent information of their abodes, modes of existence, of the theological doctrines entertained by them, and the actual diversities of their situation consequent to various degrees of moral and intellectual merit."[71]

Hare believed that in the fall of 1854 he was the recipient of a lengthy communication from his esteemed father, Robert Hare Sr. The younger Hare's reverence for his father is reflected in the fact that this communication is the centerpiece of his book. It is the most basic and the most certain description of life beyond the veil contained in the volume, and Hare refers to it throughout his book. To a great extent, much of Hare's book is a "fleshing out" of the basic data provided in this reported communication. Hare was so impressed with his "spirit father" and the lesson he received that he called on his father regularly from then on to answer questions on matters of fact, philosophy, or judgment regarding the reliability of particular spirit messages. Hare completely trusted what he believed to be his father's spirit to relay the best information about all matters, including the trustworthiness of certain spirits or mediums who he began to think were not always blessed with impeccable character.

As we shall see, the lesson that Hare received from his purported spirit father came to be more than a verbal tour of the invisible world beyond. In many of its details, the world that was presented also laid out a master plan of the Enlightenment village for which people like Hare, Pratt, and Quimby longed. The orderly, tranquil, geometric, and lawful nature of the spirit world that Hare's father described illustrated that the village Enlightenment was not merely about proper methodology for advancing knowledge and distinguishing between truth and error but also about the way the world should be and the way life ought to be lived. Science, reason, and natural law were the obvious means, but the kind of world that Hare's spirit father described was one of the intentional ends.

The reported paternal lesson was direct and factual. It was not over-endowed with the flowery prose and verse that often accompanied other communications. Hare's spirit father simply promised to do his best "according to the extent of [his] capacity and highest perception of truth,"[72] and he proceeded to survey everything from geography to economics, from marriage to music, from government to God in the world of the spirits.

According to the spirit of Hare's father—who appeared well versed in the cosmology of Emanuel Swedenborg as revamped for an American audience by the spiritualist philosopher Andrew Jackson Davis—the world in which the departed spirits of earth lived began precisely 60 miles above the earth's surface and ended 120 miles above it. In this area surrounding the earth were six concentric spheres evenly spread out, each ten miles from bottom to top. There were seven spheres in all because the earth itself was considered the first or "rudimentary" sphere. Each of the six spirit spheres was a world unto itself. Hare's spirit father emphasized that "they are not shapeless chimeras, or mere projections of the mind, but absolute entities, as much so indeed as the planets of the solar system or the globe on which you now reside. . . . Their surfaces are diversified with an immense variety of the most picturesque landscapes; with the lofty mountain ranges, valleys, rivers, lakes, forests, and the internal correspondence of all the higher phenomena of earth."[73] In this reading, there was an *increase* in visual beauty as one ascended through each of the successive layers.

These spheres surrounding the earth had no effect on basic planetary motion, and they always accompanied the earth as it revolved around the sun. However, the spirits received their warmth and light from the "spiritual correspondence" of the sun, a spiritual sun concentric with the one that warms and lights the terrestrial world. Time and seasons based on solar events were therefore different in the spirit world and really quite unimportant to beings whose reference point was eternity.

There were, according to Hare's account, laws and a government to preserve order in the spirit world. The "government of the spheres is republican," declared Hare's spirit father. Legislative, judicial, and executive powers did not need written codes or physical coercion, however: "The results of these functions are realized in simultaneous and homogeneous opinions awakened in the minds of the ruling spirits, as truth takes hold of the minds of mathematicians, *pari pasu,* as they read the same series of demonstrations. The conclusions in which the chief spirits thus unanimously concur, are by them impressed upon their constituents, who, thus impressed, are constitutionally unable to resist the sentiment which, like a magic spell, operates upon their sense of right, and overrules any rebellious passion." The system of law, order, and justice was said to be completely intuitive. Disputes did not arise, because moral and legal questions in the spirit sphere were akin to questions of "weighing, measuring, or mathematical calculation" in the rudimentary sphere. Disputes were thus settled objectively and finally by the application of the proper scientific instrument.[74] Justice was always meted out perfectly, and the natural consequences of illegal or immoral actions were the only punishments.

As for economics, it is ironic that in the same year that Karl Marx was writing his in-depth critique of economic theory in London, Hare's spirits in Philadelphia were describing a system that made the communist paradise of Marx look harsh. Here, wealth was as "unbounded and free as air or light" and was available to every member of the spirit society. In the spheres, objects of human luxury or taste existed "in profusion, the supply is of course always equal to demand." Like air, these objects "have no marketable value; there is no one who has occasion to buy, all being abundantly supplied from a common inexhaustible stock."[75] In this spirit paradise, Marx's work was already obsolete sixty miles above.

In parallel with Enlightenment village ideals, the spirit society had as its only currency, the only thing of great value, moral and intellectual attainment. The only aristocracy was that of "mind and merit." The currency was "coined in the mint of divine love, and assayed by the standards of purity and truth."[76] The quality of mind and the level of moral purity not only were the things most valued in spirit life but also formed the basis for the system of spiritual apartheid in the spheres. Spirits with lower levels of understanding or less virtuous character were unable to inhabit any except the lowest spheres until they progressed enough in learning and rectitude to be elevated. Teachers in the higher spheres would instruct those in the lower spheres in the arts and sciences and guide them into righteous thought and behavior. The elder Hare remarked that advancement for spirits in the lower spheres, "however slow it may be, is nevertheless sure, since 'Onward and Upward' is the motto emblazoned on the spiritual banner."[77]

That science and reason would invariably lead to progress and that progress itself was a natural law were foundational principles in the Enlightenment village. Likewise, there was little doubt from the proclaimed communication of Hare's spirit father—or for that matter, any spiritualist literature of the day—that the "immutable law of progression" was an unalterable principle of the spirit spheres. All inhabitants progressed in mind and character, eventually moving up the ladder of spheres to the exalted seventh sphere. True progress, however, had no terminal point. Even the seventh sphere was really just another beginning. From that level, one would be launched into the "Supernal Heavens," the "great and illimitable sphere of progression which lies outside of all other spheres, and in which the greatest conceivable degree of harmony reigns."[78] Still, Hare's spirit father made it clear that he was not aware of any spirit from earth that had made it beyond the seventh sphere. Robert Hare Jr. claimed a spirit named Maria had communicated that even "Jesus of Nazareth, the great moral reformer" had not yet progressed beyond it.[79] Other inhabitants of the seventh sphere were "the apostles, prophets, and martyrs of olden time," as well as "Confucius, Seneca, Plato, Socrates, and Solon with all the philosophers of ancient Greece and Rome."[80] The purported spirits were unanimous in their communication that infants, because of their innocence and purity, went from earth directly to the seventh sphere, where they were loved, cared for, and nurtured in a manner beyond the capabilities of mortals.

In the account Hare gave, few if any mortals, other than infants, were catapulted directly to the seventh sphere. One's initial placement in the spheres directly after death was based on earthly achievements in mind and morals. Everyone would eventually reach the Supernal Heavens, but not everyone started on the same rung of the ladder. All the spheres, however, were better and more beautiful than earth—except the second. The second sphere was darker and more barren. It was the location of a kind of spiritual boot camp for the morally depraved and ignorant. Sometimes called "Hades" in spiritualist literature, the second sphere was the abode of those who were filled with remorse for the deeds of the past life. But unlike souls in the biblical hell, the spirits in the second sphere were also filled with hope because there were teachers from the higher spheres committed to their progress "Onward and Upward." Achievements of the mind were not all considered equal in terms of spiritual reward. The "bigoted" and unjust ideas of the Calvinists and other sectarians would land them in lower spheres, but "freethinkers" with "superior liberality" would be immediately advanced.[81]

Religious instruction was a prominent part of the lessons taught in the world to come, but the teachers did not come from the ranks of orthodox Christian thinkers because they were held in very low esteem. Hare's spirit father said that "our religious teachers belong to that class of persons who were noted, during their probation on earth, for their philanthropy and deeds of moral bravery; those who . . . dared to promulgate and defend the doctrines of 'civil and religious liberty.'" He emphasized that "we have no sectarian or ecclesiastical feuds; no metaphysical dogmas." The religious teachings highlighted the wonders of nature (on earth and beyond) that pointed to the glory of the Deity and the "soul-inspiring and elevating doctrine of *universal* and *eternal* progression."[82] For the spirits, nature, reason, and religion went hand in hand.

God was rarely mentioned in the spirit communications that Hare recorded. "The Deity," as he was most often impersonally named, was responsible for all of the basic laws of nature—physical, moral, and spiritual—but like the God of the Deists, the Supreme Being had no direct involvement in the affairs of earth or the spirit spheres. God was far removed and pleased to let his laws and those who apprehended them run the world. Even though Hare's spirits said little about the Deity, Hare was not reluctant to publish his own ideas and inferences. He reasoned that God was limited in power. This was the only way he could reconcile the coexistence of evil and an all-loving God in the same universe; God simply did not have the power to stop it all. Hare, like his Mormon counterpart Orson Pratt, also considered the idea of an ex nihilo creation to be an outmoded superstition and contrary to reason, primarily because of the commonsense notion that something cannot come from nothing.[83]

Although Hare's spirits were rarely reported as offering unsolicited information about God, when Hare asked for confirmation about his own theological notions, he believed they responded in the affirmative. Hare therefore considered his own inferences and conclusions sanctioned "by Spiritualism."[84] In a remarkable theological passage that links Hare with Orson Pratt and, as we shall see, Phineas Quimby in their foundational ideas about God, Hare claimed that according to "Spiritualism," God himself was bound by natural law. "The Deity," wrote Hare, "is represented as operating by general laws, from which, consistently with his attributes, he cannot deviate, having to perform no miracle to attain his ends; and . . . through these laws he is incessantly acting for the good of mankind."[85] Also like Pratt and Quimby, Hare never found it necessary to wrestle with critical questions associated with the idea that there were laws to which God himself might have to conform. Hare never asked such questions. For him, as for Pratt and Quimby, simply invoking the word *nature* in association with these laws settled the question. If anything, nature was clearly the absolute reference point, even for God.

No matter what its ultimate origin, then, natural law in the spirit spheres and in the Enlightenment village was supreme. Natural law was not, however, limited to the law of progress. According to the description of the spirit world Hare felt he had received from his spirit father, there were other natural laws at work. For instance, an important law that orchestrated the whole cosmology of the spirit world was the "law of spiritual correspondences."[86] This law made it a near certainty that if something existed in the terrestrial sphere, it also existed in the spirit spheres but with more refinement, grandeur, beauty, intensity, and perfection. Historians who have looked at this aspect of spiritualism are confident that there is a traceable line from the law of spiritual correspondence in American spiritualism back to the Swedish seer Emanuel Swedenborg, directly through Andrew Jackson Davis.[87] Swedenborg maintained that "the whole natural world corresponds to the spiritual world, not just the natural world in general, but actually in details."[88] Davis and the spiritualists embraced this basic concept without deviation, but the finer points of the heaven they described had decidedly nineteenth-century American characteristics.

The concept of correspondence in early nineteenth-century America was not exclusive to the circles of spiritualists and Swedenborgians. American Transcendentalists, such as Ralph Waldo Emerson, based their understanding of things spiritual and unseen on correspondences with those things that were physical and seen.[89] Along less liberal lines, it was quite acceptable for orthodox Christians to think of heaven in terms that corresponded to earthly life. Heaven was regularly conceived of as a tangible place with a clearly articulated substantiality.[90] One English writer was an especially important source for the more popular, mainstream concept of "heavenly correspondence" in the American antebellum period. Isaac Taylor, a lay theologian and committed Baconian, published a small volume in 1836 that was widely circulated. Entitled *Physical Theory of Another Life,* the book featured rhetoric that was quoted in literature and sermons dealing with heaven in orthodox and heterodox circles alike. Hare himself quoted Taylor at length in his *Spirit Manifestations,* as did Pratt and Quimby. Orson Pratt acknowledged Taylor's notoriety and referred to him as "that celebrated writer."[91] Taylor inferred a great deal about the heavenly life by using the Bible and what he called the "rule of analogy." He focused primarily on the activities and employment of the occupants of heaven and asserted that there was a direct correspondence between one's occupation on earth and one's occupation in heaven. For him, earth was a grand training ground for the future life in heaven, involving an eternity of enriching and challenging work. The "rule of analogy" saw parallels between earth and heaven far beyond the line of work an individual might have, simply because work on earth entailed almost everything else imaginable in everyday life. To work, one needed fields to plant, tools to use, roads to travel, eyes to see, language to communicate, and so on. In another parallel with the spirit world, Taylor, like Andrew Jackson Davis and the spiritualists, thought heaven was a place of progress. Heavenly work would bring such fulfillment that it would lead to progress in the development of the soul. Some of the labor of heaven would actually involve working with the "millions needing to be governed, taught, rescued, and led forward, from a worse to a better, or from a lower to a higher stage of life," Taylor wrote.[92]

Although the idea of spiritual progress was not lost in Taylor's heaven, the overriding principles were "reverential submission" to God and the reign of Christ. His notions thus offered a palatable option to many in orthodox circles. Colleen McDannell and Bernhard Lang noted that Taylor's beliefs concerning heaven were incorporated into the writings of many British and American Protestants, and they placed Taylor in a line of "modern" thinking about heaven started by Swedenborg.[93] The early and wide distribution of Taylor's book indicates that spiritualist descriptions of the afterlife did not exist in isolation and may have drawn from not only Swedenborg but Taylor as well. Taylor's treatment of heaven seems to have helped confirm the popular hopes of many—including nonspiritualists—that in the next life the Enlightenment ideals not realized on earth would be realized on another plane.

The "law of spiritual correspondence" prominent in the spiritualist cosmology was, however, engrossed in details that even the most avant-garde in orthodoxy would find too speculative about biblical data, though not out of line with the hopes of village Enlightenment thinkers. In the reported lesson to his son, the spirit of Robert Hare Sr. introduced a long list of items that corresponded to life on earth, including the institution of marriage and language. Marriage in the spheres, for instance, was called "celestial marriage"; it was "the blending of two minds in one, resulting from an innate reciprocal love in each; a conjunction of negative and positive principles, forming a true and indissoluble bond of spiritual union . . . which is born of God, and is therefore eternal."[94] Like marriage, earthly language had a superior counterpart in the spheres. The language of the spheres was unified and powerful enough to "impart more ideas to each other in a single word than you can possibly convey in a hundred."[95] More important, language did not need to be spoken. Higher spirits could impress thoughts and feelings on one another and on lower spirits.

In addition to the laws of progress and correspondence, Hare reported that his spirit father introduced the "law of affinity," which reigned over all personal relationships and social status in the spheres. Individual spirits, Hare said, had a type of "halo," "aura," or "radiance" that distinguished one spirit from all others. Six societies were formed in each of the six spirit spheres, and the inhabitants of each sphere with similar "effulgence" were drawn by the law of affinity to the level in each sphere where "congenial minds and opinions are drawn toward each other . . . on the principle that 'like attracts like.'"[96] Family and friends long separated by death, it was claimed, were thus united in the spheres, being drawn together by an unalterable law of natural affinity.[97]

Science in the Spheres

Robert Hare Sr.'s reported lecture on the spirit world emerged as a thorough survey and touched most of the key aspects of the future life spiritualists disseminated. Robert Hare Jr. believed that he also communicated with his spirit brother, sister, and one of his sons, who died as an infant. He heard all of the spirits urge him to publish the results of his communications, but Hare was reluctant because most of his information had come from his claimed "relations." It was not that he did not trust them, but he wanted to be able to deflect criticism that he was sure he would encounter if he rested all his information on the authority of dead loved ones. But Hare believed that he had a "great assemblage of elevated spirits" on his side who were anxious to help. He thought that his 1854 lecture at Franklin Hall in Boston—where he demonstrated his spiritoscope to a packed house—had also been attended by "a company of the most noteworthy spirits." The visitors, he said, were interested in making great new strides in their mission to make spirit communication commonplace.[98] Hare asked his spirit father if he could assemble the spirit luminaries for a special séance—the information from which would add weight to the spiritualist case he was preparing. The response, he believed, was affirmative, and an appointment was set for "Monday, the 18th of February, 1855, at nine o'clock." So that no one could question the integrity of the session, Hare prepared sixty-four questions to be answered by the spirits. The answers would then be confirmed using Hare's apparatus *under test conditions.*"[99] At the appointed hour, a series of names were spelled out on Hare's disk: "George Washington, J[ohn] Q[uincy] Adams, W[illia]m H. Harrison, A[ndrew] Jackson, Henry Clay, Benjamin

Franklin, W[illiam] E[llery] Channing, H[enry] K[irke] White, Isaac Newton, Byron, Martha Washington, Besides relatives and friends."[100] In Hare's account, the assembly of spirits faithfully answered the questions posed on a wide variety of subjects, and Hare later published the material.[101]

Hare had thus far spent most of his time in séances in a passive, listening role attempting to get acquainted with what he was convinced was the spirit world. This time, however, he was able to interrogate the reported spirits and ask the questions most important to him. These, not surprisingly, turned out to be questions of a scientific nature. He was enormously curious about the continuity of the scientific enterprise from this world to the next, and his spirits were pleased to inform him in a unanimous voice that the spheres housed what could only be described as a scientific utopia.

Hare believed that although the spheres above were "spiritual," they were also "material." His noteworthy spirits at the "convocation" emphatically concurred. The spiritual matter of the worlds above corresponded directly to the "gross matter" of the terrestrial sphere, but the spirit matter was highly refined and rarefied. Spirit matter, although invisible to the mortal eye, followed fixed laws similar to those in the ordinary material universe. Literal "physical" science in the spheres was therefore in no way precluded. Although the terminology was confusing at times to those both inside and outside of the movement, spiritualist "doctrine" was decidedly materialistic and included unalterable physical laws.

According to the accounts of the spirits, it would be a gross understatement to say that science was simply "valued" in the spirit spheres. It is difficult to discern from Hare's accounts whether science was an object of worship or a method of worship, but either way it was inseparable from meaningful acts of reverence depicted in the spirit world. The spirits rarely described houses of religious devotion, but all of them, in Hare's telling, mentioned magnificent *temples* "devoted to the arts and sciences."[102] Hare was so favorably impressed that he wanted to form an association to render Sunday on earth a day of "scientific instruction, for those who, dissatisfied with the sectarianism of existing places of worship, pass the day without edifying occupation." The goal of the association, wrote Hare, "would be to contemplate the Deity, agreeably to the opinions entertained by the first and one of the best of philosophers, Sir Isaac Newton."[103]

The temples devoted to science in the spirit world—and Hare's hope of replicating the basic idea—were reminiscent of the "temples of reason" that the American deist Elihu Palmer attempted to organize in several major cities from 1795 to 1806. Although there may well be some direct relationship between the ideas contained in the spiritualist doctrine of the mid-nineteenth century and the crusade for popular deism five decades earlier, there is an important difference as well. That difference symbolizes a change that took place during the course of fifty years of American culture and highlights the distinction between what I am calling the "village Enlightenment" and the Enlightenment in general. Elihu Palmer's temples were "temples of reason," because "reason"—in his thinking and according to the ethos of the Enlightenment—provided the surest and most certain way to understand nature and nature's God. Reason—unlike special revelation—was the only reliable path for anyone in search of an absolute. But, ironically, over the course of only a few decades, the great Enlightenment pillar of reason lost definition in the democratic ethos it helped create in the United States. Pluralism, dissent, equality, freedom of thought, and other democratic ideals became part of everyday American life and culture. All areas of life in the young republic were affected by a multitude of individuals prepared to debate their case on any issue in the spirit of "one man, one vote." However, no one who wanted to be successful in the new democratic culture—with its strong Enlightenment heritage—would ever claim "reason" was *not* on their side. But if every person's position on a given issue was in perfect accord with reason and the positions offered were logically at odds, as they often were, what did that say about reason?[104] What, then, was the difference between reason and "opinion"—a term that carried little favor in the popular intellectual atmosphere of the day? Reason was certainly never put aside as an important ideal, but the *authority* gained by offering a position in the name of "reason" had become somewhat diminished in democratic society.[105] The term *science*, however, was growing in authority, primarily because, in its pervasive Baconian form, it could bring a decisive element to the debate. To the reasoning powers of the mind, science could add the discernment of the senses, which so many in the period agreed was, in Robert Breckinridge's words, "the ultimate certainty upon which every other certainty rests."[106] The temple of reason had been enhanced, not replaced, by a revitalized form of reason that could more effectively settle the disputes multiplying in the thick atmosphere of democracy. Any authority lost by "reason" was recaptured (at least for several decades) by "science." Through its appeal to the senses, many thought, science could temper the subjective elements that had crept into and polluted the pure activity of the mind. The people that I am associating with the village Enlightenment were able to shore up effectively the pillar of reason by attaching it firmly to the certainty of the senses.[107]

The certainty and centrality of the senses was not just a characteristic of the earthly Enlightenment village. According to Hare's spirit father, the quest for scientific knowledge through the senses was a primary activity in the spheres and the ultimate scholarly pursuit: "Our scientific researches and investigations are extended to all that pertains to the phenomena of universal nature; to all the wonders of the heavens and the earth, and to whatever the mind of man is capable of conceiving: all of which exercise our faculties, and form a considerable part of our enjoyments. The noble and sublime sciences of astronomy, chemistry, and mathematics engage a considerable portion of our attention, and afford us an inexhaustible subject for study and reflection."[108]

The spirit world and spirit beings, as Hare saw them, were inherently much better equipped for scientific work. The material substance of the spheres was more vibrant in color, texture, tone, flavor, and fragrance than the gross matter of earth, and there was a fuller range of animals, vegetables, and minerals to study. In addition, because the material properties were more radiant, the pleasure of contact with nature through science was improved. "I cannot find words to describe to you the magnificent creations of Him from whom all order, beauty, and harmony proceed," said Hare's spirit brother Charles. "I am surrounded by every thing that can delight the eye, please the ear, and gratify the taste," he added. The spirit world was by any measure more glorious than earth, but that was just one side of the equation. The spirits also had a greater capacity to appreciate all that was displayed before them because their senses were greater than those of mortals. Spirit senses were more acute in general, but they were particularly suited "for studying all the principles of the vast universe of matter."[109] The spirits were also not limited to the five senses of the mundane world. Several of Hare's spirits spoke to him about a sixth sense that one gained upon entering the spheres. It was a "peculiar sense" that laid open "the interior of nature" and allowed individual spirits to make intuitive distinctions between other spirits and between the different spheres.[110] Hare later speculated in his "Apology for My Conversion" that this sense was already with us but as yet undeveloped: "We are related to, and become acquainted with, the external world by the medium of the five senses; but who will say that there are not other senses hidden in possibility in our nature which may by means of other affinities communicate with a world far more refined in its constitution, with which we cannot now come in contact?"[111] Hare's spirit father gave an enlightening, though perhaps not completely consistent, description of the way in which this special perception aided in the learning process, particularly in the learning of science:

> We do not study those practical arts, which are essential to the earth life, such as mechanics, &c.; for we do not stand in need of their applications; our studies being wholly of a mental character, we attend to the fundamental principles only. All the more intellectual branches of the arts and sciences are cultivated in a much more perfect manner than that to which we have been accustomed upon earth. The mind being untrammeled by the gross material body, and having its intellectual energies and perceptions improved, we can by intuition, as it were, more clearly and rapidly perceive and understand the principles and truths on which the sciences are based. We can trace the various relations of each subject, so as to understand its connective importance; a knowledge at which mortals arrive only by a long and tedious process.[112]

This passage highlights another aspect of Hare's spirit world that agreed with his predispositions: the fusion of different areas of thought and study. Hare believed that traditionally diverse disciplines, such as chemistry, ethics, music, geology, economics, history, linguistics, and art, should be unified under one exalted scientific approach. On one occasion, he confessed, "I do not understand how any man of common sense can conceive that theological, metaphysical, or experimental science can be the separate object of contemplation."[113] Life in the spirit world made this all-encompassing approach to knowledge possible because it was so much easier to perceive the underlying principles and peer directly into the "interior of nature." The blending of traditional compartments of study in the spirit world was not, however, just an intellectual exercise as Hare described it; it was worked out in practice in the spheres.

Hare recorded a striking example of this blending of compartments in both theory and practice. In this case, two categories of law on earth, physical and moral, were united in the spirit world he perceived. The greatest and most certain physical law of the terrestrial domain, Newton's law of gravity, carried over into the spirit spheres. But in the spheres, it grew in grandeur by assuming moral dimensions as well. On earth, physical bodies would rise or fall in a particular medium, such as water or air, depending on the ratio—called the specific gravity—between the density of the body and the density of an equal volume of the medium. Hare's spirits maintained that this fundamental physical law actually controlled the level to which an individual spirit could rise in the spheres. Each spirit being had a "moral specific gravity" that was governed by Newton's law. The more morally pure and meritorious the spirit being, the lower its "moral specific gravity" and, hence, the higher it could rise in the spheres. A spirit ascended according to the laws of nature until it came into equilibrium with the atmosphere of the proper sphere. Hare quizzed his spirit convocation on this point in hopes of confirming the principle:

> What confines a spirit to his proper level, so that none can mount above it into a sphere to which he does not belong?
>
> *Ans.* A moral specific gravity, in which the weight is inversely as the merit, prevents the spirit from rising above his proper level.
>
> Are spirits of different densities rarer or more refined in constitution as they are higher in rank?
>
> *Ans.* Yes.[114]

This remarkable conflation of nature's moral and physical laws demonstrated that it was not necessary for God to intervene in separating the wheat from the chaff. Nature was more than capable of determining the first step in a person's final reward. The conflation was also an effective refutation of "Calvinist" or "sectarian" doctrine of the afterlife. The spiritualists vilified Calvin's idea that God condemned some to hell in a seemingly capricious manner. Equally abhorrent, however, was the Reformed concept of grace, which granted favor to those who did not deserve it. Hare and others in the spiritualist camp considered this idea immoral, holding that it accused "the Almighty of acting like an idiot."[115] Rather, God acted according to the laws of nature—laws powerful enough to control the motion of all heavenly bodies and unerringly place individuals in their proper heavenly abodes according to equitable and justifiable criteria.

Excited as he was about the unity of natural law in the spirit world and the eternal, scientific utopia presented there, Hare had not lost his curiosity about other matters. He had spent a lifetime attempting to find solutions to some of the most basic questions involving the nature of matter, heat, electricity, magnetism, and even the relationship between mind and matter. With the new connection he felt with spirits, the answers to many of those questions seemed much closer because he expected spirits to provide new data for consideration and to place decisive stamps of approval on theories that were offered. Hare was particularly grateful to the spirit of Benjamin Franklin, who, Hare reported, personally communicated that Hare's theory of electricity was the only correct one. The Franklin of Hare's experience insisted that Hare republish his treatise on electricity in his book on spiritualism, which he did.[116]

This type of theoretical vindication from the spirit world was certainly gratifying, but the vindication was not a one-way street. Hare's lifelong scientific work also helped, at least in his own mind, to vindicate the cosmology of the spirits. The theories he defended over his career, especially those related to the nature of matter, were arguably some of the best theories in the science of the period with which to argue the existence of spirits. It is no wonder it was claimed that the spirits focused their efforts on Hare's conversion, "selecting him" from among so many other scientists, because Hare's thinking on matter and its properties provided one of the best conceptual matches available to descriptions of the spirit world.

Years before he even knew about spiritualist phenomena, Hare had arrived at his very firmly held ideas about matter primarily through his experimentation with electricity. He considered alternative electrical theories posed by Benjamin Franklin, Andre-Marie Ampère, and Charles-François du Fay "irreconcilable with the premises on which they are founded, and with facts on all sides admitted."[117] The primary deficiency, he argued, was that these honored men of science did not employ theories of matter sufficiently broad to answer nagging inconsistencies in their explanations of electrical and magnetic phenomena. Hare considered himself a diehard proponent of a theory of matter that had tremendous explanatory power. As Hare saw it, matter could be broken down into two basic types: ponderable and imponderable.

The existence of ponderable matter was not in dispute in scientific circles. It was the "everyday" matter that had direct contact with the senses and could be seen, touched, and, most important, weighed. Imponderable matter was a substance that did not display the property of weight. "Ethereal matter," or "ethers," was usually what one had in mind when discussing imponderables. More scientists than not in the first half of the nineteenth century were likely to embrace the concept, but even if it was not warmly received by an individual scientist, it was usually considered part of the arsenal of explanation.[118] Of course, there were some who were adamantly opposed to the idea. The renowned English scientist and philosopher William Whewell weighed in heavily on the side of ponderability as a property *essential* to the definition of matter in an influential publication entitled "Demonstration That All Matter Is Heavy." Whewell sent Hare a copy of his paper in 1842, and Hare, in turn, wrote a well-argued letter that was published widely. Hare was not without high-powered help in his position on the existence of imponderables. On the same side of the Atlantic but on the other side of the issue as Whewell, Michael Faraday found the idea of imponderables useful in making sense of his own experiments in electricity and magnetism. However, Faraday's well-recognized humility as a scientist inclined him, unlike Hare, to hold to ideas loosely, especially such an idea as imponderable matter, which by definition was hidden from direct contact with the senses.[119] Like other issues of which he was certain, Hare put all his stock on the bipartite view of matter. As a Baconian, he was not troubled that the senses could not come into direct contact with imponderable matter. Nor did it trouble many of his scientific contemporaries. Baconianism was much stronger as a scientific mind-set than as a strict scientific method. Few had come to terms with the inconsistency of being a Baconian and believing so firmly in something with which the senses had no direct access. Ironically, this myopia demonstrated just how deeply trusted the senses were. The inferences that were drawn from experiments that did directly involve the senses were regularly acknowledged with the same authority as experimental sense data.[120]

Although generally within the mainstream of scientific discourse in maintaining the existence of "imponderables," Hare took an additional step that would have made many of his colleagues uncomfortable, especially those committed to more orthodox religious positions. As early as 1822, Hare held to two propositions about matter: (1) matter is "that which has properties," and (2) "nothing can have no property."[121] In spite of its philosophical hubris, Hare agreed wholeheartedly with the syllogistic conclusion of the two propositions: in the universe, one had a choice *only* between matter and nothing. None of Hare's biographers chose to associate him with other scientific materialists of the period, such as Joseph Priestley (one of Hare's heroes who might have influenced him on this point), perhaps because, although he was one, he never dwelt on his view of matter in the course of his scientific career. The only place he ever discussed his materialism at any length was in his book on spiritualism.

The degree of importance Hare personally placed on his commitment to a cosmos composed exclusively of matter and empty space before his conversion to spiritualism is therefore not clear. Nonetheless, he was in the materialist camp, and it certainly must have helped his acceptance of the spirit messages to learn that the superior beings from above demonstrated the truth of the materialist vision. For Hare, as for other spiritualists, spirit beings were themselves material. According to Hare, anyone believing otherwise had been hoodwinked by false biblical propositions or by misinformed clerics. Spirit was not nonmaterial, although it did not exhibit the property of weight or the ability to be detected directly by the senses designed to interact with gross matter. Spirit was a real type of imponderable matter that could be inferred with as great a degree of certainty from experimentation with spirit communication as from experimentation with electricity.

The only attempt Robert Hare ever made at synthesizing all facets of his thinking on such subjects was a thirty-three page essay entitled "Of Matter, Mind, and Spirit," contained in his spiritualist treatise *Experimental Investigation of the Spirit Manifestations*. In this essay, Hare did not rely solely on quick answers from the spirit world. Hare had found, as had other spiritualists of his day, that the reporting spirits were good at painting with very broad descriptive brushes but were somewhat reluctant to address important details. Hare thought mortal scientific reasoning about the data already in hand could fill the gaps, so he attempted to slog his way to credible answers based on the knowledge acquired in his long life. As might be expected, however, his essay was not of the quality of his earlier scientific writings. He was seventy-five years old and had never attempted anything that required such a high degree of philosophical sophistication. In addition, the spiritualist context had been a part of his life for less than two years—not much time to reflect deeply on all of the implications.

Hare began his essay by restating his basic case for matter as a substance with ponderable and imponderable forms and his case for matter as an exclusive universal substance. After that, his arguments were far less informed and not nearly so sharp. One area he explored was the relationship between mind and matter. According to Hare, there was no "great distinction" between the two because they were both fundamentally material substances. They really differed in only one respect: one had the property of "will," and the other did not. The presence of "will" ensured that mind could "actuate motion," the only material substance that could do so. Here Hare completely ignored the mind as the possible source of reason and emotion. Perhaps he later noticed the lapse because he inserted a brief paragraph toward the end of the essay on the "soul," in which he offered a utilitarian definition that called "the word soul" simply a term that helps us distinguish "a being capable of passion, and competent to reason, from a corpse." But he never offered anything about the cause of passion or reason.[122] The key to the universe was to be found in matter and the cause of its motion, not in such secondary "properties" as passion and reason.

In Hare's thinking, mind was the only material substance capable of overcoming the powerful Newtonian principle of inertia. Material mind could exert its property of "will" and cause "inert" matter to begin or change motion. This was the source of all "causes" produced by rational beings, including the "great first cause" that was the mind of God and its initial action on a universe of inert matter. Hare was willing to go further than his spirits in offering an explanation of the cause of motion. Hare's spirit father told him that "although advanced spirits are much more conversant with the forces operating in nature than the most intellectually developed man in the form, still they do not, nor can they ever, as long as eternity rolls on, understand the hidden sphere of cause."[123]

In his essay, Hare went even further down this "causal" road upon which even the spirits feared to tread. After determining that the mental property of "will" was the cause of motion, he asked the next logical question: how was the "will-power" transmitted over great distances or, for that matter, even over very short distances? Solving the action-at-a-distance problem was not a complex task. One needed only to identify a medium through which "will" might travel between two points. This was obviously not a problem for Hare, who firmly believed in infinite amounts of imponderable matter throughout the universe. Just as the light of the sun traveled in undulating waves through the intermediate "ether" to illuminate planets in the far reaches of the solar system, so the will of God could be transmitted through a corresponding ether to people and places of infinite space. Hare even equated the universal force of gravity with the will of God as a physical force: "It is through this [ether] that gravitation exists as one of the effects of divine will, since, although it appears to be a property of matter, it is inferred to be no less the effect of habitual exercise of volition."[124] To maintain the deistic-style God who was not directly involved in the affairs of the cosmos, Hare reasoned that if gravity is an exercise of God's will, it is analogous to involuntary muscle contractions in humans. Just as the human mind causes the heart to beat even when one is thinking about other things, so the mind of God exerts its will through universal gravitation without his direct attention.

The analogies Hare used to explain his ideas were not merely analogies of illustration; they were also analogies of correspondence. The solution to the problem of action at a distance on the cosmic scale thus applied to the mind-body problem on a human scale. Hare wrote, "The human will, within its comparatively minute, humble sphere of action, must require also a medium analogous to that through which God acts; otherwise, how does a thought so quickly move the toe?"[125] The human mind actuated motion in the body by exerting its will through the nerves that were filled with an "ethereal fluid." The universal presence of a medium that could act as a "will" conductor had the potential of solving a multitude of problems. For instance, Hare considered "mesmeric phenomena" to be a perfect example of how the ethereal fluid could conduct "will-power" outside one's own body; hence, "the will of one individual dominates over the limbs of another."[126]

The ethereal fluid, like everything else, enjoyed greater repute in the world of spirits and was the substance in which all the amazing phenomena described by the reported spirits found their explanation. This made possible some of the activities that Hare's spirit father related. The spirit government, he reported, transmitted new legislation directly to the minds of the governed; teachers transferred ideas directly and without adulteration to the minds of students; indeed, the whole system of spirit language had no need for the spoken word.

Ethereal fluids once again proved seductive substances for those in the business of bringing science and new religion together in the antebellum period. Hare quickly related ether to spiritualism and gave it tremendous power in the spirit cosmology. Like Pratt and Quimby, Hare elevated ether to unwarranted heights, making it the ultimate universal substance to fill menacing conceptual gaps in the world of the spirits or almost anywhere else they might be found.

Conclusion

In spite of the astonishing descriptions of the spirit world—and the few but valiant attempts at systematic explanation—provided by Hare and others, the spiritualist movement in America was not able to maintain the momentum it had during the 1850s. By the beginning of the next decade, its popularity had declined, although serious circles of devotees continued their communication with the spirits and the exposition of the messages received.[127] Strong organization, institutionalization, and a central charismatic figure never materialized for the spiritualists. Still, spiritualism had made its mark. Because of the size of the movement and its popular appeal, those who explored spiritualism were not necessarily considered outside the bounds of common sense. The steady flow of eyewitness claims to the reality of the phenomena, the openness to objective verification, the scientific claims of demonstration, and the notable people who had become convinced were enough to keep "common sense" an applicable term, at least for a séance or two. It was certainly possible to maintain one's dignity, justify one's sanity, and at least check out the claims being made. Attending a séance was not a significant commitment; no one was likely to take an offering, make an "altar call," or urge one to join a church. Ultimately, all of this played into spiritualism's astounding popularity in this way: a seeker could get a fair amount of "supernatural" excitement for very little sacrifice of money, reputation, or time. After a couple of séances, people had a wide range of reactions. But far fewer emerged from their contact with the "spirits" with the missionary zeal of a Judge Edmonds or Samuel Brittan than came out, like Abraham Lincoln, thoroughly intrigued and yet uncommitted.

Moreover, few people, at least in the 1850s, went past the initial claims of objectivity to test the claims in a positive scientific fashion—that is, to investigate without the primary goal of debunking it. Hare was one of those, but he came around too late in life to make a lasting impact on the movement. Had he been a younger man and had he been able to organize and institutionalize the "temples of science" that he envisioned, the pre–Civil War movement might have had a different and longer life.

Like spiritualists who had been in the movement longer, Hare hoped to see at least some of the millennial vision of the spirit world descend to the ponderable sphere. The great law of progress was already being realized in small degrees on several fronts, especially in technology and the institution of republican government. Another pillar of spiritualist theology, however, held even more promise for the earthly: the law of harmony. By nature, the young democratic culture created dissonance, and the nation stood in sore need of harmony as the divisions grew on the eve of civil war. The "brotherhood" described in the spirit spheres seemed the answer to all of society's ills and could bring harmony to spouses, families, neighbors, races, and nations. The social reform movements that the earthbound spiritualists joined and often led were attempts to take the first step on this path. But the harmony of which the spirits spoke was not limited to personal, civic, race, gender, or international relations—as Andrew Jackson Davis, the preeminent spiritualist philosopher, made abundantly clear in his early writings.[128]

Like Davis, Robert Hare also noticed that harmony was a multifaceted concept. Hare had a penchant for thinking through to the foundations of issues, and he thought social harmony could result only from the harmony of ideas. In good Baconian fashion, he took the relationship one step further, positing that the harmony of ideas could come about solely through scientific understanding, in which opinion and error were replaced with fact, truth, and natural law. The millennial kingdom he sought was not one of harmonious human relationships alone but also included knowledge of the truth on every issue, answers for every mystery, and perfect integration of all data into one grand theory. In Hare's mind, these goals could never be reached in a universe in which any "substance," such as spirit, soul, or mind, could exist outside the rule of natural law. Harmony was possible only in a material cosmos in which natural law had a chance to bring all matter in line.

Spiritualism in its phenomenal and philosophical forms, with its attendant scientism and materialism, proved to be one of the strongest expressions of the village Enlightenment. Half a century earlier, the evangelists of the traditional Enlightenment, such as Elihu Palmer, Thomas Paine, and Ethan Allen, sought to bring much the same Enlightenment message to the masses but were not nearly so successful. It is ironic that many of the ideals of the Age of Reason finally found a popular audience when they were presented by the "spirits" to "scientific" Americans waiting breathlessly in dimly lit rooms. But that was the power of what I am calling the village Enlightenment and one of its most prominent citizens, Robert Hare.

3 Science, Matter, and Mind Cure: Phineas Parkhurst Quimby

A quiet and isolated revolution in the popular healing arts began in 1830, when a twenty-eight-year-old clockmaker, very ill, possibly with tuberculosis, went for a carriage ride in the country outside Belfast, Maine. He would rather have been riding directly on horseback because an acquaintance of his had cured himself of a serious ailment by means of a brisk ride, but he was too weak to manage a remedy that strenuous. Even the carriage ride proved to be too much. His horse was not cooperating on this occasion, and he found himself leading it up a long hill about two miles from home. The climb exhausted him, and he had only enough energy to crawl back into the carriage. He decided to sit there the rest of the day because the horse was still uncooperative and he was so drained of strength that he could scarcely lift his whip to encourage the animal.

The situation confirmed to him again that he was most likely in his last days of life. All through the illness, he had been under the care of physicians, who told him that his liver was affected, his kidneys were diseased, and his lungs were nearly consumed. The prescribed calomel therapy was slowly poisoning him, and he had lost many of his teeth from its effects. Although by this time he had lost hope of recovery, he at least had hope of making it back home that day when he observed a farmer plowing a field adjacent to the road. He had to wait patiently until the farmer had plowed around a three-acre lot before coming close enough to hear his frail plea for help. He finally got the farmer's attention, and—still too weak to lift his whip, even after the long rest—he asked the farmer to start his horse.

Exactly what happened as the horse began to move is not clear, but we do know it was the start of a new religious movement ushered in by the carriage driver himself, Phineas Parkhurst Quimby. Quimby concluded this story, which can be found in an article he wrote in 1863 entitled "My Conversion," by explaining that as the horse began to move "excitement took possession of my senses, and I drove the horse as fast as he could go, up hill and down, till I reached home and, when I got into the stable, I felt as strong as I ever did."[1]

This episode in self-healing was probably the first time Quimby considered the idea that there might be an important causal connection between state of mind and state of body. Reflecting on the incident years later, Quimby wrote with certainty that it was his mental state of excitement that was the cause of this sudden and dramatic physical transformation. This notion that the mind was the key to bringing about changes in the world of matter—especially in diseased bodies—and that this causal relationship was incontrovertibly demonstrable—especially in the healing of those bodies—was the cornerstone of what would become his "Science of Health and Happiness."

Today, over a century and a half after Quimby's hilltop experience, the church section of the telephone directory in almost all of the major cities in the United States reveals the eventual widespread flowering of Quimby's ideas in churches with such names as Religious Science, Divine Science, Science of Mind, and Unity. If this variety of American religion, often referred to as the metaphysical movement, mind cure, or New Thought, had any identifiable beginning at all, Phineas P. Quimby is the most likely candidate for the movement's unwitting founder. The most persuasive reason for the designation is that he was the teacher and healer of the most important early personalities in movements that came after him. The list includes such notables as the popular New Thought authors Julius and Annetta Dresser (parents of the prolific New Thought philosopher and Quimby supporter Horatio Dresser) and Warren Felt Evans, as well as the matriarch of Christian Science herself, Mary Baker Eddy.

Quimby's legacy is much more than a dry identification of the clinical importance of the relationship between mind and body; he inspired religious movements rather than new schools of medical thought. Quimby was in line with what Alexis de Tocqueville observed about Americans in general, that they think "everything in the world can be explained and nothing passes beyond the limits of intelligence."[2] Quimby not only practiced a new form of healing but also did his best to construct a comprehensive explanation of the healing phenomenon and the cosmos in which it took place.

The cosmology that he ultimately constructed has a historical irony associated with it. As I demonstrate in this chapter, it is clear from Quimby's writings that his system of thought was thoroughly devoted to materialism.

The mental healer Phineas Parkhurst Quimby, circa 1860. (Courtesy of Devorss and Company, Marina del Rey, California)

The irony is that the movements that can in some sense be traced back to him are fundamentally nonmaterialistic in their view of ultimate reality.[3]

Quimby's materialism did not, however, diminish his religious teaching. As his collected writings reveal, his attempt at explanation also resulted in a thoroughly religious product—Catherine L. Albanese called it a "homespun theology"[4]—which had at its center two divine images, one called "Science" and the other "Wisdom." In time, Quimby's explanation of the mental healing phenomenon and the religious worldview that grew out of it became as important as the healing practice itself. He employed his personal theological construct to address issues far beyond the healing of sick bodies. According to the principles derived from his homespun view of the world, he commented on issues ranging from the nature of the mind to the meaning of democracy, from an explanation of spiritualism to a new theory of cardiovascular physiology. On a still grander scale, his enlightened way of seeing the world was set forth as a millennial harbinger, a tool for healing and restoring sick societies as well as sick bodies.

Whatever issues he addressed, whether they were sacred or mundane, Quimby started and ended with "Science." Science was the name of his system of thought, the indestructible center, and, on occasion, even "the one living and true God to worship." Quimby's uncommon amalgam of religion, science, and a host of Enlightenment ideals makes him my third exemplar of the American Enlightenment villager.

From Clock Making to Christian Science

Phineas Parkhurst Quimby (1802–66) was born in Lebanon, New Hampshire, but moved with his family to Belfast, Maine, at the age of two and remained there most of his life. Because of his family's poverty, he spent no more than six weeks in school but became a clockmaker's apprentice while still a boy. The New Thought philosopher Horatio Dresser described the young Quimby as a man with meager education who, if he had had the chance, would have sought training in the special sciences, as "that was the tendency of his mind." Quimby's son, George, wrote that his father "had a very inventive mind, and was always interested in mechanics, philosophy and scientific subjects. . . . He was very argumentative, and always wanted proof of anything, rather than an accepted opinion. Anything which could be demonstrated he was ready to accept; but he would combat what could not be proved with all his energy, rather than admit it as truth."[5]

Although Quimby never did receive any formal training in the sciences, his apprenticeship in the art of clock making allowed him to become a sort of first cousin to the natural philosopher. This was clearly his most important connection, although indirect, with the orthodox science of the period. By Quimby's day, there was a substantial tradition going back more than two hundred years in which clockmakers moonlighted as inventors and makers of scientific instruments. In many cases, clockmakers "controlled the rhythm of applied mechanics" and were often the first to apply new mechanical and physical theories. Many of them were close associates of important natural philosophers and scientists, and, as science lost its aristocratic exclusivity, the clockmakers themselves were directly involved in scientific discovery. Quimby's inventiveness (four of his inventions received patents) and his inquisitiveness about new phenomena (he was one of the first makers of daguerreotypes) strongly hint at his personal identification with the tradition of clockmaker as applied scientist. His work building and repairing clocks may also have given him some indirect conceptual insight into the interaction of the physical and spiritual worlds. The clock—complex, precise, orderly, and predictable—was often used in his day as an important symbolic representation of God's glorious design in creation, on the one hand, and as an expression of the marvels of Newtonian mechanics, on the other. The clock put Quimby in conceptual contact with both spheres.[6]

Just how Quimby may have integrated his early religious views with his work as a clockmaker has to be inferred because neither Quimby nor any of those close to him directly addressed the religious training or exposure he may have received as a child or young adult. There are, however, a number of clues in Quimby's later writings that suggest he had a lifelong interest in religious matters. He had a solid working knowledge of the Bible and knew enough about some basic Christian theological points to offer criticisms. Quimby also paid attention to the new and more sensational religious movements and ideas as they came on the scene. In his collected writings, he regularly referred to such groups as the adventist Millerites, Mormons, and spiritualists. Quimby also demonstrated in his early writings a close familiarity with such men as LeRoy Sunderland, Charles Buchanan, and John Bovee Dods, whose controversial publications and lectures—containing ideas considered "humbugs" by mainstream Protestant culture—often wove religious and scientific concepts together. Against this backdrop, Quimby faithfully carried out his work as mechanic of the clock until he was thirty-six years old. It was at that age, eight years after his initial hilltop healing, that his worldview and his fortunes began to change.

The French mesmerist Charles Poyen entered at this point. In a small lyceum lecture hall in Belfast, Maine, in 1838, the self-proclaimed professor of animal magnetism lectured and performed demonstrations in the new science of mesmerism, which, at the time, was virtually unknown in the new republic.

Mesmerism was "discovered" by a Viennese physician, Franz Anton Mesmer, who, in 1779, claimed that all bodies, both celestial and animal, were subject to mutual influence by means of a fluid that fills all space. The mutual influence between bodies followed laws that were analogous to magnetic phenomena, hence the term *animal magnetism* for animal bodies. Mesmer used these principles as the basis of a new healing science, which he demonstrated throughout Europe. Mesmerism became more than a new healing art, though. Europeans, especially the French, thought that the new science "offered a serious explanation of Nature, of her wonderful, invisible forces, and even, in some cases, of the forces governing society and politics," according to the historian Robert Darnton.[7]

Charles Poyen carried the French enthusiasm for mesmerism to North America. Poyen did not simply claim animal magnetism to be an interesting, curious, and entertaining phenomenon. With evangelical zeal, he proclaimed, as Robert C. Fuller explained, the revelation of "lawful principles long hidden beneath the appearances of the outer world," and he thought himself "to be unveiling the hidden secret of human happiness and well-being." As Poyen's reputation spread throughout New England, many people came to his lectures to volunteer as subjects in hopes of obtaining medical cures. Magnetic treatments were a regular part of the act, and reports of success were not uncommon.[8]

Through Poyen's performances in Belfast, Maine, the recently imported science of animal magnetism encountered the spirit of American Baconianism in the person of Phineas P. Quimby. Quimby was so enthralled with this remarkable new science that he dropped everything to follow Poyen from town to town, learning both mesmerism and show business. Through observation, inquiry, and experimentation, Quimby soon became adept at wielding the mysterious power. He teamed up with Lucius Burkmar, a young man particularly susceptible to mesmeric trance, and took his own show on the road. Before small-town audiences, Quimby would demonstrate his new science by putting Burkmar into a trance, in which the young man would take clairvoyant journeys, read minds, and diagnose and prescribe treatment for illnesses. Cures abounded, including another one for Quimby himself, who claimed that, with Burkmar's clairvoyant assistant, he had been healed of a serious kidney ailment. Newspapers began to take note, and crowds began to gather. Quimby's son, George, claimed that "it is not stating it too strongly to assert that with him [Burkmar] he made some of the most astonishing exhibitions of mesmerism and clairvoyance that have been given in modern times."[9]

Then, at some point during his stint as an itinerant lyceum performer, Quimby began to doubt that animal magnetism could account for the success in curing the sick. Through extensive experimentation with the phenomenon on Burkmar and others, he decided that clairvoyant diagnosis and prescribed treatment had little to do with the patient's recovery. Burkmar was not detecting the actual disorder, nor was his prescribed treatment the source of the cure. He was, instead, reading the patient's belief about his or her own physical condition. Quimby reasoned that the patient, amazed at Burkmar's accurate diagnosis, would then put full trust in the suggested remedy. The actual cure would come by *believing* that the remedy would cure, not by the remedy itself.

Drawing on this insight, Quimby soon concluded not only that the patients were cured by correcting the errors in their beliefs or ideas but also that the errors in belief were the cause of the illness in the first place. In an answer to the question "Is disease a belief?" Quimby wrote, "I answer it is, for an individual is to himself just what he thinks he is, and he is in his belief sick. If I am sick, I am sick for my feelings are my sickness, and my sickness is my belief, and my belief is my mind; therefore all disease is in the mind or belief. Now as our belief or disease is made up of ideas which are matter, it is necessary to know what ideas we are in; for to cure the disease is to correct the error; and as disease is what follows the error, destroy the cause, and the effect will cease." It was from this basic observation that Quimby began to develop not only his healing practice but also an involved and often confusing theology that spoke to the physical, moral, and conceptual ills of the day.[10]

After his personal discoveries about the nature of illness, the mind, and the cosmos, Quimby abandoned the lyceum circuit because people began regularly seeking him out for therapy. He set up a practice in Belfast but soon moved to Portland, where he practiced his mental-healing techniques for nearly seven years and treated, according to one estimate, over twelve thousand people, a handful of whom became notable students of his ideas and eventually helped carry them to wider circles of disciples.

Patient, Heal Thyself

Quimby's therapeutic foundation that "disease is in the mind or belief" is not unfamiliar to those of us acquainted with psychosomatic disorders and the like. However, unlike most modern physicians, Quimby did not consider the mental roots of disease as one among many possible sources. For Quimby, *all* physical maladies were the result of wrong belief; there were no exceptions. In carrying this idea to what he considered its logical conclusion, Quimby dogmatically spurned all of medical science, calling it a "theory based on the lowest grade of ignorance and superstition." Going a step further, he maintained not only that the physicians were wrong and unable to help the sick (except by the occasional unwitting application of a form of Quimby's treatment) but also that they (along with the priests) were the very source of almost all human misery. Quimby estimated that "nine-tenths of the sick at this time would be well and hearty if the medical faculty were annihilated." He came to these conclusions about conventional medicine early on, while still in what Horatio Dresser called his "mesmeric period." Quimby reasoned that

> the world is full of theories and humbugs. No two men can agree precisely in any science about which there is much controversy as to the laws by which it is made up. The difficulties arising in medical science, are from the uncertainties of its practice. It is not like many of the physical sciences, about which there may be uniform and constant results. Even in this enlightened age, there seem to be no settled rules of practice. Every physician of course defines his own position or rather works out the position of his brother; and then declares his system entirely opposite. The whole practice of the schools and the faculty seems to have been a continual introduction of Theories contradicting each other—each order as they rise and fall opposing all others.[11]

Quimby's disdain for medical science and the popularity of his unusual methods of treatment make much more sense when one considers the dismal state of mid-nineteenth-century medicine. When a person fell seriously ill, the courses of action were few and frightful. Although other choices were available, regular physicians were still using bloodletting, calomel, blisters, and crude surgery. A young physician, fresh out of medical school, observed in 1835 that "the practice of that time was heroic: it was murderous. I knew nothing about medicine, but had sense enough to see that doctors were killing their patients, that medicine was not an exact science, that it was wholly empirical and that it would be better to trust entirely to Nature than to the hazardous skill of the doctors." By turning to Quimby, patients were at least assured that the treatment itself would not make them worse. The worst aftereffects of Quimby's treatment were dashed hopes and the charge from skeptics that the patient had fallen prey to humbuggery, a far cry from a gangrenous infection or mercury poisoning. Such therapies as Quimby's must have been exceedingly attractive given the alternatives.[12]

Quimby's method of healing the sick was very different from that of the orthodox physician. Stewart W. Holmes, one of the few people outside of the metaphysical movement to study the work of Quimby seriously, described better than most how with no instruments, no medications, and no formal training, Quimby would treat the patient:

> Sitting down quietly beside the patient, without exchanging a word with him, he divined clairvoyantly what was wrong and what had been the origin of the disease. His findings he then revealed to the sufferer, pointing out how the belief in the disease had originated, perhaps in some fright, perhaps in a remark made by someone whose opinion was valued, and then how the abnormality operated,—or was manifested. He explained that the reality of the symptoms was conditional on the patient's belief in them. Then he formed a mental image of the patient in "normal," healthy condition and concentrated on this so strongly that the patient's mind, prepared by his explanation of the principles involved, accepted the image. Finally, with varying degrees of speed and permanence, the sick person's organism manifested this healthy belief. In other words, he was restored to health.[13]

Quimby's method of treatment, although unorthodox, appears to be straightforward enough. However, below the level of application lies a rather tangled body of theory developed by Quimby to undergird, explain, and defend his practice. Untangling and explaining the details of his ideas is an awkward task since, as Charles S. Braden wrote, he "seems to have been groping for a consistent theory, but never quite to have achieved it," probably because "he himself was not clear in his own thought."[14] Quimby left no doubt, however, about the basic premise of his thought, which is repeated continually in one form or another throughout his collected writings:

> We can create this idea called matter and condense it into any form that our belief is capable of forming. And if our power of imitation is sufficient, we can form any idea we choose. Every disease is a manufactured article of our own make and children being but a lump of our own ideas, their mind or matter is as much under our control as their education. We can teach our children to be just what we wish and even give form to their matter and cer-

tain actions to their bodies. So we can create tumors, coughs, and every disease that flesh is heir to. Mind or matter is like mortar or potter's clay. And
no one can deny that the clay in experienced or scientific hands can be made
into better vessels than in the hands of an unscientific person.[15]

For Quimby, the matter that we bump into everyday in the physical world
was simply the manifestation—or "condensation"—of the mind. Mind was
the cause; matter was the recognizable effect in the physical realm. However,
what appeared to be a distinct mind-matter dualism in this passage quickly
became muddled in his notion that mind was something called "spiritual
matter." He maintained that "mind was something that could be changed,
so . . . I came to the conclusion that mind was something and I called it
matter, because I found it could be condensed into a solid. . . . and by the
same power under a different direction it might be dissolved and disappear."
Using a model based on a common chemistry demonstration performed on
the lyceum circuit—the precipitation of a solid from a solution and back
again—Quimby concluded that mind was a sort of solution, which contained
invisible or "spiritual" matter. "Belief," then, came into play as that which
had the power to cause the spiritual matter (or mind) to condense in one of
two ways. Right belief would bring about the precipitation of life, health, and
happiness, including, of course, the cure for the particular illness being
treated. Wrong belief, or error, precipitated misery, sickness, and death.[16]

In practice, Quimby's treatment focused on one thing—changing the
patient's belief. To accomplish this, he used two methods, one of which was
described by Holmes above. In the first, he would simply talk to the patient,
reason away false ideas about his or her own physical condition, and expect
that the cure would naturally follow. In the second, he would use a more
direct mind-on-mind operation during which he would not speak at all. He
would sit silently and read the patient's feelings, which were "daguerreo-
typed" on his mind. Then he would mentally correct the belief and send it
back to the patient. He continued this until "the patient's feelings sympa-
thized with his, the shadows [grew] dim and finally the light [took] its place
and there [was] nothing left of the disease." The details of this silent method
of treatment indicate that although Quimby renounced his earlier practice
of mesmerism as "one of the greatest humbugs of the age," his methods and
theory still retained, as Catherine L. Albanese argued, "something of the
mesmeric model." Mesmeric notions, such as magnetic fluid, clairvoyance,
and action at a distance through a medium, all remained entrenched in the
system in one form or another.[17]

From the description of Quimby's thought thus far, one might not re-gard it as necessarily religious. In fact, the whole system so far described could be categorized as a sort of curious but practical homespun philosophy. Con-sidering Quimby's copious and consistent rhetoric against the "priests" and their "doctrines" that "humbug the people" and keep them in their misery, one might come to the conclusion—as some latter-day disciples did—that he was overtly antireligious. This does not stand up in the face of some of Quimby's more perspicuous passages, however. He was an advocate of reli-gion insofar as it was scientific; that is, insofar as it was what he considered the "real" religion of Jesus:

> The introduction of religion based on science is the commencement of the new world. The science which shall devour our errors is the teaching of this great truth. The sick are those who are bound in prison before the flood and the opening of the prison doors is the understanding of this truth. Peter is the science that holds the keys or theory. All that are loosed by this truth are loosed in heaven or in their belief. To preach Christ is to put heaven in prac-tice, to liberate the poor and sick who have been bound by the false ideas of the world.
> . . . Then a new world begins and a new religion springs up based on sci-ence. Under this religion, no man will say to another, Do what is right, for all will do right because he will feel right in so doing.[18]

Charles Braden, convinced that much of Quimby's thought was religious in nature, wrote that his ideas "were not orthodox ideas according to the theo-logical standards of his day, but that he held profound religious convictions none can deny who has read the *Manuscripts.*" Concerning Quimby's numer-ous invectives against the Christian thought and practice of his day, Braden correctly observed that "what he is really saying is that he is attacking not re-ligion itself, but a false idea of religious truth, replacing the error with the truth, which is his declared method of cure. And a careful reading of his *Manuscripts* quite bears this out. Though he uses other terminology than the traditional orthodox religious leaders do, it is difficult to avoid the conviction that Quim-by was really a deeply religious person, who merely found himself unable to accept religion in its traditional forms."[19] As I have already noted, his collected writings are rife with scriptural quotations and allusions and filled with reflections on Jesus Christ, God, wisdom, and other religious themes. The first person to edit Quimby's writings, Horatio Dresser, estimated that at least half of the manuscripts are filled with references to religious problems and the Bible.[20] Quimby was not just fascinated with revisions of traditional Christian beliefs. His collected writings contain a number of articles about the ideas and practices of spiritualists. Although he denied the reality of spirit manifestations, Quimby shared with the spiritualists, not to mention the Mormons, a range of fundamental ideas, including the materiality of spirit, a cosmology of progress, the importance of demonstration, and a vision for personal and societal harmony through natural law.

More to the point, his concept of *science* was overtly religious. While his religious ideas about science came as a later outgrowth of his discoveries and theories on healing, the ideas began to coalesce early in his work with clocks, in his inventions, and in his apparent obsession with all things scientific. For Quimby, science was there from the beginning, lending authority, credence, and proof to the developing system.

Science as Theological Absolute

Of the studies that have addressed the early history of New Thought and Christian Science, only one has touched, even indirectly, on the importance of the scientific reckoning in the emerging mind-cure movement. Stewart Holmes, writing in 1944, awarded Phineas Quimby the title "Scientist of Transcendentalism" because he "demonstrated visibly, on human organisms, the operational validity of Emerson's hypotheses." Holmes did not intend to trumpet the "truth" of the ideas of either Quimby or Ralph Waldo Emerson. But he was expressing his view that "while Emerson arrived at his theories deductively and never submitted them to anything approaching laboratory proof, Quimby forged his theories—and thence his view of ultimate reality—from years of patient experiment with individual persons; something lawful and orderly occurred when he applied his technique."[21] Holmes had noticed something important. Quimby's use of science goes far beyond the picture of the noble enterprise that Holmes sketched, though. Quimby appeared to be obsessed with the concept of science. It emerges from his writings as a theological absolute, with universal authority in all matters, natural and spiritual, and with enough force of meaning to be carried to the present day by those who share Quimby's legacy.

To say that science saturates Quimby's writings is not an overstatement. The term is used so often and in so many ways that the prospects for extracting a precise or comprehensive definition are problematic at best. Part of the problem is that, by contemporary twentieth-century standards, Quimby used *science* in decidedly nonscientific ways. He used the term interchangeably with *charity, love, freedom, revelation from God, God, Christ, the Son, kingdom of God, kingdom, power, law,* and *Truth* (most often equating the terms directly with an inclusive disjunction, such as "Science or God"). The confusion of Quimby's usage lends credence to Horatio Dresser's statement that Quimby was not a regular reader of philosophy or theology.[22] Take, for example, his use of the term in the following rambling passage:

> When He [Jesus] was accused of curing disease through Beelzebub or ignorance, He said "If I cast out devils (or diseases) through Beelzebub or ignorance, my kingdom (or science) cannot stand; but if I cast out devils (or disease) through a science or law, then my kingdom or law will stand for it is not of this world." . . . He [Jesus] must have known what that power or science is and the difference between His science and their ignorance. His science was His kingdom; therefore it was not of this world, and theirs being of this world, He called it the kingdom of darkness.[23]

In spite of the definitional difficulties inherent in working with his texts, Quimby used the term *science* so often that certain patterns do emerge. The most obvious is that Quimby used "Science" as the name for his system of thought and practice. Although such names as the Science of Health, Science of Happiness, Science of Life, Science of Jesus, and Christian Science pepper his writings, the simple designation "Science" appears most frequently. This practice of using science-soaked titles was one of the more conspicuous legacies he bequeathed to those who followed in his mind-cure footsteps. The other attributes of the term *science,* although more slippery than the first, likewise do not completely defy description. An examination of the term in context yields characteristics that I describe as monistic, divine, living, certain, and pragmatic.

The monism inherent in Quimby's use of the term *science* was almost completely unqualified. Science was "wisdom reduced to self-evident propositions" and was therefore the same throughout the world of matter, mind, or spirit.[24] I do not intend to suggest that Quimby was a monist in terms of rejecting categorically all distinction between matter and mind or matter and spirit. What I am claiming, instead, was that for Quimby science was methodologically monistic and therefore held true in all domains, whether physical or metaphysical. In contrast, his student Mary Baker Eddy and her Christian Science departed from him and other proponents of mind cure on this point by categorically rejecting all science of the physical world. Eddy saw no place for physical science in her system, claiming her own "divine science wars with so-called physical science, even as truth wars with error."[25] In Quimby's system, where mind was primary and causative and matter was secondary and resultant, one would expect the same distinction that Eddy made, but Quimby's dedication to the legitimacy of the physical sciences never wavered. His writings are replete with illustrations drawn from physics, chemistry, astronomy, geology, physiology, and mathematics, which are used to support his spiritual insights. To him, all these sciences rested on the same foundation as his own Science of Health and Happiness because all of them had the key to truth—proof by demonstration. The sciences he ultimately rejected, such as medicine, phrenology, spiritism, and mesmerism, he negated on the premise that they are not really sciences at all. They were filled with error and opinions and, like orthodox religion, could not "stand the test of investigation."[26]

The only qualification apparent in Quimby's monistic approach to science was that his Science of Happiness, although built on the same foundation as other true sciences, required senses beyond the five we usually recognize: "A man may be scientific in many sciences—chemistry, mathematics, astronomy, botany—all that are acknowledged and admitted by even the natural man, though not understood. But the Science of Happiness was not acknowledged by the wisdom of the five senses, so it requires more senses to put man in possession of this Science that will teach him happiness." In a remarkable adherence to Baconian directives, Quimby did not abandon the all-important "senses" when investigating a world that was beyond our natural abilities to detect. Rather, he introduced a new set of senses that could be "detached" from, and exist outside of, the body. These extrasensory senses, along with all the mesmeric baggage they carry, became Quimby's instruments for exploring the unseen world of the mind.[27]

Nowhere was Quimby's obsession with science more evident than when he paid it the ultimate tribute by raising it to the level of the divine. In some passages, he equated science directly with God, using the two as interchangeable terms, "God or Science." In others, he made the connection even more unequivocally. On a single page of his collected works, he did this four times, writing "God is Science"; "there is but one living and true God or Science"; "Science is the one living and true God to worship"; and "Science is the God or Christ." At other times, instead of making science out to be God, he made science one of God's attributes, such as "the voice of God" or "God's religion." Despite the theological confusion, it is clear that for Quimby science was divine; if it did not occupy the very throne of God, it surely issued forth from near that location.[28]

Once it is established that Quimby considered science and God to be in some sense one and the same, it should follow that science was living and certain. For Quimby, it was. Consider Quimby's rendition of 1 Corinthians 13: "Science suffers long before it becomes a fact. It envieth not other science, it praiseth not self, is not puffed up, doth not behave unseemly, is not easily provoked, thinketh no evil, rejoiceth not over trouble but rejoiceth in the truth. Science never fails but prophesies. The knowledge of this world fails but science never fails." This passage is representative of many that speak of science as if it were some sort of animate entity. The passage also points to the absolute certainty wrapped up in Quimby's concept of science: "science never fails." "Men never dispute about a fact that can be demonstrated by scientific reasoning," claimed Quimby. In his reckoning, "science holds no doubt." Science was demonstrable to everyone and perfectly predictable. Unlike the God of Calvinism, Quimby's God of Science was in no way capricious. Science was certain, acted in accord with the orderly laws of wisdom, and was available to every person.[29]

Finally, Quimby's science was pragmatic. It was "wisdom reduced to practice," and the healing of sick bodies was its most important demonstration. It was applicable in any situation and was always able to help people "get the most happiness out of the least labor." True to the popular fascination with the utilitarian aspects of the science of the day, Quimby used the daguerreotype, steam engine, telegraph, and various other machines as important illustrations of his insights. The practical nature of Quimby's program did not stop there, though. In keeping with the millennialist movements of his day, Quimby's science had the practical benefit of being able to heal society at large, as surely as it could heal the body. "Science," he declared, "is the axe in the hands of Wisdom to hew down this wilderness and destroy its inhabitants and introduce a better state of society." With an even greater apocalyptic sense, he lamented, "How long shall it be till the wisdom of this world shall become reduced to a science so that it can be taught for the healing of the nations?" But, he added in the same passage, when the "Kingdom of Science" comes, "then will arise a new heaven and a new earth to free man from disease or error, for this old world or belief shall be burned up with the fire of science and the new heaven or science shall arise, wherein shall not be found all these old superstitions, bigotry and disease, but where there is no more death nor sighing from some ache or pain which arises from superstitions of the world."[30]

Although Quimby's "Kingdom of Science" had not yet arrived in the way that he envisioned, his concept of science had a significant impact on the mind-cure movements that followed, most obviously in the elevation of science to such an authoritative position. The pervasive use of the term throughout metaphysical literature, as well as its multifarious uses in organizational names, book titles, and key concepts—e.g., Religious Science, Science of Mind, Science of Being, Spiritual Science, Science of Health, and Mental Science—suggests that the love affair with the idea of science initiated by Quimby did not dim in the least after his death. Horatio Dresser, a leader in New England's New Thought movement well into the twentieth century, continued to trumpet Quimby's idea of science with little deviation. Writing almost sixty years after the mental doctor's demise, Dresser reaffirmed that Quimby's science was the

> fundamental knowledge of this our real nature, with its inner states and possibilities. It is light in contrast with the wisdom of the world. It is harmony in contrast with disease or discord. It corrects all errors, holds no doubts, proves all things, explains all causes and effects. It is Divine wisdom "reduced to self-evident propositions." It is the basis of all special branches of knowledge—when those other sciences are rightly founded. It is Christ, the wisdom of Jesus. It is in all, accessible to all. We all become parts of it in so far as we discern real truth. In fact, Quimby often says the real man "is" Science.[31]

Certainly few practitioners of antebellum science would recognize Quimby's concept of science as relevant to what was going on in their investigations. But strange as it may seem, some of the rules were the same. In many respects, Quimby was a paradigmatic Baconian. Insofar as he understood, Quimby was showing a spirited enthusiasm for natural science, propounding a scrupulous empiricism, and expressing an intense distrust of speculation. However, he unwittingly fell into the hole that existed in the commonsense philosophy upon which American Baconianism was based: that which is common sense to one person is not necessarily common sense to another. Those ideas that Quimby considered "self-evident propositions" and demonstrable truths were, to his critics in conventional medical practice, colossal humbugs. Yet his critics were also victims of the commonsense predicament. Holding tenaciously to their own commonsensical, self-evident notions, Quimby's critics may have missed a golden opportunity to harness the curative power of suggestion decades ahead of the now-recognized pioneers in psychosomatic medicine.[32]

In retrospect, Quimby had expressed an important insight into the practical connection between state of mind and state of body. However, the theoretical extrapolations that he derived from his experiences with healing were grounded in something less than epistemological terra firma. He was clearly guilty of the same offense of which many spiritualists, phrenologists, and various medical sectarians—not to mention a number of "orthodox" scientists—of his day were guilty: making grand inductive leaps from a few observed phenomena to all-encompassing laws of nature and supernature.

Quimby was leaping to conclusions alongside these others, but his notion of science was significantly different. Today, as in Quimby's day, the term *science* has two root meanings. The term can emphasize the *method* by which knowledge is obtained or the *knowledge* that is obtained by the method. While Quimby had no problem using the term in both senses, it was his uncommon and unbridled emphasis on science as *knowledge* that most set him apart from the antebellum scientific culture. Even those religious people who thought science was a useful tool for investigating the trappings of spiritual reality, such as Protestant theologians and spiritualists, used the term in its methodological sense almost exclusively.[33]

For Quimby, however, science was equivalent to infallible knowledge, or what he referred to with reverence as "Wisdom." Science was one of the theological absolutes that grounded his radically different view of the world. Without the authority of something comparable to the *scriptura* or *traditio* that grounded the denominational churches, Quimby's ideas would likely have carried little weight. They were, after all, the simple musings of an uneducated craftsman. By contrast, science—popular and trustworthy in the public mind and infallible in Quimby's—provided the perfect foundation for his thought. In the antebellum Protestant culture, it was the only thing that approached scriptural revelation in authoritative stature.

In this light, it is not hard to understand how Quimby could elevate science to the level of God and how, in Quimby's mind, they shared so many of the same attributes. If, as Stewart W. Holmes argued, Quimby deserves the title of "Scientist of Transcendentalism," it appears that he also deserves the title of "Transcendentalist of Scientism," for in making science equal to God and declaring science to be as effective in the metaphysical sphere as in the physical, Quimby transcendentalized it.

Quimby saw science and religion not only as altogether compatible but as one and the same, contrary to any "warfare" approach to interpreting the interaction of science and religion. In the midst of the nineteenth-century American love affair with science and the Baconian philosophy, Quimby journeyed from his background as an amateur scientist and inventor to experimentation with mesmerism and mental healing and ultimately to the foundation of a spiritual science that was "the greatest of the sciences or the kingdom of God."[34] When one takes into consideration the tremendous

influence of Baconianism and popular science on many aspects of life in antebellum America, it seems far less puzzling that they were incorporated into
Quimby's brand of Christian Science and that they remain today in the teachings of the religious movements that can be traced back to this mental healer.

Making Sense of the Cosmos: Progress, Wisdom, and Matter

There is a danger in attempting to explain Phineas Quimby's thought in a
coherent and methodical manner: the reader may get the impression that
Quimby's thinking was more coherent and methodical than it actually was.
Both Quimby and his patients referred to his problem in communicating
ideas. Quimby wrote several articles that focus on his trouble in expressing
his ideas with words. In one such article he began, "In introducing my ideas
to the world I labor under the disadvantage as anyone does who seeks to bring
into language what has never been embodied in thought or words." In another important article—likely one of the last Quimby wrote and probably
the introduction to the book that he never put together—he wrote of himself, "People not familiar with Dr. Quimby's ideas think that he does not
understand the meaning of language and therefore does not express himself
clearly upon these subjects which he undertakes to elucidate."[35] In a passage
that reveals the reaction of some of his patients to his frequent rambling, he
said, "The question is often asked, Why does not Dr. Quimby make his cures
and hold his peace, for his talk only confuses the mind of the patient and
makes hard feeling and it does no good. In this way he is misunderstood, from
the fact that his ignorance of language makes it hard to get the idea which
he would convey for he has never been educated. . . . Now to all the above I
plead guilty."[36]

By his own admission, and certainly by his patients' complaints, Quimby was very *unclear* in his thought. One therefore cannot approach Quimby's
extant writings in the same way one approaches a systematic treatise on its
subject. Because Quimby often seemed to change his mind about points he
had previously made, used the same words to mean several different things,
and regularly introduced unrelated tangents, the only hope is to look for
repetition of key ideas. When this method is applied, other themes emerge
from his writings almost as conspicuously as that of science, his primary
organizing concept.

Although most of the time these secondary themes rest under the authority of Quimby's view of science, they are indispensable if one wishes to un-

derstand Quimby's handcrafted view of the cosmos. I focus here on two of these themes that might be considered—apart from science—the most important premises on which Quimby rests his cosmological thought: "progress" and "wisdom."

In his 1980 study of the history of the idea of progress, Robert Nisbet, in accord with a host of historians who preceded him, proclaimed the nineteenth century as the period in which the idea of progress in Western thought reached its zenith in both the scholarly and the popular mind. Nisbet wrote that the concept of progress for the nineteenth century was "distinct and pivotal in that it becomes the developmental *context* for other ideas," such as freedom, equality, and popular sovereignty.[37] If Nisbet is correct, Quimby's thinking might be good material for reflecting on the concept of progress in the popular mentality of antebellum America. Quimby, in his characteristic exuberant manner, not only addressed Nisbet's list of identified themes but also went on to address a great deal more within the context of his own view of progress.

Quimby used the term *progress* so often that the readers of his collected writings cannot miss its importance. Progress seems ubiquitous and, not surprisingly, was often directly associated with science. After all, science in the early nineteenth century was widely considered one of the best and most visible proofs of the certainty of progress. Quimby therefore did not hesitate to claim that science *is* progress or to assert that progress is at least a vital part of science. Along these lines, he wrote that "science has proved to all persons understanding it, that the true wisdom of Science is progression, [and it follows that] to oppose progression is to oppose science."[38]

Quimby also saw a relationship between progress and God, just as he did between science and God, with the same degree of conflation. On one occasion, he said explicitly that God is a progressive being and on several others implied that God is progress. The notion that it was not just ideas, humans, animals, and technology that were moving onward and upward but God as well was one of the most important theological breaks Quimby made with orthodox Christianity. The idea of the progress of God was also one of the most significant theological connections between Quimby and Joseph Smith in Mormonism, though one cannot ascertain how deep the similarities are because Quimby did little more than assert a nonstatic deity and did not build on the idea.[39]

If God, science, and the cosmos were in a state of flux, it is reasonable to ask if anything was static in Quimby's universe. Given what we have seen thus far concerning progress, the notion of progress itself would appear to be a prime candidate. But Quimby wrote that even progress itself was in a state of "progression," an observation that confuses the issue considerably.[40]

Quimby did, however, allow stasis into his system by introducing two different concepts. The first was his idea of the "natural man." The natural man, for Quimby, was one who had not yet discovered Quimby's principles of science, one who lived in the world governed by error, ignorance, and superstition. The natural man listened to the physician and the priest, accepting their every word concerning the state of his body and the state of his soul. In a key passage, Quimby explained that the natural man was

> naturally indolent, brutish and willful, content to live like a brute. He is pleased at any bauble or trifling thing. He has imitation and tries to copy whatever pleases him. In this he shows his reverence for his superiors. As he does not possess wisdom or science, he is often deceived. Thus he is made timid and willing to be led. His courage is the courage of ignorance, and when he sees superior numbers, he curls down like a dog when whipped by his master. Easily led and easily deceived, no confidence is to be placed on his word, for his word is always like the wag of a dog's tail to show his submission. But when his ends are answered, his next act might be to injure the very one that had just saved him from some trouble. He is easy in his manners if all goes well, but if needed for anything he, like the dog, is ready at the whistle of his master or anyone that will pat him, to bite his own master or anyone else.
>
> Now because the brutes can be taught something, it does not follow that they can be taught science. They have their bounds which they cannot pass. So the natural man has his bounds which he cannot pass.[41]

For Quimby, the natural man was the static man, the part of his cosmology that was not in a state of flux. He was limited by his ignorance and had no science, no wisdom, no progress within him. Quimby even called on the still popular notion of the "chain of being" to show that "there is a gradual progression from the mineral to the animal kingdom" but that the natural man was left out of this innate upward climb: "To suppose that [the natural] man as we see him is superior to the brute or any other living creature is not the case. [The natural] man is matter; so are the brutes and all living creatures, and to say that one has any superiority over any other matter is false. You might as well say that the soil of California is more intelligent than the soil of Maine."[42]

Juxtaposed to the natural man was his opposite, the "scientific man," who was a person of progress, a "book of nature, understood, so that he can prove all he says. He is made not of opinions but of wisdom, and never refers to old authors but proves all things by his science." To illustrate the difference between the two scientifically, Quimby used the two branches of physics with which he was familiar, statics and dynamics. The natural man was dead weight, destined to be motionless forever unless acted on by an outside force. The scientific man was mass in motion, whose direction was necessarily onward and upward. The transformation of a person from the natural to the scientific state was what Quimby considered being "born again" and was as close to a concept of salvation as he came. Quimby denied at every turn that the transformation he spoke of would have anything at all in common with the "Calvinist Baptist" (to Quimby, the greatest of the enemies of his science), but even for him the concept of faith was unavoidable. Quimby argued that investigation, experimentation, and sound reasoning were enough to lead any person to the truth of his science. In reality, however, faith on the part of the seeker was the only means of leaping from the demonstrable healings Quimby claimed to perform to the worldview he constructed to account for these demonstrations and hence was the only way of getting from the natural to the scientific state. Although he was effective in eliminating grace from the salvation scheme, faith remained a necessary but unrecognized part of Quimby's idea of transformation.[43]

The "saved" in Quimby's and Calvin's theologies were on a similar positive trajectory, both on their way onward and upward "from glory to glory." However, those outside of the fold in each system had very different fates. For most Christians at the time, hell was still the ultimate destination for the unbeliever—a definitive downward trajectory in this life and the life to come. Quimby rejected all such punishment and downward motion. He left the recalcitrant natural man who refused the Science of Health and Happiness to continue indefinitely in his brutish state, destined to stay in the same place, on the same plane forever, a fixed point in Quimby's otherwise ever-progressing universe.

The second important premise on which Quimby's cosmological construction rested was also the second static entity in his universe—"wisdom." The static nature of wisdom in Quimby's scheme was of a higher order of magnitude than the simple nonprogressive nature of his "natural man," though, because it was truly cosmic in character and size. The concept of wisdom might even be considered Quimby's other absolute, often rivaling science in his writings for center stage. He was not, however, as obsessed with the term *wisdom* as he was with the term *science*. *Wisdom* appeared less often and with less fanfare than *science* did, but its fixed position in Quimby's universe and the role it played in his philosophy made it stand out sharply.

As with the concept of the natural man, Quimby was consistent about the nondynamic character of wisdom. His customary attachment of the word *progress* to almost everything in his writings was conspicuously absent where wisdom was concerned, and he left little doubt that this was conscious and deliberate. On at least one occasion, he stated unequivocally that "wisdom cannot change."[44]

A full description of wisdom would mean repeating many characteristics that have already been attributed to Quimby's concept of science. Wisdom, too, was monistic, divine, living, certain, and pragmatic. Not surprisingly, Quimby often equated wisdom with both God and science: "As God is Wisdom, [so] Wisdom is Science." Although the similarities between the concepts of wisdom and science are obvious and significant, there were some important differences. Quimby reserved certain attributes for wisdom alone, and it is some of these attributes that best reflect Quimby's cosmological construction. The distinctions were not always clear, however, and to avoid having continually to tease wisdom and science apart, I, for the most part, ignore the overlap and focus on wisdom alone.[45]

Before writing his series of articles between 1859 and 1865, Quimby almost never used the term *wisdom*, and even the few times it did appear, it was used only in the common dictionary sense. In contrast, the term *science* appeared in Quimby's "Lecture Notes"—probably written during his early demonstrations with Lucius Burkmar from 1843 to 1847—and even then it was beginning to take on some of the attributes discussed in his later articles. The concept of wisdom, then, may very well be a product of Quimby's final years, a concept that emerged to help glue his system together as he struggled to come up with a grand worldview that could account for all he saw and experienced in his healing practice.

If, for Quimby, science, progress, and wisdom were all equal to God, then wisdom seems to have been "more equal" than the others—especially in terms of common nineteenth-century theistic or deistic notions. For example, Quimby, with true Enlightenment devotion, regularly referred to wisdom as the "First Cause." Even in his healing practice, he saw all the effects that he helped bring about in his patients' bodies—through the condensation of mind (spiritual matter) into matter in its proper state of harmony—as causally linked in a great unbreakable chain to wisdom, the First Cause. He wrote that wisdom had known only one law—the law of action and reaction. Causes initiated in the spiritual world had thus manifested themselves in visible effects in the physical realm: "Wisdom must act on mind and mind on matter. As weight and velocity make mechanical power, so mind and matter make spiritual power governed by a wisdom superior to both."[46]

Quimby assigned other godlike attributes to wisdom, including an existence without beginning or end. Because wisdom existed outside of matter, it would "exist when opinions are gone. . . . Wisdom is eternal without beginning or end." It was that which Jesus "introduced, the Science of God . . . based on eternal wisdom." Quimby's theological pronouncements concerning wisdom were linked at this point to his cosmological speculations. He reasoned that because wisdom was eternal, "space and the universe" must also be eternal since they were the dwelling place of wisdom.[47]

Wisdom was also omniscient according to Quimby's logic. It was all-knowing, at least in the sense that wisdom held the blueprints for everything. Anybody, anything, and any idea that ever was, is, or would be must have already existed in wisdom. It was in this sense that Quimby said "wisdom creates." He was steadfast throughout his writings in his position that "something cannot come from nothing." Anything that was made was therefore not created from nothing but was a recombination of elements that already existed under the purposeful direction of wisdom:

> I assume that every element when disturbed is combined with other elements to produce some idea and when the idea is destroyed, the elements of which it is composed return to their original state. If life is a combination of elements which when they are dissolved destroys life, then life is not an element of itself but a result of a combination. And let me ask what was it that made the elements a combination? It must be something that is outside these gases. I contend that wisdom contains all this, and everything in the form of gases or fluids are subject to it.[48]

It is difficult to know what Quimby thought "wisdom contains." Sometimes it appeared to be the blueprints for elemental combinations, and at other times it appeared that wisdom contained the actual thing in itself in some unspecified form. In any case, he called on this transcendental wisdom regularly—without paying homage to the correspondence theories of either Plato or the Swedish seer Emanuel Swedenborg—to account for the material existence and appearance of people, things, and ideas. He claimed, "Every person who was or ever will be existed as much before he ever came to our senses as afterwards, the same as any mathematical problem or truth. Man's intelligence is a truth that existed before he took form or was seen by the natural eye." He also declared that "every machine and every mathematical calculation that has ever been reduced to practice existed before it was formed."[49]

Wisdom was also omnipresent. Quimby was certain that "wisdom fills all space." On the surface, his concept of wisdom seems to resemble the notion of the ubiquitous nature of God common among his Protestant contemporaries. Theirs was a God of spirit, whose immateriality made possible his omnipresence throughout the material world. The orthodox theologians did not have to contend with the problem of how God might occupy the same space at the same time as material objects, because their God was of a wholly different nature, not restricted by space-time limitations and therefore not excluded from any part of the universe because a material object already occupied the same coordinates. Quimby's wisdom was similar in many respects. However, for Quimby, wisdom had another remarkable attribute that separated it from the Christian God. Not only did wisdom fill all space, but "wisdom [was] solid" as well. Quimby reasoned that "what is immortal must be solid because it cannot be affected by blows, so that nothing can pierce it or break it through. This I call wisdom. It has no beginning nor ending. It cannot be stretched for it fills all space and there is no place to receive it. So it is like space, and the universe is eternal." The logical paradox laid to rest by the Christians met Quimby at this juncture. How could anything else with a like nature exist in space if wisdom, a solid, filled it completely? To be consistent, Quimby either had to deny the materiality or the solidity (synonymous terms in his day) of everything else except wisdom or had to affirm that all that was material or solid was in some way a part of the one great solid. It was a tribute to his chronic struggle to make sense, however, that he held to both positions.[50]

In the first model, Quimby tried to remove the substance from the common conception of matter. Unlike his student Mary Baker Eddy, however, he was not very consistent in his attempt to reconceptualize the material world. The attempt was there nonetheless, and the following statements illustrate this: "I believe matter to be nothing but an idea." "God . . . has no matter, only as an idea." "Lucretius . . . proved that matter is nothing but an idea." "Matter is only an idea that fills no space." "With God all matter is imagination, for to him it is but shadow." These statements that appear to be direct denials of matter were, in context, really only a way of making room for the true material substance: wisdom. In this model, what looked like matter was actually insubstantial, the shadow cast by wisdom, the only solid in Quimby's universe. "Wisdom is the solid or substance. Matter or mind is the shadow of the spiritual wisdom," he wrote. Wisdom could be a solid and fill all space to the exclusion of matter, because matter, at least in this model, was of a different nature, a shadow that could not occupy "any real space."[51] In one article, Quimby described and briefly illustrated this model:

> Does man see himself or any other person or any true substance, or is it the shadow of the substance that he sees? My own observation has satisfied me that what I see is nothing but shadow or some intelligence which is behind the shadow, as man looking in a glass sees himself, but the substance is not seen by the reflection although you would think life was in a shadow. *Everything is reversed by man's ignorance of himself. This reversed shadow is taken for the substance* and it has its identity and its life is dependent on the substance and its acts depend on the wisdom that governs it. . . . I commune with the substance whenever I sit down by the sick who have been deluded with this horrid [Christian] belief. They have spiritual eyes or sympathy but cannot see, so they rely on their eyes or shadows and being blind they wander about like sheep without a shepherd, and having deceived themselves, they try to deceive others.[52]

Quimby perceived that the true nature of things had been reversed, especially by the Christians of his day. He turned the common theological notion that God was immaterial and the creation material on its head. For Quimby, in what seems to be a variation on Platonism, God or wisdom was the solid and the creation but shadow.

Quimby's reversal of traditional Christian ideas, however, was not limited to the trading off of shadow and substance. It extended into physical theory as well because he also inverted Isaac Newton's still popular concept of particulate matter. Newton, in an oft-quoted passage from his treatise on *Opticks,* wrote "that God in the Beginning form'd Matter in solid, massy, hard, impenetrable, moveable Particles . . . and these primitive Particles being Solids, are incomparably harder than any porous Bodies compounded of them; even so very hard, as never to wear or break in pieces; no ordinary Power being able to divide what God Himself made one in the first Creation."[53] Quimby took some of the qualities of Newtonian matter (solid, massy, hard, and impenetrable) and attached them not to elementary particles but to wisdom, which he saw as filling all space. This picture of a universal, monolithic solid would have unnerved most of his contemporaries. It must have especially unnerved his student Mary Baker Eddy, who kept the universal but replaced the monolithic solid with the monolithic mind.

Since the nature of Quimby's thinking was never as monolithic as the nature of his concept of wisdom, he had another way out of the problem of one solid substance occupying the same space as another solid substance at the same time. This second solution, instead of denying the solidity or materiality of "matter," made individual solid objects a part of the one great solid in some way or another. This solution has an obvious logical problem of its own that Quimby did not address. How can a solid that fills *all* space even have parts? With no attempt at explanation and with no announced retreat on the idea that wisdom fills all space, Quimby, unwittingly or not, confronted the paradox with characteristic imprecision. When it served to salvage his immediate line of thought, he simply transformed the solid into a fluid. Although still referred to as a "solid," wisdom was now able to surround and saturate matter like a sponge immersed in a pail of water. The model he employed here was significantly different from the substance-shadow model. On this point, Quimby showed just how close he remained to his mesmeric roots by loading up his all-pervasive and divine "wisdom" with many of the trappings of an ethereal or magnetic fluid. In this model, matter appeared to be something more than mere shadow and was capable of being both immersed in and filled with wisdom. Quimby wrote that matter "is a vacuum, ready to be filled by wisdom"; that "[wisdom] is in and through all matter, which is called solid"; and that wisdom "penetrates through the pores of all matter."[54]

Quimby was familiar with various fluid theories because he discussed them extensively in his "Lecture Notes." There he described at length some of the ideas set forth by such itinerant lyceum magnetizers as Charles Poyen and Robert Collyer and some popular works analyzing mesmerism by such authors as Chauncey Townshend of Trinity Hall, Cambridge, and John Bovee Dods of Boston. The nature and role of the invisible fluid employed by these popularizers and proponents of mesmerism were fundamentally the same as those given by Franz Anton Mesmer himself in his famous "Dissertation on the Discovery of Animal Magnetism." In that work, Mesmer listed twenty-seven principles that formed the basis of his science, the first two of which were affirmed by everyone Quimby cited: "(1) There exists a mutual influence between the Heavenly bodies, the Earth and Animate Bodies. (2) A universally distributed and continuous fluid, which is quite without vacuum and of an incomparably rarefied nature, and which by its nature is capable of receiving, propagating and communicating all the impressions of movement, is the means of this influence."[55]

Since these fluid/ether theories are inseparable from the notion of wisdom that sits so close to the center of Quimby's cosmology, it is particularly ironic to note that one of the primary objectives of his "Lecture Notes" was

not to argue in favor of such theories but to denounce them as "humbugs."
In his early days, Quimby saw fluid theories as both experimentally and theoretically untenable. They could not explain that which was observed to occur in such phenomena as mesmerism and clairvoyance. Quimby opted instead for a theory of the direct action of mind on mind, without a fluid
medium, as a more satisfying explanation. "We have endeavored in every
portion of our work to keep distinctly in view the theory of 'mind acting
upon mind,'" wrote Quimby, and "not through a medium, because we see
no necessity of an agent different from itself, but by any direct action." He
lamented that "the followers of Mesmer" unduly complicated the issue by
insisting on an "imponderable" intermediary. Quimby maintained that if the
fluid theory had been tested experimentally, "the theory of fluid would have
been abandoned long ago; for it would have been ascertained that all the fluid
which really exists is in the mind of the operator, being like Berkeley's com-
position of matter, made up of ideas, impressions etc."[56]

In another section of the lecture notes in which he was criticizing a pamphlet on animal magnetism by John Dods, Quimby wrote, "If this 'elastic,
invisible ether pervading all Nature' causes all these phenomena, it is Godlike power, second only to its Author. . . . If I could believe in the 'Fluid
Theory' it would be far more marvelous and astonishing to trace out such
laws as must govern this 'invisible ether' than the experiments which follow.
Or perhaps it may be a principle without the pale of the law, governing itself
under the direction of the operator, in part, at some times and at others,
entirely at its own control."[57]

In these remarks—likely written at least twelve years before he started
producing his "wisdom"-centered articles in 1859—Quimby divulged his
personal fascination with invisible fluids and foreshadowed almost exactly
the place they would have in his later writings. He unabashedly exploited all
the attributes of the "fluids" and "ethers" in his later writings, but he all but
banished the words, opting instead for the philosophically problematic label of "solid." Quimby most likely thought the terms *fluid* and *ether* were still
too closely connected with animal magnetism—which he held in disdain
until his death—for him to use them in his manuscripts. He slipped on only
one telltale occasion, when he stated that "the scientific [person is] in ether."[58]

In spite of the truth-in-labeling problem, the fluid nature of wisdom was
at least as important as all of wisdom's more traditional divine attributes. At
one point, Quimby even called wisdom the Holy Ghost, which, in fluidlike
fashion, was able to fill human beings as wisdom filled matter. Even more like
the Holy Ghost, wisdom was an intelligent fluid able to impart knowledge

and life itself to the matter it filled. And, like the Holy Ghost, it could direct matter toward happiness and harmony. Wisdom was a powerful invisible force that governed the matter filling endless space, yet it was "full of love, compassion and every attribute that wisdom can suggest." At another point, Quimby even elevated wisdom above God by declaring that "God is the name of that essence that flows from wisdom."[59]

Aside from its teleological nature, Quimby's all-pervasive rarefied fluid was, in many respects, playing the same role that ethers did in other arenas. Ethers were not just filling the lyceum halls when itinerant mesmerists were presenting their wares. They also had a prominent theoretical place in the more widely esteemed sciences of the antebellum period. Generally considered different in mechanical properties from other types of matter, ethers were usually seen as mediums by which action could be transmitted between bodies without the bodies' making direct contact. As waves were transmitted by water, so etheric media could carry or propagate light, heat, electricity, and other influences that traveled through otherwise empty space. Buoyed by the venerable names of Rene Descartes and Isaac Newton, both of whom employed a form of the concept, European and American scientists investigated the existence and explanatory utility of ethers. According to G. N. Cantor and M. J. S. Hodge, ether theories played crucial conceptual roles in many scientific enterprises from 1740 to 1900. Ethers provided mechanisms that kept the other scientific ideas, such as "contact causes," alive in the otherwise great void of space. They kept alive mechanical theories of the propagation of light, heat, and other influences that traversed distances, and they helped avoid the conceptual problems involved with the notion of action at a distance. Ethers helped unify "disparate phenomena and diverse branches of science," from the ideas of transmission of impulses through nerves in physiology to the theory of gravitational attraction between heavenly bodies in physics.[60]

In step with the orthodox science of his day, although on a much less sophisticated scale, Quimby's writings show that he, too, was concerned with such problematic ideas as causes, unity, mechanical theories, and action at a distance. The etheric fluids in his system were employed to solve some of the same problems. He went a giant step further than most ether theorists of his day, however, by endowing his ether with supreme intelligence and a panoply of divine attributes. Quimby's etheric wisdom was yet another god of the gaps. It literally filled all space and accounted for most phenomena that were otherwise inexplicable. His ether had the added advantage of being able to bring to life the cold passive matter that Newtonian mechanics postulated because as wisdom filled all matter, it brought intelligence along. Matter was alive with wisdom. Accordingly, gravitation was not to be considered a mysterious force that caused all material particles in the universe to attract one another. Rather, they were "held together by their own sympathy, wisdom or attraction." The vital physiological action of the circulation of the blood was not to be considered a function of impersonal hydraulic theory. In reality, it was an "overruling wisdom" that was directly choreographing circulation.[61]

Although one could draw some conceptual relation between scientific ether theories of the time and Quimby's intelligent, etheric "Wisdom," it still seems too speculative an idea even for those, like Quimby, whose Baconianism sometimes had ad hoc rules. Justifying this idea in some way or another was a high priority, and not just for Quimby. Orson Pratt and Robert Hare likewise postulated concepts of matter that could carry knowledge. Although it may have been a speculative notion, in the minds of Quimby, Pratt, and Hare it had a basis in fact. All three used the same phenomenon as evidence: the nature of odor.

Phineas Quimby thought that the way in which humans and animals detected odor provided proof, not just an analogical example, of the notion that matter could carry knowledge. In an essay originally entitled "The Senses and Language," Quimby examined what he considered the roots of spoken language. He found odor and the sense of smell to be the primordial basis for communication. In his thinking, it was not just that an odor could communicate the presence of food, smoke, or flowers nearby, an idea with which no one would argue. Quimby took it a step further by maintaining that feelings and ideas, too, could be carried by odor, or what he sometimes called "atmosphere." For instance, he wrote that "the atmosphere of a lion was certain death to the other animals so that their fright threw off an odor that did not attract the lion till the object of his prey came in contact with his sight." As language developed for humans, Quimby argued, the odor actually "contained the thing created"; indeed, this form of communication "created the power of creating." Quimby noticed that smelling something could not be explained in mechanical terms alone. Smells were not just received and acknowledged by humans, they also caused such reactions as hunger or fear and brought images and memories to mind. Odors, Quimby thought, created ideas and feelings in humans. He therefore concluded that odors, like spiritual matter, carried all the attributes of mind.[62]

In a remarkably similar vein, Orson Pratt, too, compared spiritual matter to odor. Spirit, he contended, was exactly like the particles of odor. Spirit "can exist in connexion with the body or separate from it; and yet it forms no part of the fleshly tabernacle." In "odorous particles," one could not directly detect the usual properties associated with matter, such as resistance to muscular effort, visibility, and extension. Yet "immaterialists, without any hesitation, pronounce them to be matter." Using the example of "odor" or "atmosphere" was a popular way of defending the material nature of spirit or mind. Parley Pratt and Brigham Young employed it in Mormon circles, and Robert Hare used it to defend the spiritualist concept of material spirit. For all of these nineteenth-century religious thinkers, odor or atmosphere provided a fairly precise model of material spirit. Odor was invisible and filled space, and it was immediately evident that odor interacted with gross matter in olfactory sensation. Just as important, odor was associated with information, intelligence, and knowledge. Odor was able to communicate. It could carry information about the presence of a skunk, an apple, or a fire. All these materialists considered it reasonable to claim that "odoriferous particles," as well as all other matter, did not simply carry knowledge but were themselves knowledge-filled and intelligent.[63]

Because Quimby's etheric wisdom, like odor, could go anywhere, it did not exist in ordinary matter alone. It also resided in and quickened his other material substance, mind, which Quimby called "spiritual matter." As we have seen, one of Quimby's fundamental tenets was that mind was something material. It was one of those points on which he was clear and consistent. He was also clear, however, that mind was *not* to be confused with wisdom. Quimby made this distinction on numerous occasions. For example, in one dialogue he summarized his thoughts on the nature of mind and wisdom and the distinction between them:

> Patient: "I have been thinking of what you said to me yesterday and now I want to know why you so persistently insist upon saying that my disease is in my mind, when I know that it is in my body."
> Dr. Quimby: "What do you call the mind?"
> Patient: "The intellectual ability, and you know very well that does not have consumption."
> Dr. Quimby: "I differ from the world from the application of the word mind."
> Patient: "What right have you to differ? What do you depict the mind to be?"
> Dr. Quimby: "I say that mind is spiritual matter."
> Patient: "But it is not so."
> Dr. Quimby: "Cannot the mind change?"
> Patient: "Certainly."
> Dr. Quimby: "Can wisdom change?"
> Patient: "No, I suppose not if it is true."

Dr. Quimby: "Then mind cannot be wisdom, for mind changes. Consequently, it must be matter or a substance that can change and take form."[64]

The distinction between mind and wisdom was important to Quimby. Mind was, in some sense, a cause, but it was not to be confused with the eternal, unalterable First Cause, wisdom: "Wisdom [is] superior to the word mind, for I always apply the word mind to matter but never apply it to the First Cause." Quimby removed the mystery from mind. While the philosophers and theologians of his day continued to struggle with all of the perplexities of the mind-matter dualism Descartes bequeathed to them, Quimby solved the problem by proclaiming mind to be matter. That he usually called mind "spiritual" matter does not cloud the issue. Spiritual matter, for Quimby, was simply matter not yet condensed, and he often referred to mind as matter without the "spiritual" qualification. Since mind was really matter, it would follow that wisdom could fill, quicken, and direct the mind in the same way it did gross matter. Quimby wrote, "Mind is always under the control of some spiritual wisdom superior to the natural man," and in another section, he declared, "Matter is a medium for wisdom and when I say matter I embrace mind in it, so it is not necessary to repeat the two every time I allude to mind."[65]

But what of spirit? How did Quimby deal with the concept, and what place did it play in his cosmological construction? He knew the question was important because it confronted him regularly and not just because the nature of spirit was a common question of orthodox theological speculation. Quimby lived through the heyday of the spiritualist movement in America, and he was not only frequently charged with engaging in spiritualist practice but also repeatedly called upon by patients, detractors, and the spiritualists themselves to show how his system was different. It is clear that he had a great deal to say about the topic because he dedicated more than sixteen articles to it in his collected works. The various spirit-caused phenomena that were supposed to have occurred in spiritualist circles—such as rapping, writing, noises, healings, furniture movement, and visual manifestations—were particularly suited for Quimbyesque commentary. In the same way he dealt with disease, he considered these "so-called" spirit manifestations the result of a "person's belief . . . founded on the fact that they want to have it true." He directly experimented with the phenomena himself and claimed to be considered a "medium" by the spiritualists themselves. When all was said and done, though, he concluded that what he saw and heard in the séances was brought about by his belief, not by real spirit visitors.[66]

Quimby treated spiritualism in the same divided way that he treated mesmerism, though. He denounced it as humbug but continued to carry some of the common conceptual baggage, in this case, the spiritualist notion of the nature of spirit. He treated Mormonism in exactly the same way. Quimby, like most of the spiritualists and Mormons, claimed that spirit was a material substance although in a more subtle state. Sounding no different from Orson Pratt and Robert Hare, Quimby emphatically wrote, "I will state my belief and bring proof to substantiate it as true. Spirit is only matter in a rarefied form."[67]

Although spirit never played a significant role in Quimby's scheme, his pronouncement on the material nature of that which was traditionally considered immaterial was one more indication that the *mental* doctor viewed the world in *material* terms. For him, even thoughts, knowledge, ideas, reason, and the soul "must be of matter." The only thing in Quimby's cosmos that retained a hint of immateriality was wisdom, and even that was elusive. On the one hand, he referred to wisdom as a "solid," but on the other hand, he seemed certain that wisdom was not matter. He ascribed to wisdom many of the qualities of a traditionally immaterial God but also ascribed to it the properties of ethers that in his day were generally regarded as matter in a subtle or rarefied state. In spite of the ambiguity in the case of wisdom, his materialism seems otherwise comprehensive.[68]

In many respects, however, materialism was not the end in itself for Pratt, Hare, or Quimby. Rather, the ultimate goal was to have a cosmos ruled by science to ensure that the Enlightenment pillars of reason and natural law predominated. The conceptual elimination of the nonmaterial guaranteed that there would be no corner of the universe in which "Science," the guardian of truth and the source of harmony, could not be the final arbiter.

Conclusion

In studying his writings, no scholar has missed Phineas P. Quimby's commitment to science. His materialism, however, has generally been, for various reasons, overlooked, ignored, or transformed by those who have examined the mental doctor's ideas. The root of the problem may lie in the circumstances surrounding the first codification of Quimby's writings. Materialism clearly did not suit the purpose of Horatio Dresser, the compiler and editor of the *Quimby Manuscripts,* first published in 1921. Horatio Dresser, the son of two prominent students of Quimby, Julius and Annetta

Dresser, embarked on his editorial project for a specific reason. He wanted to emphasize the similarities between the teachings of Phineas P. Quimby and Mary Baker Eddy to show that Eddy had stolen her basic ideas from Quimby, a charge Eddy and her followers fought tenaciously and continue to fight even today. That Mary Baker Eddy had actually overturned one of Quimby's main philosophical tenets would not have helped Dresser's case. Dresser's editing and commentary on Quimby's manuscripts therefore resulted in spiritualizing the materialism the mental doctor had set forth. On several occasions, Dresser directly inserted the word *spiritual* as a modifier in front of the word *matter* in Quimby's text. On at least three other occasions, Dresser seemed to find it necessary to help the reader by explaining just what Quimby meant by *matter*. He even went so far as to say that the fact that Quimby never explicitly denied the reality of matter was just a "back-handed way of declaring what to him was the greatest truth: there was no reality save that which exists in God or Science. His realization of this truth was so strong that he did not need denials."[69] Dresser was certainly right that Quimby never denied the reality of matter, but he was wrong about the reason. Without Dresser's transformational editing and comments, Quimby's commitment to materialism is difficult to deny.[70]

Quimby's materialism also calls into question the common characterization of his thought as belonging in some way to the family of Ralph Waldo Emerson, Henry David Thoreau, and others, as Stewart W. Holmes did in calling Quimby the "Scientist of Transcendentalism." It was really only Dresser's spiritualized Quimby that fit this classification. Not surprisingly, Holmes and others, such as Robert C. Fuller, Charles S. Braden, Lester M. Hirsch, and Ferenc M. Szasz, who used Dresser's edition of the *Manuscripts* exclusively, connected Quimby in various ways to the Transcendentalist heritage.[71]

Quimby's materialism was too bold to be ignored, though. As Catherine L. Albanese noticed, Quimby had "managed to turn in a decidedly physical reading of metaphysical reality." With the materialism expressed climactically in Quimby's obsession with things scientific, it appears that his basic worldview was really only a forced fit into Romantic or Transcendentalist categories. Given his scientism, the materialism blends with his tendencies toward a deistic conception of the divine to suggest that Quimby might be better characterized as a less sophisticated second cousin to Thomas Jefferson, Benjamin Franklin, Thomas Paine, Ethan Allen, and Elihu Palmer than to Ralph Waldo Emerson, Henry David Thoreau, or Bronson Alcott. Quimby's continual exaltation of Newtonian mechanics, first causes, progress, experimentation, reason, and the practical application of his theories, as well as his overt antielitism and anticlericalism, places him much more in line with what I am calling the village Enlightenment. Quimby brought together several streams of popular thought and packaged them into a new view of the world that he believed could address pressing problems of the day better than all competing views. When G. Adolf Koch wrote that "the history of the eighteenth century with respect to deism was the story of its gradual filtration from the philosopher to the common man," he stopped too early, and he needed to speak of more than deism. The effects of the Enlightenment's filtration continued to be felt well into the first half of the nineteenth century, and the mental doctor from Belfast, Maine, may very well be just such a "common man." His scientific healing practice and religious ideas were an important embodiment of the village Enlightenment.[72]

Conclusion:
The Enlightenment Village

Nineteenth-century popular religion in America was not kind to the general "warfare" approach to science and religion. The "honeymoon" between the spheres in the antebellum period was real, and it was based on much more than some warm feeling that there ought to be cooperation between science and religion. Rather, the honeymoon was based on the idea that harmony had to reign epistemologically. Without using a great deal of sophisticated jargon, thinkers and writers in popular religious movements, orthodox or not, made it clear that for something to be "truly true," an overall harmony had to obtain. If it was perceived that one's religious ideas were out of step with science, those beliefs were in deep trouble—they could not possibly be true. If, however, one could make the case that one's religious ideas and science matched perfectly (even with a great deal of stretching on the part of either science or religion), all of the rights, privileges, and benefits of one of antebellum culture's greatest sources of authority were there for the taking.

Even those in quasi-religious movements knew the key to success was harmonization with science. Take, for example, the well-known nineteenth-century American phrenologist Orson S. Fowler. Phrenology, in popular terms, was the belief that the surface shape of the skull could give important information about a person's emotions, character, and intelligence. Like a number of the most committed devotees of such practices, Fowler took the beliefs to the next level by claiming that phrenological ideas and practices revealed great new truths that in turn confirmed and harmonized with the great truths of religion and science. "*Phrenology is truth,*" wrote Fowler in his 1843 defense of phrenological theory entitled *The Christian Phrenologist.* "It is a *demonstrative* science. It is a science built upon FACTS and *consisting in* facts—facts of every kind and infinite in number."[1]

According to Fowler, because of the undeniable scientific truth of phrenology, religious doctrine and revelation had either to measure up or to "*go by the board*." To achieve harmony, there could be no middle ground, no gray areas or compromise. Religious revelation was either in harmony with science or "at war with *truth* and must suffer defeat." But if phrenology was "found to *harmonize* with Revelation," wrote Fowler, it stood "on the rock of *truth,* and is supported and defended by *nature*." Fowler reasoned that because of the obvious harmony, the factual nature, and the demonstrability of the great truths of phrenology, people "cannot *help* believing it." Using the certainty of the senses as the analogical coup de grace in the argument, he wrote, they could not help believing it, "any more than they can avoid seeing what they look at, or feeling fire when they touch it. *All must and will* believe it."[2] Fowler's lifework was an overall pursuit of harmonious relationships—between individuals, between nations, between mind and body, between humankind and nature. What brings him under the umbrella of the village Enlightenment, like Quimby, Pratt, and Hare, was that he did not for a moment neglect the goal of harmony in the world of ideas. The epigraph he chose as the guiding principle for his book was, "Truth is a unity, and always consistent with herself."

Few people in antebellum America would have agreed more wholeheartedly with Fowler's epigraph than Orson Pratt, Robert Hare, and Phineas Parkhurst Quimby. A millennial excitement clung to all three men and all three of their movements, so that the new ideas were deemed certain to lead the way back to ancient truths. They were in a new world, a new republic, and a new scientific era, and they felt new sense of courage to challenge what were in their view the falsehoods carried to the modern era by corrupt clerics. They considered themselves loosed from medieval intellectual shackles and endowed with the freedom to promulgate new ideas. They were convinced that Baconian scientific reasoning could make unerring choices between competing ideas. Looking forward with great enthusiasm to the withering away of sin, death, disease, disputes, and war, they all envisioned the final reign of nature through reason.

All of this said, it should be clear that popular religion was not and is not simply a synonym for mindless religion. There is certainly plenty of room to disagree with the arguments, dissect the reasoning, and counter the presuppositions of people like Pratt, Hare, and Quimby. However, there is no room for doubting that arriving at the "truth" through reason was paramount for them. They were not engaged in intellectual games or whipping up ecstatic experiences to get people beyond rationality in order to achieve enlightenment. Nor were they searching for answers to great cosmic questions in categories of illusions or in old scholastic categories of intangible substances. They looked to reason, science, and the senses for truth and wrestled the question of ultimate reality into submission by naming it matter.

Pratt, Hare, and Quimby each developed or embraced a system of thinking in which the popular odds and ends of religion, philosophy, and science seemed to rush together for them into one conceptual scheme. Orson Pratt could see himself as a latter-day Newton offering a new and improved way to explain the motion of the heavenly bodies because he was not shackled by the inadequate first principles that sent the original Newton down a wayward path. From the same materialist foundation, Phineas Quimby was able to solve what was thought to be the insoluble problem of Cartesian dualism. Mind-body interaction was not a problem because both were fundamentally material substances. Mind was simply matter in a more rarefied form. Likewise, Robert Hare could answer the problem of "action at a distance"—a loose end in Newton's cosmology—by proclaiming the invisible ether that permeated all space was a "will" conducting material substance. Action therefore did not take place mysteriously over a distance; action was carried physically between bodies by the oceans of intelligent material particles that constituted the universal ether.

Because Pratt, Hare, and Quimby were seeking the "unity of truth," they made no attempt to distinguish these scientific and philosophical conclusions from religious ideas. They ultimately had to be one and the same. The historian Jon Butler found this type of popular religious creativity "extending across antebellum society" in the 1850s, when Pratt, Hare, and Quimby were writing, and he even thought that it "rivaled the American ingenuity and adaptability evident in exploration, politics, and technology."[3] The Enlightenment had been assimilated into the "village" setting, although not without some changes. Nonetheless, the twin pillars of nature and reason were raised on the village green, and so were the hopes of such figures as Pratt, Hare, and Quimby, who found in their enlightened approach to the cosmos the answers to all-important questions. Nathan O. Hatch properly called this assimilation of Enlightenment rationality into popular religion a "blurring of worlds."[4] But for the citizens of the Enlightenment village, the blurring of worlds seemed to make the world they lived in perfectly clear.

Notes

INTRODUCTION

1. John William Draper, *The History of the Conflict between Religion and Science* (New York: D. Appleton, 1898), 364.

2. The lecture was published independent of the larger work as Andrew Dickson White, *The Warfare of Science* (New York: D. Appleton, 1876), 7.

3. David C. Lindberg and Ronald L. Numbers, "Beyond War and Peace: A Reappraisal of the Encounter between Christianity and Science," *Perspectives on Science and Christian Faith* 39 (September 1987): 140, 141; James R. Moore, *The Post-Darwinian Controversies: A Study of the Protestant Struggle to Come to Terms with Darwin in Great Britain and America, 1870–1900* (Cambridge: Cambridge University Press, 1979), 99. See also David C. Lindberg and Ronald L. Numbers, eds., *God and Nature: Historical Essays on the Encounter between Christianity and Science* (Berkeley: University of California Press, 1986).

4. Herbert Hovenkamp, *Science and Religion in America, 1800–1860* (Philadelphia: University of Pennsylvania Press, 1978), 49. Ironically, Lindberg and Numbers pointed out that Hovenkamp himself illustrated the negative influence of the "warfare" thesis in that although he described the harmony of the antebellum period, he characterized the advent of Darwinism in America as a "pitched battle" between religion and science, a view that Lindberg and Numbers considered simplistic. David C. Lindberg and Ronald L. Numbers, introduction to *God and Nature*, ed. Lindberg and Numbers, 6.

5. Theodore Dwight Bozeman, *Protestants in an Age of Science: The Baconian Ideal and Antebellum American Religious Thought* (Chapel Hill: University of North Carolina Press, 1977), xv.

6. George M. Marsden, "Understanding Fundamentalist Views of Science," in *Science and Creationism,* ed. Ashley Montague (New York: Oxford University Press, 1984), 98. See also Walter H. Conser Jr., *God and the Natural World: Religion and Science in Antebellum America* (Columbia: University of South Carolina Press, 1993), 2.

7. For an overview of the relationship between these nineteenth-century movements and science, see Arthur Wrobel, ed., *Pseudo-Science and Society in Nineteenth-Century America* (Lexington: University Press of Kentucky, 1987).

8. Jon Butler, *Awash in a Sea of Faith: Christianizing the American People* (Cambridge, Mass.: Harvard University Press, 1990), 255–56.

9. Robert V. Bruce, *The Launching of Modern American Science, 1846–1876* (Ithaca, N.Y.: Cornell University Press, 1987), 3–6.

10. See, for instance, Robert Dale Owen, *The Debatable Land between This World and the Next* (New York: G. W. Carleton, 1872), 46 (spiritualism as "Science of the Soul"); and Parley P. Pratt, *Key to the Science of Theology* (Liverpool and London: F. D. Richards, 1855), xiv (Mormonism as "the divine science"). *Christian Science* was a term used for mind-cure practices both before and after Mary Baker Eddy started her work of the same name. See, for example, Phineas Parkhurst Quimby, *Phineas Parkhurst Quimby: The Complete Writings,* ed. Ervin Seale, 3 vols. (Marina Del Rey, Calif.: DeVorss, 1988), 2:40; and Charles Fillmore's early New Thought journal entitled *Christian Science.*

11. Although the case against the "warfare thesis" is sufficiently strong already, one might consider the historical attempts to bring ultimate harmony between religion and science by these new religious movements as a way to broaden the base of opposition. They certainly provide salient counterexamples from the margins of American religion that add to the case already made using counterexamples from traditional Protestant and Roman Catholic sources.

12. David Jaffee, "The Village Enlightenment in New England, 1760–1820," *William and Mary Quarterly* 47 (July 1990): 327–28.

13. Henry F. May, *The Enlightenment in America* (Oxford: Oxford University Press, 1976), 361.

14. Ibid., 361–62.

15. Nathan O. Hatch, *The Democratization of American Christianity* (New Haven, Conn.: Yale University Press, 1989), 34–35.

16. Catherine L. Albanese, *Nature Religion in America: From the Algonkian Indians to the New Age* (Chicago: University of Chicago Press, 1990), 149.

17. Charles S. Braden, *Spirits in Rebellion: The Rise and Development of New Thought* (Dallas: Southern Methodist University Press, 1963), 28–40.

18. Bozeman, *Protestants in an Age of Science,* xii. See also George H. Daniels, *American Science in the Age of Jackson* (New York: Columbia University Press, 1968), 63–85. Compare Braden's confusion over science in New Thought with the way in which Stephen Gottschalk used popular Baconian thinking to make sense of the concept of science in Mary Baker Eddy's writing. Stephen Gottschalk, *The Emergence of Christian Science in American Religious Life* (Berkeley: University of California Press, 1973), 72–74.

19. Marsden, "Understanding Fundamentalist Views of Science," 98.

20. C. Leonard Allen, "Baconianism and the Bible in the Disciples of Christ: James S. Lamar and *The Organon of Scripture,*" *Church History* 55 (March 1986): 66. The best study to date on the topic of the influence of American Baconianism and Protestant theology is Bozeman, *Protestants in the Age of Science.*

21. Arthus Wrobel, introduction to *Pseudo-Science,* ed. Wrobel, 8, 17.

22. Daniels, *American Science in the Age of Jackson,* 63.

23. Bozeman, *Protestants in an Age of Science,* 21.

24. Daniels, *American Science in the Age of Jackson,* 65–67.

25. Ibid., 66.

26. George H. Daniels, "The Process of Professionalization in American Science: The Emergent Period, 1820–1860," in *Science in America since 1820,* ed. Nathan Reingold (New York: Science History Publications, 1976), 66.

27. Donald Zochert, "Science and the Common Man in Antebellum America," in *Science in America since 1820*, ed. Reingold, 7–32.

28. William Ellery Channing, *Milwaukee Sentinel*, August 17, 1841, quoted in Zochert, "Science and the Common Man in Antebellum America," 7.

29. Donald M. Scott, "The Popular Lecture and the Creation of a Public in Mid-Nineteenth-Century America," *Journal of American History* 66 (March 1980): 800.

30. Josiah Holbrook, quoted in Carl Bode, *The American Lyceum: Town Meeting of the Mind* (New York: Oxford University Press, 1956), 12.

31. Bruce, *Launching of Modern American Science*, 116.

32. Ibid.

33. Quoted in ibid., 80.

34. Quoted in ibid., 29.

35. Quoted in ibid., 131.

36. Daniels, *American Science in the Age of Jackson*, 47.

37. Zochert, "Science and the Common Man in Antebellum America," 32.

38. Bozeman, *Protestants in an Age of Science*, xiii.

39. Quoted in Zochert, "Science and the Common Man in Antebellum America," 30.

40. James G. Carter, "The Two Books of Francis Lord Verulam: Of the Proficiencie and Advancement of Learning, Divine and Human," *American Journal of Education* 4 (1829): 193, quoted in J. J. Chambliss, "James G. Carter on Baconian Induction," *History of Education Quarterly* 3 (December 1963): 200.

41. Zochert, "Science and the Common Man in Antebellum America," 31.

42. Scott, "Popular Lecture," 802–3. See also Daniels, *American Science in the Age of Jackson*, 40–41.

43. Daniels, "Process of Professionalization in American Science," 66.

44. *Milwaukee Gazette*, February 3, 1846, quoted in Zochert, "Science and the Common Man in Antebellum America," 25.

45. *Milwaukee Courier*, October 5, 1842, quoted in ibid., 32.

46. Zochert, "Science and the Common Man in Antebellum America," 7.

47. Daniels, "Process of Professionalization in American Science," 63.

Chapter 1: Mormon Cosmic Philosophy

1. Orson Pratt, "History of Orson Pratt," *Deseret News Weekly* 8 (1858): 178.

2. Breck England, *The Life and Thought of Orson Pratt* (Salt Lake City: University of Utah Press, 1985), 132.

3. Edward Tullidge, *Life of Brigham Young* (New York: n.p., 1876), 74; T. B. H. Stenhouse, *Rocky Mountain Saints* (New York: D. Appleton, 1873), 9; Wilford Woodruff quoted in the *Latter-day Saints' Millennial Star* 43 (November 7, 1881): 707.

4. David J. Whittaker, "Orson Pratt: Prolific Pamphleteer," *Dialogue: A Journal of Mormon Thought* 15 (Fall 1982): 32.

5. *The Pearl of Great Price* (Liverpool: F. D. Richards, 1851), 38.

6. Orson Pratt, *The Orson Pratt Journals*, comp. Elden J. Watson (Salt Lake City: Elden J. Watson, 1975), 8–9.

7. Ibid., 9.

8. Orson Pratt, *Divine Authenticity of the Book of Mormon* (Liverpool: R. James, 1850), 83.

9. O. Pratt, *Journals*, 6.

10. Ibid., 8.

11. Ibid., 7.

12. Whitney R. Cross, *The Burned-over District: The Social and Intellectual History of Enthusiastic Religion in Western New York, 1800–1850* (Ithaca, N.Y.: Cornell University Press, 1950); O. Pratt, *Journals*, 6.

13. Parley P. Pratt, *Autobiography of Parley P. Pratt* (Salt Lake City: Deseret Book, 1985), 1; England, *Life and Thought of Orson Pratt*, 11.

14. P. Pratt, *Autobiography*, 1.

15. Whittaker, "Orson Pratt," 30.

16. Orson Pratt, *A Interesting Account of Several Remarkable Visions, and the Late Discovery of Ancient American Records Giving an Account of the Commencement of the Work of the Lord in This Generation* (Edinburgh: Ballantyne and Hughes, 1840); Whittaker, "Orson Pratt," 28.

17. Quoted in Milando Pratt, "Life and Labor of Orson Pratt," *Contributor* 12 (January 1891): 85–87.

18. England, *Life and Thought of Orson Pratt*, 94.

19. Orson Pratt, *Prophetic Almanac for 1845* (New York: Prophet Office, 1844), 5–10.

20. For more on the history of the almanac in America, see Robb Sagendorph, *America and Her Almanacs: Wit, Wisdom, and Weather, 1639–1970* (Boston: Little, Brown, 1970); Moses Coit Tyler, *A History of American Literature, 1607–1765* (Ithaca, N.Y.: Cornell University Press, 1949), 363–72; and Milton Drake, *Almanacs of the United States, Part I* (New York: Scarecrow, 1962), i–xiv.

21. Orson Pratt, "Lectures on Astronomy," delivered in Salt Lake City, 1851–52, in *Wonders of the Universe, or a Compilation of the Astronomical Writings of Orson Pratt*, comp. Nels B. Lundwall (Salt Lake City: Nels B. Lundwall, 1937), 1.

22. Orson Pratt, "Concentration of the Mind, Remarks by Elder Orson Pratt, Delivered in the Tabernacle, Great Salt Lake City, February 12, 1860," in *Journal of Discourses, by Brigham Young, President of the Church of Jesus Christ of Latter-day Saints, His Two Counselors, the Twelve Apostles, and Others*, 26 vols. (Liverpool: F. D. Richards, 1855–66), 7:157 (*Journal of Discourses* hereafter referred to as *JD*).

23. Tullidge quoted in England, *Life and Thought of Orson Pratt*, 155; Peter Crawley and Chad J. Flake, *A Mormon Fifty: An Exhibition in the Harold B. Lee Library in Conjunction with the Annual Conference of the Mormon History Association* (Provo, Utah: Friends of the Brigham Young University Library, 1984), item 35.

24. Whittaker, "Orson Pratt," 29.

25. Orson Pratt, "The Pre-existence of Man," *Seer* 1 (August 1853): 117.

26. Orson Pratt, letter to Brigham Young, quoted in Gary James Bergera, "The Orson Pratt–Brigham Young Controversies: Conflict within the Quorums, 1853 to 1868," *Dialogue: A Journal of Mormon Thought* 13 (Summer 1980): 11.

27. The unrevised and revised texts of this confession can be found in "'Let Brother Pratt Do as He Will': Orson Pratt's 29 January 1860 Confessional Discourse—Unrevised," *Dialogue: A Journal of Mormon Thought* 13 (Summer 1980): 50–58.

28. See Smith's revelations recorded in *The Doctrine and Covenants of the Church of Jesus Christ of Latter-day Saints* (Salt Lake City: Church of Jesus Christ of Latter-day Saints, 1876), 93:33, 131:7.

29. See O. Pratt, *Journals,* 91, 191, 270–73, 401–3, 554–56.

30. Orson Pratt, quoted in *Wonders of the Universe,* vii.

31. Donald Skabelund, "Cosmology on the American Frontier: Orson Pratt's Key to the Universe," *Centaurus: International Magazine of the History of Mathematics, Science, and Technology* 11, no. 3 (1965): 193.

32. England, *Life and Thought of Orson Pratt,* 66–67.

33. O. Pratt, *Interesting Account of Several Remarkable Visions,* 1, 15.

34. Daniels, *American Science in the Age of Jackson,* 63.

35. Bozeman, *Protestants in an Age of Science,* 160.

36. See Orson Pratt, *Great First Cause; or the Self-Moving Forces of the Universe* (Liverpool: R. James, 1851); and Orson Pratt, *Absurdities of Immaterialism, or, A Reply to T. W. P. Taylder's Pamphlet, Entitled, "The Materialism of the Mormons or Latter-day Saints, Examined and Exposed"* (Liverpool: R. James, 1849).

37. Daniels, *American Science in the Age of Jackson,* 63.

38. Ibid., 63–64.

39. O. Pratt, *Absurdities of Immaterialism,* 9; Orson Pratt, *Reply to a Pamphlet Printed in Glasgow, with the "Approbation of Clergymen of Different Denominations," Entitled "Remarks on Mormonism"* (Liverpool: R. James, 1849), 10 (last two quotes).

40. In applying inductive scientific method to the "facts" of scripture, Pratt anticipated the influential Princeton theologian Charles Hodge, who made this method the basis for his magnum opus in systematic theology. See Charles Hodge, *Systematic Theology* (New York: Scribner, 1872–73).

41. It is interesting to note that the account of the coming forth of the earliest and most important Mormon revelation—the Book of Mormon—has more in common with the way in which the "facts" of nature were discovered in the antebellum period than with traditional Christian accounts of men writing under the inspiration of the Holy Spirit. Joseph Smith dug up the tangible, revelation-laden gold plates in a day when scientists, not to mention treasure hunters, spent a good deal of their time probing the earth for geological data and paleontological oddities. Although certainly tempered by the fact that one had to accept Smith's divinely inspired translation of the "Reformed Egyptian" characters, as well as the story of the plates being taken back by the angel Moroni, the empirical portion of the account may have been enough to convince such Baconian-minded people as Orson Pratt that Mormonism was offering something more empirical than were the competing Christian sects of the day.

42. Brigham Young, "Remarks by President Brigham Young, Delivered in Salt Lake City, May 14, 1871," in *JD* 14:115–17. An in-depth study of the significance of the Baconian mindset and the influence of the Pratt brothers and Sidney Rigdon could be as helpful in understanding the early church as D. Michael Quinn's *Early Mormonism and the Magic World View* (Salt Lake City: Signature Books, 1987).

43. *Deseret News,* August 1, 1855, reprinted in Orson Pratt, *Key to the Universe, or a New Theory of Its Mechanism* (Liverpool: Author, 1879), 83.

44. Skabelund, "Cosmology on the American Frontier," 193.

45. See Quinn, *Early Mormonism and the Magic World View,* 197. Quinn writes that "almost half of the first apostles—Brigham Young, Heber C. Kimball, Orson Hyde, Luke S. Johnson, and Orson Pratt—gave specific evidence of a belief in various magical practices . . . at least two-thirds of Mormonism's first apostles may have had some affinity for magic" (195).

46. For more on the linkage between Orson Pratt's theory of matter and occult and hermetic philosophy, see John L. Brooke, *The Refiner's Fire: The Making of Mormon Cosmology, 1644–1844* (Cambridge: Cambridge University Press, 1994), 275; Erich Robert Paul, *Science, Religion, and Mormon Cosmology* (Urbana: University of Illinois Press, 1992), 129–30; and Quinn, *Early Mormonism and the Magic World View*, 220.

47. Kirkwood's presentation was eventually published as Daniel Kirkwood, "On a New Analogy in the Periods of Rotation of the Primary Planets," *American Journal of Science and Arts*, 2d ser., 9 (May 1850): 395–99. His discovery was reported in several other publications: "Kirkwood's Analogy," in *Annual of Scientific Discovery* (Boston: Gould, Kendall, and Lincoln, 1850), 335–38; [C. Piazzi Smyth], "On a New Analogy in the Periods of Rotation of the Primary Planets Discovered by Daniel Kirkwood of Pottsville, Pennsylvania," *Edinburgh New Philosophical Journal* 49 (July 1850): 169–70; and "Astronomy," *Scientific American* 6 (October 12, 1850): 26. For an account of how Kirkwood's analogy helped revive the nebular hypothesis in the United States, see Ronald L. Numbers, *Creation by Natural Law: Laplace's Nebular Hypothesis in American Thought* (Seattle: University of Washington Press, 1977), 41–54.

48. "Kirkwood's Analogy," 335.

49. Numbers, *Creation by Natural Law*, 48.

50. *Deseret News*, August 1, 1855, reprinted in O. Pratt, *Key to the Universe*, 89–90.

51. Ibid., vii.

52. Skabelund, "Cosmology on the American Frontier," 194.

53. Edmund Whittaker, *A History of the Theories of Aether and Electricity*, vol. 1, *The Classical Theories* (London: Thomas Nelson and Sons, 1951; reprint, New York: Dover Publications, 1989), 303 (page references are the same in both editions).

54. Skabelund, "Cosmology on the American Frontier," 194.

55. Ibid.

56. Ibid., 201.

57. Ibid., 200; William J. Christensen, "Critical Review of Orson Pratt Senior's Published Scientific Books" (M.A. thesis, University of Utah, 1929), 43. Both Skabelund and Christensen provide a detailed technical critique of Pratt's *Key to the Universe*.

58. O. Pratt, *Key to the Universe*, v.

59. Ibid., 14.

60. See Smith's prophetic utterances in Doctrine and Covenants, 130:20–21, 121:30–32, and 88:36–43.

61. O. Pratt, *Key to the Universe*, 74.

62. Orson Pratt, *New and Easy Method of Solution of the Cubic and Biquadratic Equations, Embracing Several New Formulas, Greatly Simplifying This Department of Mathematical Science. Designed as a Sequel to the Elements of Algebra, and for the Use of Schools and Academies* (London: Longmans, Green, Reader, and Dyer, 1866). For evaluations of his mathematical work, see Edward Hogan, "Orson Pratt as Mathematician," *Utah Historical Quarterly* 41 (Winter 1973): 59–68; Thomas Edgar Lyon, "Orson Pratt—Early Mormon Leader" (M.A. thesis, University of Chicago, 1932), 99–117; and Christensen, "Critical Review of Orson Pratt Senior's Published Scientific Books."

63. C[harles] Piazzi Smyth, *Our Inheritance in the Great Pyramid*, 3d ed. (London: Daldy, Isbister, 1877).

64. Orson Pratt, "The Great Prophetic Pyramid—An Important Discovery by Prof. O. Pratt, Sen.," *Latter-day Saints' Millennial Star* 41 (May 5, 1879): 281.

65. Ibid., 282.

66. Ibid., 282, 283.

67. Ibid., 283.

68. Orson Pratt, *Divine Authority, or the Question, Was Joseph Smith Sent of God?* (Liverpool: R. James, 1848), 11.

69. *The Pearl of Great Price* (1856), 36.

70. O. Pratt, *Divine Authority*, 1.

71. Edward W. Tullidge, *The Life of Joseph the Prophet* (New York: Tullidge and Crandall, 1878), 94.

72. O. Pratt, *Divine Authenticity of the Book of Mormon*, 56.

73. O. Pratt, *Absurdities of Immaterialism*, 1.

74. Ibid., 11.

75. Orson Pratt, *The Kingdom of God* (Liverpool: R. James, 1848–49).

76. T. W. P. Taylder, *The Materialism of the Mormons, or Latter Day Saints, Examined and Exposed* (Woolwich: R. Jones, 1849), 8.

77. Parley P. Pratt, *The Millennium, and Other Poems: To Which Is Annexed, A Treatise on the Regeneration and Eternal Duration of Matter* (New York: W. Molineux, 1840).

78. Peter L. Crawley, "Parley P. Pratt: Father of Mormon Pamphleteering," *Dialogue: A Journal of Mormon Thought* 15 (Fall 1982): 16.

79. Parley Pratt was at the forefront of writing tracts designed to respond to the avalanche of published assaults on Mormonism in the early years. Some of his responses include *Mormonism Unveiled: Zion's Watchman Unmasked, and Its Editor, Mr. L. R. Sunderland, Exposed; Truth Vindicated; the Devil Mad, and Priestcraft in Danger!* (New York: n.p., 1838); *Plain Facts, Showing the Falsehood and Folly of the Rev. C. S. Bush, (a Church Minister of the Parish Peover,) Being a Reply to His Tract against the Latter-day Saints* (Manchester: W. R. Thomas, [1840]); *A Reply to Mr. Thomas Taylor's "Complete Failure," &c., and Mr. Richard Livesey's "Mormonism Exposed"* (Manchester: W. R. Thomas, 1840); *An Answer to Mr. William Hewitt's Tract against the Latter-day Saints* (Manchester: W. R. Thomas, 1840); and *Truth Defended, or a Reply to the "Preston Chronicle," and to Mr. J. B. Rollo's "Mormonism Exposed"* (Manchester: P. P. Pratt, 1841).

80. Taylder, *Materialism of the Mormons*, 14; O. Pratt, *Absurdities of Immaterialism*, 2.

81. Taylder, *Materialism of the Mormons*, 14; O. Pratt, *Absurdities of Immaterialism*, 3

82. O. Pratt, *Absurdities of Immaterialism*, 2–8. Pratt also extended the argument to others, such as Isaac Taylor, John Mason Good, John Abercrombie, Thomas Brown, David James, Stephen Charnock, and Joseph Butler—all of whom he quoted as proponents of immaterialism. See Isaac Taylor, *Physical Theory of Another Life* (New York: D. Appleton, 1836); John Mason Good, *The Book of Nature* (Boston: Wells and Lilly, 1826); John Abercrombie, *Inquiries concerning the Intellectual Powers and the Investigation of Truth* (Edinburgh: Waugh and Innes, 1830); Thomas Brown, *Lectures on the Philosophy of the Human Mind by the Late Thomas Brown* (Edinburgh: W. and C. Tait, 1820); Stephen Charnock, *Discourses upon the Existence and Attributes of God* (New York: Robert Carter and Brothers, 1853); and Joseph Butler, *The Analogy of Religion, Natural and Revealed, to the Constitution and Course of Nature* (New Haven, Conn.: A. H. Maltby, 1822).

Orson Pratt stood out among the early Mormon writers because of his research and citations. In *Absurdities of Immaterialism*, he also quoted Joseph Priestley, *Disquisitions relating to Matter and Spirit* (London: J. Johnson, 1777; reprint, New York: Arno, 1975); Erasmus Darwin, *Zoonomia, or, The Laws of Organic Life* ((London: J. Johnson, 1794–96); Dionysius Lardner, *Popular Lectures on Science and Art, Delivered in the Principle Cities and Towns of the United States* (New York: Greely and McElrath, 1846); Isaac Newton, *Principia Mathematica*, trans. Andrew Motte (London: Printed for B. Motte, 1729); and John Robison, *A System of Mechanical Philosophy, with Notes by David Brewster* (Edinburgh: J. Murray, 1822).

83. O. Pratt, *Absurdities of Immaterialism*, 11.

84. For instance, Timothy Dwight, the president of Yale, used this line of argument in his popular work that circulated widely in the United States entitled *Theology, Explained and Defended, in a Series of Sermons* (Glasgow: Blackie and Sons, 1836), 121–26.

85. Taylder, *Materialism of the Mormons*, 16.

86. O. Pratt, *Absurdities of Immaterialism*, 7.

87. Ibid., 8. Neither Pratt nor Taylder makes a point of distinguishing between mind, spirit, or soul. Both found these distinctions secondary to the issue at hand: the materiality or immaterial of these substances.

88. Ibid.

89. Taylder, *Materialism of the Mormons*, 19.

90. O. Pratt, *Absurdities of Immaterialism*, 8–9.

91. Ibid., 24.

92. Ibid., 23–24.

93. Ibid., 15.

94. Because of its chronological primacy, it is possible that Mormon theology was a source for the idea of spiritual matter in later movements.

95. Joseph Smith's successor, Brigham Young, took the idea of spirits in apparently inanimate objects to an almost animistic level. On one occasion, he wrote, "There are a multitude of spirits in the world. . . . Is there life in these rocks and mountains? There is. Then there is a spirit peculiarly adapted to those rocks and mountains. We mark the progress of the growth of grass, flowers, and trees. There is a spirit nicely adapted to the various productions of the vegetable kingdom. There is also a spirit to the different ores of the mineral kingdom, and to every element in existence." Brigham Young, "When I Contemplate the Subject of Salvation: A Sermon Delivered on 12 February 1854," in *The Essential Brigham Young* (Salt Lake City: Signature Books, 1992), 82.

96. O. Pratt, *Absurdities of Immaterialism*, 16–17.

97. The historian John L. Brooke makes a good case for tracing this concept of intelligent matter in Mormon thought back to medieval and Reformation-era occult activity, such as hermeticism, alchemy, and magic, although he writes that "Orson Pratt's hermeticism was distant, muffled by his immersion in nineteenth-century science, but still unmistakable (*Refiner's Fire*, 275).

In the history of philosophy, the closest one comes to Orson Pratt's view of sentient particulate matter would be the position that has come to be known as panpsychism or hylozoism. According to Paul Edwards, "Panpsychism is the theory according to which all objects in the universe, not only human beings and animals but also plants and even objects we usually classify as 'inanimate,' have an 'inner' or 'psychological' being."

Panpsychists who call these sentient objects "living"—which accounts for most panpsychists—would be more specifically labeled hylozoists. Paul Edwards, "Panpsychism," in *Encyclopedia of Philosophy*, ed. Paul Edwards (New York: Macmillan, 1967), 6:22–31. See also Charles Hartshorne, "Panpsychism," in *A History of Philosophical Systems*, ed. Vergilius T. Ferm (Freeport, N.Y.: Books for Libraries Press, 1970), 442–53; and Sterling McMurrin, *The Theological Foundations of the Mormon Religion* (Salt Lake City: University of Utah Press, 1965), 7, 45.

If anything, the early Mormon thinkers fell into the category of hylozoism. From his first comments on "intelligent matter," Joseph Smith was interpreted as implying that matter was in some sense alive. Parley Pratt, Orson Pratt, and Brigham Young all stated this directly, although there is no evidence that Joseph Smith or anyone in the early movement was directly influenced by panpsychists in the philosophical world. Panpsychist tendencies were, however, alive and well in a less sophisticated form in the folk magic and occultism of the period. Quinn, *Early Mormonism and the Magic World View*, xii, 184.

98. One of the notable characteristics of LDS religious thought to this day is that it has not developed and does not aspire to develop a metaphysical foundation. The modern Mormon philosopher Sterling McMurrin wrote that "metaphysics has never received a technical structuring and systematic formulation, as Mormon intellectual effort in the past has been directed especially toward the constructive elaboration of theological doctrine with comparatively little attention to its philosophical implicates or assumptions." In another work, McMurrin also said that the "highly speculative materialism of Orson Pratt" stands out because "in a general way [it] profoundly influenced Mormon thought though it was never accepted as an official Church position." Max Nolan confirmed this some years later, writing that materialism has been a "curiously neglected issue" except for the case of Pratt, who produced "the most sustained attempt to philosophically explicate this material metaphysics." Sterling McMurrin, *The Philosophical Foundations of Mormon Theology* (Salt Lake City: University of Utah Press, 1959), 6; McMurrin, *Theological Foundations of the Mormon Religion*, 45; Max Nolan, "Materialism and the Mormon Faith," *Dialogue: A Journal of Mormon Thought* 22 (Winter 1989): 71–72. See also Dennis Rasmussen, "Metaphysics," in *Encyclopedia of Mormonism*, ed. David H. Ludlow (New York: Macmillan, 1992), 2:894–95.

99. England, *Life and Thought of Orson Pratt*, 163.

100. O. Pratt, *Great First Cause; Orson Pratt, The Holy Spirit* (Liverpool: Latter-day Saints Book and Millennial Star Depot, 1856); *Seer* (Washington, D. C., and Liverpool), 1853–54.

101. Isaac Newton, *Opticks: Or, a Treatise of the Reflexions, Refractions, Inflections and Colours of Light*, foreword by Albert Einstein, introduction by Edmund Whittaker, preface by I. Bernard Cohen, analytical table of contents by Duane H. D. Roller (based on the 4th ed., London, 1730) (New York: Dover Publications, 1952), Query 28, 369–70.

102. O. Pratt, *Great First Cause*, 16.

103. Ibid., 9.

104. Ibid.

105. Paul, *Science, Religion, and Mormon Cosmology*, 48.

106. The most difficult scientific challenge to Orson Pratt's system did not surface until after the apostle's death. Pratt's system was dependent on a view—handed down from Democritus and perpetuated by Newton—of the solid impenetrable atom as the most

basic unit of matter. Beginning in 1897, discoveries by J. J. Thomson, Ernest Rutherford, Neils Bohr, and others resulted in conceptions of the atom that looked less and less like Pratt's ultimate particles, whose "essence was solidity."

107. O. Pratt, *Absurdities of Immaterialism*, 31.

108. O. Pratt, *Great First Cause*, 16; O. Pratt, *Holy Spirit*, 49.

109. Ibid., 15.

110. Orson Pratt, "A Discourse by Elder Orson Pratt, Delivered in the Tabernacle, Salt Lake City, Sunday Afternoon, August 8th, 1880," in *JD*, 21:233–34. Brigham Young was in full agreement, but as usual he blurred many of the fine distinctions made by the more philosophically minded Pratt. See Brigham Young, "A Discourse by President Brigham Young Delivered in the Temple Court, Great Salt Lake City, March 23, 1856," in *JD* 3:277.

111. O. Pratt, *Absurdities of Immaterialism*, 23.

112. Orson Pratt, "The Figure and Magnitude of Spirits," *Seer* 1 (March 1953): 33.

113. O. Pratt, *Absurdities of Immaterialism*, 12, 13.

114. O. Pratt, "Figure and Magnitude of Spirits," 33.

115. P. Pratt, *Key to the Science of Theology*, 43, 44; Parley P. Pratt, "Spiritual Communication: A Sermon Delivered by Elder P. P. Pratt, Senr, before the Conference at Salt Lake City, April 7, 1853," in *The Essential Parley P. Pratt*, Classics in Mormon Thought Series (Salt Lake City: Signature Books, 1990), 174; Brigham Young, "The Resurrection: A Discourse by Brigham Young, President of the Church of Jesus Christ of Latter-day Saints, Delivered in the New Tabernacle, Salt Lake City at the General Conference, October 8, 1875," in *Essential Brigham Young*, 219.

116. Book of Moses 3:7.

117. O. Pratt, *Absurdities of Immaterialism*, 24. His brother Parley could not have agreed more. He echoed the idea soon after Orson did that "this subtle fluid or spiritual element is endowed with the powers of locomotion in a far greater degree than the more gross and solid elements of nature" (P. Pratt, "Spiritual Communication," 174).

118. Vern G. Swanson, "The Development of the Concept of a Holy Ghost in Mormon Theology," in *Line upon Line: Essays in Mormon Doctrine*, ed. Gary James Bergera (Salt Lake City: Signature Books, 1989), 89.

119. Joseph Fielding Smith, "How Can a Spirit Be a Member of the Godhead?" *Answers to Gospel Questions* (Salt Lake City: Deseret Book, 1958), 2:145, quoted in Swanson, "Development of the Concept of a Holy Ghost in Mormon Theology," 89.

120. Orson Pratt made a distinction that would have made other Mormons uncomfortable. He considered the Holy Ghost a personage made up of particles of the infinite Holy Spirit whenever the Holy Spirit decided it wanted to form such a personage. For distinctions the Mormons make between the Holy Spirit and the Holy Ghost, see James E. Talmadge, *A Study of the Articles of Faith, Being a Consideration of the Principal Doctrines of the Church of Jesus Christ of Latter-day Saints* (Salt Lake City: Church of Jesus Christ of Latter-day Saints, 1979), 159–60.

121. Doctrine and Covenants, 20:28

122. Quoted in Swanson, "Development of the Concept of a Holy Ghost in Mormon Theology," 91.

123. John A. Widtsoe, *Rational Theology; as Taught by the Church of Jesus Christ of Latter-day Saints* (Salt Lake City: Deseret News, 1915); Brigham H. Roberts, *Seventy's Course in Theology*, 5 vols. (Salt Lake City: Deseret News, 1907–12); James E. Talmadge, *Jesus the*

Christ: A Study of the Messiah and His Mission according to Holy Scriptures Both Ancient and Modern (Salt Lake City: Deseret News, 1915).

124. My observation on J. F. Smith's statements is supported by Swanson, "Development of the Concept of a Holy Ghost in Mormon Theology," 98; O. Pratt, *Holy Spirit*, 56; and Orson Pratt, "The Holy Spirit and the Godhead: A Discourse by Elder Orson Pratt, Delivered in the Open Air, on the Temple Block, Great Salt Lake City, February 18, 1855," in *JD* 2:338.

125. O. Pratt, "Holy Spirit and the Godhead," 338.

126. Ibid. (emphasis added).

127. Ibid.

128. O. Pratt, *Holy Spirit*, 49–50.

129. Brigham Young from "Minutes of the Meeting of the Presidency & Twelve Presidents of Seventies and Others Assembled in President Young's Council Room," in *Wilford Woodruff Journal*, January 27, 1860, LDS Archives, quoted in Bergera, "Orson Pratt–Brigham Young Controversies," 18.

130. Brigham Young, *Woodruff Journal*, March 4, 1860, quoted in Bergera, "Orson Pratt–Brigham Young Controversies," 18. There is no punctuation in the original journal entry.

131. The rationalistic Pratt must have been a man of great patience to put up with what he would have considered intellectual suicide coming from Young. In a public sermon, Young committed himself, a materialist, to the idea that there was no such thing as empty space: "I never studied philosophy to any great extent, but on one occasion I had a kind of confab with Professor Orson Pratt, who endeavored to prove that there was empty space, I supposed there was no such thing. He thought he had proved it; but I thought he had not proved a word of it, and told him the idea was folly. After hearing a good many arguments from him, and other men, his colleagues in learning, I wished them to tell me where empty space was situated, that I might tell the wicked. . . . where to go, for they will be where God is not, if they can find empty space. . . . There is no such thing as empty space." Brigham Young, "True and False Riches: A Sermon Delivered on 14 August 1853," in *JD* 1:276.

132. A meeting recorded in the *Office Journal of President Brigham Young*, January 28, 1860, LDS Archives, quoted in Bergera, "Orson Pratt–Brigham Young Controversies," 20.

133. O. Pratt, *Holy Spirit*, 53. Parley Pratt helped popularize the idea of the Holy Spirit as ethereal fluid in his famous *Key to the Science of Theology*, in which he claimed the Holy Spirit was able to "penetrate the pores of the most solid substances" and pierce the "human system to its most inward recesses," thereby discerning the "thoughts and intents of the heart." Parley Pratt also introduced the "fluid" theme in the Mormon practice of the "laying on of hands" to impart the Holy Spirit to a new believer. In expounding on this practice, Parley continued with the fluid theme and demonstrated his reliance on popular notions of mesmerism and animal magnetism, which he said contained many "great truths" and "display much intelligence" but would eventually fall because they "have not the keys to the science of Theology—the Holy Priesthood." P. Pratt, *Key to the Science of Theology*, 39–40.

Parley Pratt also thought that "sacred history and also the experience of the present age" had proved that the laying on of hands was not the only means of spiritual communication. "Spiritual fluid" could also be communicated "between minds of strong and mutual faith" with no contact at all (P. Pratt, *Key to the Science of Theology,* 117–18, 97). All of the material quoted here was deleted and replaced by other text in the current edition of Parley Pratt's work. Apostle Charles W. Penrose did this without noting any of the alterations in order to expunge all of the material referring to the Holy Spirit as a spiritual fluid pervading the universe. See Jerald and Sandra Tanner, *Changes in the Key to Theology* (Salt Lake City: Utah Lighthouse Ministry, 1965).

134. Orson Pratt, *Spiritual Gifts* (Liverpool and London: Latter-day Saints Book and Millennial Star Depot, 1856), 77.

135. Ibid., 78.

136. Paul, *Science, Religion, and Mormon Cosmology,* 138.

137. O. Pratt, *Spiritual Gifts,* 78–79.

138. See Gary L. Bunker and Davis Bitton, "Mesmerism and Mormonism," *Brigham Young University Studies* 15 (Winter 1975): 146–70; and Gary L. Bunker and Davis Bitton, "Phrenology among the Mormons," *Dialogue: A Journal of Mormon Thought* 9 (Spring 1974): 42–61.

139. B. Young, "When I Contemplate the Subject of Salvation," 83.

140. O. Pratt, *Great First Cause,* 10.

141. O. Pratt, *Holy Spirit,* 49. With the particles of the Holy Spirit in direct control of all natural laws, a miracle—by definition a suspension of those laws—was no longer a mystery. As the Father and Son willed, so the Holy Spirit guided the materials of the universe. "By the power of their word, the Spirit could suspend its operations in one way, and operate in another, directly opposite, causing what the world generally calls a miracle," Pratt declared. Ibid., 55. In an article on the resurrection of the body, Pratt argued that given the forces behind it, the idea of a miracle was wrongheaded. "A deviation from [a] law is called a miracle; while the law itself, which is still more marvelous, is looked upon as nothing but a common occurrence." In reality, it was "the laws of nature" that were the most astonishing and the most marvelous. O. Pratt, "Resurrection of the Saints," *Seer* 2 (June 1854): 279.

142. As Pratt stated in *The Holy Spirit,* there is no difference in substance between the Holy Spirit and the Holy Ghost. The Holy Ghost is the name for the finite personage of spirit formed by an aggregate of particles of the Holy Spirit in one place in space.

143. O. Pratt, *Great First Cause,* 16 (emphasis added).

144. Ibid.

145. O. Pratt, "Holy Spirit and the Godhead," 345.

146. Ibid.

147. Orson Pratt, "The Pre-existence of Man," *Seer* 1 (March 1953): 132–33. See also Orson Pratt, "The Powers of Nature," *Seer* 2 (March 1854): 225–27.

148. O. Pratt, "Holy Spirit and the Godhead," 346. Ironically, Brigham Young himself came close to this same idea in an 1854 sermon: "We render praise, and honor, and thanksgiving to the Fathers, and the Son, and the Holy Ghost; or in other words, *Holy Spirits*" (B. Young, "When I Contemplate the Subject of Salvation," 79).

149. Eber D. Howe, *Mormonism Unvailed: Or, A Faithful Account of That Singular Imposition and Delusion, from Its Rise to the Present Time, with a Sketch of Its Propagators* (Painesville, Ohio: E. D. Howe, 1834); I. Woodbridge Riley, *The Founder of Mormonism: A Psychological Study of Joseph Smith, Jr.* (London: W. Heinemann, 1903). See also Robert N. Hullinger, *Joseph Smith's Response to Skepticism* (Salt Lake City: Signature Books, 1992),

xiii–xvii; and William O. Nelson, "Anti-Mormon Publications," in *Encyclopedia of Mormonism*, ed. Ludlow, 1:45–52.

150. Fawn Brodie, *No Man Knows My History* (New York: A. A. Knopf, 1945); Marvin S. Hill, *Quest for Refuge: The Mormon Flight from American Pluralism* (Salt Lake City: Signature Books, 1989); Jan Shipps, *Mormonism: The Story of a New Religious Tradition* (Urbana: University of Illinois Press, 1985); Quinn, *Early Mormonism and the Magic World View;* Brooke, *Refiner's Fire;* Hullinger, *Joseph Smith's Response to Skepticism;* Richard T. Hughes, "Soaring with the Gods: Early Mormons and the Eclipse of Religious Pluralism," in *The Lively Experiment Continued,* ed. Jerald C. Brauer (Macon, Ga.: Mercer University Press, 1987), 135–59.

151. Klaus J. Hansen, *Mormonism and the American Experience* (Chicago: University of Chicago Press, 1981), 43. For special focus on the religious environment of the time, see also Milton V. Backman Jr., *American Religions and the Rise of Mormonism* (Salt Lake City: Deseret Book, 1965).

152. Mario S. De Pillis, "The Quest for Religious Authority and the Rise of Mormonism," *Dialogue: A Journal of Mormon Thought* 1 (Spring 1966): 82.

153. For more on the Mormon response to pluralism in general, see Hill, *Quest for Refuge.*

154. Alexander Campbell, *Delusions: An Analysis of the Book of Mormon; with an Examination of Its Internal and External Evidences, and a Refutation of Its Pretences to Divine Authority* (Boston: B. H. Greene, 1832), 13.

155. O. Pratt, *Divine Authority,* 1, 16.

156. See Paul, *Science, Religion, and Mormon Cosmology,* 140.

157. Jaffee, "Village Enlightenment in New England," 328.

158. Bergera, "Orson Pratt–Brigham Young Controversies," 42.

159. Ibid. See Joseph Fielding Smith Jr., *Doctrines of Salvation,* 3 vols. (Salt Lake City: Bookcraft, 1954–56), 1:8; and Bruce R. McConkie, *Mormon Doctrine,* 2d ed. (Salt Lake City: Bookcraft, 1966), 317–21, 238–39.

160. Bergera, "Orson Pratt–Brigham Young Controversies," 49. See, for example, Charles W. Penrose, "Discourse Delivered by Elder Charles W. Penrose, Delivered in the Tabernacle, Salt Lake City, Sunday Afternoon, November 16, 1884," in *JD* 26:18–29; Roberts, *Seventy's Course in Theology,* 198; and Hyrum L. Andrus, *God, Man and the Universe* (Salt Lake City: Bookcraft, 1968), 109–43.

161. Erich Robert Paul confirmed this view when he wrote that "Orson Pratt personified the natural theologian with a Mormon flavor: his entire life was dedicated to the vision that true science (natural philosophy) and revealed religion (Mormonism) were in total harmony; therefore, both reflected the presence of the Divine in His works (nature) and in His word (scripture). Conflict between science and religion, as Pratt defined it, was an utter impossibility" (Paul, *Science, Religion, and Mormon Cosmology,* 128).

162. Orson Pratt, *Deseret News* 22 (1873): 586, quoted in Paul, *Science, Religion, and Mormon Cosmology,* 128.

Chapter 2: Spiritualism and Science

1. Bruce, *Launching of Modern American Science,* 3.

2. Edgar Fahs Smith, *The Life of Robert Hare: An American Chemist, 1781–1858* (Phila-

delphia: J. B. Lippincott, 1917), 6. The reason Hare was boarding and not living at his parent's home in the city is unknown.

3. Quoted in George P. Fisher, *Life of Benjamin Silliman, M.D., LL.D., Late Professor of Chemistry, Mineralogy, and Geology in Yale College* (New York: C. Scribner, 1866), 33.

4. Ibid., 34.

5. On the life and career of Benjamin Silliman, see Chando Michael Brown, *Benjamin Silliman: A Life in the Young Republic* (Princeton, N.J.: Princeton University Press, 1989); John F. Fulton and Elizabeth H. Thomson, *Benjamin Silliman, 1779–1864: Pathfinder in American Science* (New York: Schuman, 1947); Fisher, *Life of Silliman;* and John C. Greene, "Benjamin Silliman," in *Benjamin Silliman and His Circle: Studies on the Influence of Benjamin Silliman on Science in America, Prepared in Honor of Elizabeth H. Thomson,* ed. Leonard G. Wilson (New York: Science History Publications, 1979), 11–27.

6. E. Smith, *Life of Robert Hare,* 499.

7. John Young, *The Christ of History: An Argument Grounded in the Facts of His Life on Earth* (New York: Robert Carter, 1856).

8. Benjamin Silliman, letter to Robert Hare, 1857, quoted in E. Smith, *Life of Robert Hare,* 500–501.

9. See Ralph Henry Gabriel, *Religion and Learning at Yale: The Church of Christ in the College and University, 1757–1957* (New Haven, Conn.: Yale University Press, 1958), 114; Hovenkamp, *Science and Religion in America,* 119–45; Bozeman, *Protestants in an Age of Science,* 79; and John C. Greene, *American Science in the Age of Jefferson* (Ames: Iowa State University Press, 1984), 413.

10. Jon Butler, *Awash in a Sea of Faith,* 255.

11. Biographical information about Robert Hare can be gleaned from E. Smith, *Life of Robert Hare; Dictionary of American Biography,* s.v. "Hare, Robert"; Daniels, *American Science in the Age of Jackson,* 210; Greene, *American Science in the Age of Jefferson,* 176–87; Edgar Fahs Smith, *Chemistry in America: Chapters from the History of the Science in the United States* (New York: D. Appleton, 1914; reprint, New York: Arno, 1972), 152–205; *Encyclopedia of Occultism and Parapsychology,* 2d ed., s.v. "Hare, Robert, M.D."; Wyndham D. Miles, "Robert Hare," in *American Chemists and Chemical Engineers,* ed. Wyndham D. Miles (Washington, D. C.: American Chemical Society, 1976), 195–96; *Dictionary of Scientific Biography,* s.v. "Hare, Robert," 6:114–15; and Wyndham D. Miles, "Robert Hare," in *Great Chemists,* ed. Eduard Farber (New York: Interscience Publishers, 1961), 420–33.

12. E. Smith, *Life of Robert Hare,* 2.

13. Ibid., 7.

14. Ibid., 4.

15. Miles, "Robert Hare," in *Great Chemists,* ed. Farber, 423.

16. E. Smith, *Chemistry in America,* 184.

17. Robert Hare Jr., *Memoir of the Supply and Application of the Blow-Pipe. Containing an Account of the New Method of Supplying the Blowpipe Either with Common Air or Oxygen Gas: and Also of the Effects of the Intense Heat Produced by the Combustion of Hydrogen and Oxygen Gases* (Philadelphia: H. Maxwell, Columbia House, 1802).

18. One letter submitted to the University of Pennsylvania trustees on behalf of Hare was signed by fifty students who had taken a special course from him at the College of William and Mary. They acknowledged his lecture abilities were lackluster but said that Hare was "well adapted for the purpose of elucidating the subject." They were much more

enthusiastic when describing the "laborious and unparalleled exertions which he made for the class in the laboratory." Quoted in E. Smith, *Life of Robert Hare,* 56.

One of Hare's colleagues, George Wood, remarked that the apparatus for demonstration and experimentation in Hare's laboratory was "by the admission of all who had inspected it, unequaled in extent, variety, and splendor. . . . Individuals who have visited the schools of Germany, France, and Great Britain agree in the statement, that they have nowhere met with a laboratory so amply furnished with all that is calculated to illustrate the science of chemistry as that of Dr. Hare." Quoted in Miles, "Robert Hare," in *Great Chemists,* ed. Farber, 428.

19. This incident involved Edward Clarke of Cambridge University, England, who gave no credit to Hare—he actually ignored all previous research on the device—in his book on the "gas blowpipe" published in 1819. Silliman spearheaded the American response because he had great affection for his friend, first-hand knowledge of Hare's primacy, and a vehicle to spread the word—his journal, which in 1820 had some circulation in Britain. Silliman's letter to the scientific community was also published in American newspapers. His case was solid. He cited Hare's previous publications on the oxyhydrogen blowpipe in European journals and pointed out names of eminent European scientists who had spoken or had written about Hare and his discovery years earlier. Edgar Fahs Smith wrote, "The protest was full and spirited. [Edward] Clarke received it, but remained silent" (E. Smith, *Life of Robert Hare,* 14).

20. *Dictionary of American Biography,* s.v. "Hare, Robert."

21. Daniels, *American Science in the Age of Jackson,* 210.

22. Ibid.

23. Hare's clash with William C. Redfield, a New York naval engineer and later first president of the American Association for the Advancement of Science, is particularly illustrative. In a debate over the agency of electricity in the generation of storms (Hare believed electricity played a primary role), Hare's published academic attacks seemed out of place in the traditional gentlemanly, dispassionate world of the natural philosopher. Redfield replied that, among other things, the strenuous effort Hare had undertaken to confute his doctrines was disproportional to the low estimation in which Hare professed to hold them. To Hare, however, any public divergence from the truth— "error"—required a vigorous response. Hare wrote, "I cannot give this alleged theory the smallest importance, while the unequal and opposing forces, on which it is built, exist only in the imagination of an author who disclaims the agency either of heat or electricity." Redfield's "arguments," concluded Hare, "will amount to a *reductio ad absurdum.*" Quoted in E. Smith, *Life of Robert Hare,* 464. Neither man was convinced by the other's published efforts, but there was always the avenue of verbal exchange. This, however, turned out to be a one-sided affair. Edgar Fahs Smith recorded that those present at the meeting of the American Association for the Advancement of Science in New Haven in 1849 said they would never forget "the zeal and energy with which Dr. Hare, in an off-hand speech, fluent and animated, assailed the views of Mr. Redfield, who was all the while a quiet and silent listener." No reason was given, but Redfield had decided not to engage in an oral controversy with Hare. Redfield's responses were always written and not available for verbal public contests. Ibid., 472–73. Ironically, Redfield's theory prevailed and became an important advance in meteorological science.

24. Roger J. Boscovich, *A Theory of Natural Philosophy* (1763; reprint, Boston: MIT Press, 1966), 48–49.

25. Daniels, *American Science in the Age of Jackson*, 128.

26. Robert Hare's works include *A Brief View of the Policy and Resources of the United States: Comprising Some Strictures on "A Letter on the Genius and Dispositions of the French Government"* (Philadelphia: Bradford and Inskeep, 1810); *Proofs That Credit as Money in a Truly Free Country Is to a Great Extent Preferable to Coin* (Philadelphia: J. C. Clark, 1834); *Suggestions respecting the Reformation of the Banking System* (Philadelphia: J. C. Clark, 1837); *A Brief Exposition of the Injury Done to the Community and Especially to the Poor, by the Prohibition of Bills under Five Dollars, While Such Bills Are Permitted to Circulate in Adjoining States, in a Letter to William B. Reed, Esq., also, a Subsequent Letter, on the Failure of the Late Effort to Resume Specie Payments, to Which Is Annexed, a Scheme for a National Currency* (Philadelphia: n.p., 1841); and *Oregon: The Cost and the Consequences* (Philadelphia: J. C. Clark, 1846), which he wrote under the pseudonym "Disciple of the Washington School."

27. Eldred Grayson, *Standish the Puritan: A Tale of the American Revolution* (New York: Harper, 1850); Eldred Grayson, *Overing, or, the Heir of Wycherly: A Historical Romance* (New York: Cornish, Lamport, 1852).

28. Joseph McCabe, *Spiritualism: A Popular History from 1847* (London: T. F. Unwin, 1920), 69.

29. Robert Hare, *Experimental Investigation of the Spirit Manifestations, Demonstrating the Existence of Spirits and Their Communion with Mortals. Doctrine of the Spirit World respecting Heaven, Hell, Morality, and God. Also, the Influence of Scripture on the Morals of Christians* (New York: Partridge and Brittan, 1855), 16.

30. E. Smith, *Life of Robert Hare*, 483.

31. Hare, letter to the president of the AAAS, August 18, 1855, reproduced in *Experimental Investigation of the Spirit Manifestations*, 430.

32. Quoted in Emma Hardinge Britten, *Modern American Spiritualism: A Twenty Years' Record of the Communion between Earth and the World of Spirits* (1870; reprint, Hyde Park, N.Y.: University Books, 1970), 119.

33. Quoted in E. Smith, *Life of Robert Hare*, 495.

34. The testimony of John D. Fox, quoted in E. W. Capron, *Modern Spiritualism: Its Facts and Fanaticisms, Its Consistencies and Contradictions* (Boston: Bela Marsh, 1855), 43.

35. Dellon Marcus Dewey, *History of the Strange Sounds or Rappings, Heard in Rochester and Western New York, and Usually Called the Mysterious Noises!* (Rochester, N.Y.: D. M. Dewey, 1850); Eliab Wilkinson Capron and Henry D. Varron, *Singular Revelations: Explanations and History of the Mysterious Communion with Spirits, Comprehending the Rise and Progress of the Mysterious Noises in Western New York* (Auburn, N.Y.: Capron and Barron, 1850). For accounts in the newspapers of the southern states, see Robert W. Delp, "The Southern Press and the Rise of American Spiritualism, 1847–1860," *Journal of American Culture* 7 (Fall 1984): 88–95. For newspaper stories in Wisconsin, see Mary Farrell Bednarowski, "Spiritualism in Wisconsin in the Nineteenth Century," *Wisconsin Magazine of History* 59 (Autumn 1975): 2–19; and Philip Shoemaker, "Seers and Seances: The Course of Spiritualism in Nineteenth-Century Wisconsin," *Journal of Religious Studies* 7 (Fall 1979): 39–57.

36. George Templeton Strong, *The Diary of George Templeton Strong*, ed. Allan Nevins and Milton Halsey Thomas, 4 vols. (New York: Macmillan, 1952), 2:15–16.

37. Andrew Jackson Davis, *The Principles of Nature, Her Divine Revelations, and a Voice to Mankind* (New York: Lyon and Fishbough, 1847).

38. Catherine L. Albanese, "On the Matter of Spirit: Andrew Jackson Davis and the Marriage of God and Nature," *Journal of the American Academy of Religion* 60 (Spring 1992): 4. See also Alice Felt Tyler, *Freedom's Ferment: Phases of American Social History from the Colonial Period to the Outbreak of the Civil War* (1944; reprint, New York: Harper and Row, 1962), 80–81.

39. Ernest Isaacs, "The Fox Sisters and American Spiritualism," in *The Occult in America: New Historical Perspectives,* ed. Howard Kerr and Charles L. Crow (Urbana: University of Illinois Press, 1983), 90.

40. Bret E. Carroll, *Spiritualism in Antebellum America* (Bloomington: Indiana University Press, 1997); Mary Farrell Bednarowski, "Nineteenth Century American Spiritualism: An Attempt at a Scientific Religion" (Ph.D. diss., University of Minnesota, 1973); R. Laurence Moore, *In Search of White Crows: Spiritualism, Parapsychology, and American Culture* (New York: Oxford University Press, 1977); Ernest Isaacs, "A History of Nineteenth Century American Spiritualism as a Religious and Social Movement" (Ph.D. diss., University of Wisconsin, 1975), 166.

41. R. Laurence Moore, "Spiritualism and Science: Reflections on the First Decade of the Spirit Rappings," *American Quarterly* 24 (October 1972): 476.

42. Capron, *Modern Spiritualism,* 391.

43. Charles Chauncey Burr and Herman Burr, *Knocks for the Knockings* (1850), quoted in A. H. Mattison, *Spirit Rappings Unveiled!* (New York: J. C. Derby, 1855), 176. See also C. Chauncey Burr, letter to the *New York Tribune,* January 2, 1851, reproduced in Capron, *Modern Spiritualism,* 416–19.

44. Austin Flint, M.D., Charles A. Lee, M.D., and C. B. Coventry, M.D., of the University of Buffalo, letter to the *Buffalo Commercial Advertiser,* reproduced in Capron, *Modern Spiritualism,* 310–13. In 1888, a troubled Margaret Fox announced that she had always made the rapping sounds by throwing her big toes out of joint, but one year later she recanted, saying she was tricked into making the confession by unscrupulous people seeking to make money from such an exposé.

45. E. W. Capron related a story of a member of Congress from New York, A. P. Hascall, who had become a writing medium. One day Hascall asked the spirits to write a speech for him. Hascall started to write and after finishing a page thought it a well-reasoned work but, unfortunately, completely contrary to his own beliefs. As an experiment, he continued to write so that the spirit could finish. Upon writing the last line, he discovered the speech was signed "James O'Conner," a name Hascall had never heard. Capron, *Modern Spiritualism,* 335–36.

46. Andrew Jackson Davis pioneered this method in the United States, employing it well before the rapping phenomena came onto the scene.

47. Capron, *Modern Spiritualism,* 187–89.

48. *Encyclopedia of Occultism and Parapsychology,* 2d ed., s.v. "Spiritualism"; Russell M. Goldfarb and Clare R. Goldfarb, *Spiritualism and Nineteenth-Century Letters* (London: Associated University Presses, 1978), 38–39. After examining all the claims about the num-

ber of spiritualist believers in the United States coming from both detractors and sup-porters and taking into account census figures, Ernest Isaacs estimated that 1.0 million was a safe number. That meant that one out of every twenty-eight people was commit-ted to the movement in some way. Isaacs, "History of Nineteenth Century American Spiri-tualism," 137–38. The historian Whitney Cross, using different methods, arrived at the figure of approximately 1.5 million in *The Burned-over District,* 349. E. Douglas Branch estimated the number of spiritualist sympathizers to be 1.0 million at the height of the movement in *The Sentimental Years* (New York: D. Appleton-Century, 1934), 366–79.

49. Strong, *Diary,* 2:244–45.

50. Capron, *Modern Spiritualism,* 175.

51. Ibid., 335–55. Tallmadge also displayed his courage by using his political influence to introduce into Congress a petition with fifteen thousand names requesting that Con-gress appoint a scientific committee to investigate the spirit phenomena. After some ridi-cule, the request was tabled and never sent to committee. During the debate, one senato-rial wag said that he wondered to which committee it should be sent? The Committee on Foreign Relations?

52. Peggy Robbins, "The Lincolns and Spiritualism," *Civil War Times Illustrated* 15, no. 5 (1976): 4–10, 46–47.

53. Franklin was such a frequent spirit visitor that he was even credited with inventing rapping as a means communicating with mortals. Franklin was an excellent symbol for the movement because he shared with the spiritualists a fascination with religious eclec-ticism, science, and social progress. See Werner Sollors, "Dr. Benjamin Franklin's Celes-tial Telegraph, or Indian Blessings to Gas-lit American Drawing Rooms," *American Quar-terly* 35 (Winter 1983): 459–80.

54. For a thorough list of these publications, see Ann Braude, "News from the Spirit World: A Checklist of American Spiritualist Periodicals, 1847–1900," *Proceedings of the American Antiquarian Society* 99 (1989): 399–462.

55. See, for example, Robert W. Delp, "American Spiritualism and Social Reform, 1847–1900," *Northwest Ohio Quarterly* 44 (Fall 1972): 85–99; Michael Anthony O'Sullivan, "A Harmony of Worlds: Spiritualism and the Quest for Community in Nineteenth-Century America" (Ph.D. diss., University of Southern California, 1981); Howard Kerr, *Mediums, and Spirit-Rappers, and Roaring Radicals: Spiritualism in American Literature, 1850–1900* (Urbana: University of Illinois Press, 1972); and Isaacs, "History of Nineteenth Century American Spiritualism," 238–61.

56. Ann Braude, *Radical Spirits: Spiritualism and Women's Rights in Nineteenth-Cen-tury America* (Boston: Beacon, 1989).

57. Carroll, *Spiritualism in Antebellum America,* 65–71; Isaacs, "History of Nineteenth Century American Spiritualism," 166–208; Bednarowski, "Nineteenth Century American Spiritualism," 77–115; R. Moore, *In Search of White Crows,* 3–39.

58. 1 John 1:1–4.

59. Hare, *Experimental Investigation of the Spirit Manifestations,* 131.

60. Ibid., 35, 36.

61. Ibid., 38.

62. Ibid., 38, 36.

63. Ibid., 39.

64. Ibid., 40–41.

65. Ibid., 41

66. Ibid., 42.

67. Ibid., 46. Before this occurrence, Hare displayed his skepticism in a letter to Amasa Holcombe dated February 8, 1854: "You believe fully that tables move without human contact, because you have *seen them move;* I am skeptical, because I have never seen them move without human contact, although I have been at several circles. You have been much more lucky than I have been as to the manifestations, whether mechanical or mental" (ibid., 133).

68. However, some Christian ministers opposed to spiritualist practices were quick to point out the fallacy involved: just because spirits existed and communicated was no proof that they were telling the truth. Perhaps they were demons leading unsuspecting souls to destruction. For more on the orthodox opposition to spiritualism, see R. Moore, *In Search of White Crows,* 40–69.

69. Adin Ballou, *An Exposition of Views respecting the Principle Facts, Causes, and Peculiarities Involved in Spiritual Manifestations; Together with Interesting Phenomenal Statements and Communications,* quoted in Hare, *Experimental Investigation of the Spirit Manifestations,* 324.

70. J. F. Lanning, letter to Robert Hare, Philadelphia, June 7, 1855, quoted in Hare, *Experimental Investigation of the Spirit Manifestations,* 12.

71. Hare, *Experimental Investigation of the Spirit Manifestations,* 86.

72. Ibid., 87.

73. Ibid.

74. Ibid., 88.

75. Ibid., 89.

76. Ibid.

77. Ibid., 96.

78. Ibid., 95.

79. Like many of the Deists and Unitarians, the spirits honored Jesus as a great person and moral teacher but did not equate him with the Almighty. Hare's sister actually went so far as to say that "Christ never uttered the language recorded as his" in the Bible (ibid., 425).

80. Ibid., 108.

81. Ibid., 122.

82. Ibid., 92.

83. Ibid., 28.

84. Ibid., 403.

85. Ibid.

86. Ibid., 95.

87. Albanese, "On the Matter of Spirit," 6; Marguerite Block, *The New Church in the New World: A Study of Swedenborgianism in America* (New York: Holt, Rinehart and Winston, 1932), 136; Al Gabay, "Alfred Deakin and Swedenborg: An Australian Experience," in *Swedenborg and His Influence,* ed. Erland J. Brock (Bryn Athyn, Pa.: Academy of the New Church, 1988), 383; Isaacs, "History of Nineteenth Century American Spiritualism," 209. The idea was also not lost on John Humphrey Noyes, who said that spiritualism was simply "Swedenborgianism Americanized." John Humphrey Noyes, *History of American Socialisms* (1870; reprint, New York: Dover Publications, 1966), 540.

88. Emanuel Swedenborg, *Heaven and Hell* (1758), 2d ed., trans. George F. Dole (New York: Swedenborg Foundation, 1979), 89.

89. For more on the concept of correspondence in the thinking of American Transcendentalists, see Catherine L. Albanese, *Corresponding Motion: Transcendental Religion and the New America* (Philadelphia: Temple University Press, 1977).

90. Colleen McDannell and Bernhard Lang, *Heaven: A History* (New Haven, Conn.: Yale University Press, 1988), especially chapters 7 through 9, dealing with the Swedenborgian conception and later Christian renditions.

91. O. Pratt, *Absurdities of Immaterialism*, 3.

92. Taylor, *Physical Theory of Another Life*, 168.

93. McDannell and Lang, *Heaven*, 281, 181.

94. Hare, *Experimental Investigation of the Spirit Manifestations*, 91. A similar concept with the same name was defended by Orson Pratt and the Mormons. In another interesting parallel to Mormon teaching, Hare added the concept of *plurality* in celestial marriage (ibid., 123). Phineas Quimby, too, thought eternal marital bliss important enough to address in one of his articles; however, he called it "scientific marriage" (Quimby, *Complete Writings*, 2:4). The source for all of this was most likely Emanuel Swedenborg. See his *Marital Love*, trans. W. F. Wunsch (New York: Swedenborg Foundation, 1975).

95. Hare, *Experimental Investigation of the Spirit Manifestations*, 96.

96. Ibid., 97.

97. Ibid., 89, 91, 96, 97, 110, 111.

98. Ibid., 101–2.

99. Ibid., 114.

100. Ibid., 113.

101. *Convocation of Spirits: Sixty-four Queries Addressed to a Convocation of Worthies from the Spirit World; Also, the Replies Given by Them, and Confirmed under Conditions Which No Mortal Could Pervert*, reprinted in Hare, *Experimental Investigation of the Spirit Manifestations*, 113–19.

102. Ibid., 107.

103. Ibid., 237.

104. Alexis de Tocqueville noticed that "reason" had its problems "among democratic peoples"; because of a lack of authority, ideas and beliefs were always in danger of becoming "no more than a sort of mental dust open to the wind on every side and unable to come together and take shape." Alexis de Tocqueville, *Democracy in America*, ed. J. P. Mayer, trans. George Lawrence (Garden City, N.Y.: Anchor Books, 1969), 433.

105. See, for instance, the paean to *"Reason"* in the first passages of Davis, *Principles of Nature*, 1, 5.

106. Robert J. Breckinridge, *The Knowledge of God, Objectively Considered, Being the First Part of Theology Considered as a Science of Positive Truth, Both Inductive and Deductive* (New York: Robert Carter and Brothers, 1858), 324.

107. One need not look only to Palmer's "temples of reason" as a starting point to illustrate the movement away from the authority of pure reason. The place of reason in the work of other popularizers of American deism of Palmer's time, such as Thomas Paine's *The Age of Reason* (1793; reprint, Secaucus, N.J.: Citadel, 1974) and Ethan Allen's *Reason the Only Oracle of Man; or, a Compenduous System of Natural Religion* (Bennington,

Vt.: Haswell and Russell, 1784), could be used just as effectively as starting points in the argument.

108. Hare, *Experimental Investigation of the Spirit Manifestations*, 90.

109. Ibid., 112.

110. Ibid., 121, 110. I use the word *intuitive* because Hare used it on a regular basis and one of the main chapters in *The Experimental Investigation of the Spirit Manifestations* is entitled "Intuitive Evidence of the Existence of Spirits." At first it seems to be a word that should be foreign to a Baconian's vocabulary because intuition is considered a way of perceiving without the senses. The use of the word also must have confused the first readers of Hare's manuscript because there is a note about the term added to the bottom of the page where that title appears. Hare explained, "It is suggested that these words may be misapprehended. I use them in the sense given by Johnson: 'Sight of any thing, commonly mental view [*sic*].' I understand that evidence to be intuitive which is obtained by the simultaneous action of the mind and the sight, and, of course, of any other of the senses" (35). Hare saw the term as the strongest expression of the human ability to perceive evidence, that is, reason in lockstep with the senses.

111. Ibid., 128.

112. Ibid., 90.

113. Ibid., 29.

114. Ibid., 116.

115. Ibid., 231.

116. Ibid., 427. It was a particularly humble act for the "spirit" of Franklin to do so because Hare's treatise on electricity spent not a little time refuting Franklin's own view.

117. Robert Hare, "Objections to the Theories Severally of Franklin, Dufay, and Ampere, with an Effort to Explain Electrical Phenomena, by Statical or Undulatory Polarization" (1848), reprinted in *Experimental Investigation of the Spirit Manifestations*, 459.

118. For more on the debates over imponderables and ethers, see Larry Laudan, "The Medium and Its Message: A Study of Some of the Philosophical Controversies about Ether," in *Conceptions of Ether: Studies in the History of Ether Theories, 1740–1900*, ed. G. N. Cantor and M. J. S. Hodge (Cambridge: Cambridge University Press, 1981), 157–85; J. L. Heilbron, *Weighing Imponderables and Other Quantitative Science around 1800* (Berkeley: University of California Press, 1993); Nancy J. Nersessian, "Aether/Or: The Creation of Scientific Concepts," *Studies in the History and Philosophy of Science* 15, no. 3 (1984): 175–212; and P. M. Heimann, "Ether and Imponderables," in *Conceptions of Ether*, ed. Cantor and Hodge, 61–83.

119. William Whewell, "Demonstration That All Matter Is Heavy," *Transactions of the Cambridge Philosophical Society* 7, no. 2 (1841): 197–207; Geoffrey Cantor, *Michael Faraday, Sandemanian and Scientist: A Study of Science and Religion in the Nineteenth Century* (New York: St. Martin's, 1991), 179–84.

120. George Daniels correctly pointed out that the issue of "imponderables" was one of the first and most significant cracks in the armor of Baconianism. The next generation of scientists was much more open to the idea that one did not necessarily need direct sensory impressions to admit something was true in science. See the chapter "The Limits of Baconianism: History and the Imponderables," in Daniels, *American Science in the Age of Jackson*, 118–37. Also, the issue of "imponderables" may have been a special case

for the Baconians for two reasons: (1) Newton himself, the cofigurehead of the Baconian movement, held out the possibility of their existence, and (2) ethers and imponderable substances already had a long history in scientific thought (certainly predating the Scottish philosophy that would eventually call the idea into question).

121. Robert Hare, "Letter in Opposition to the Conjecture That Heat May Be Motion and in Favor of the Existence of a Material Cause of Calorific Repulsion," *American Journal of Science* 4 (1822): 148. Hare's definition of matter was also contained in the chemistry text he authored and used at the University of Pennsylvania, *A Compendium of the Course of Chemical Instruction in the Medical Department of the University of Pennsylvania*, 3d ed. (Philadelphia: n.p., 1836), 2.

122. Hare, *Experimental Investigation of the Spirit Manifestations*, 392.

123. Ibid., 95.

124. Ibid., 395

125. Ibid.

126. Ibid.

127. In her book *Radical Spirits*, Braude mentions a spiritualist "resurgence during the 1880s" but does not provide comparative data. However, she does point to the continued vitality of spiritualism from 1870 to 1890 by examining census data and the brisk sales of spiritualist literature (25–26, 192).

128. For a complete exposition of Davis's "Harmonial Philosophy," see Andrew Jackson Davis, *The Great Harmonia: Being a Philosophical Revelation of the Natural, Spiritual, and Celestial Universe*, 5 vols. (New York and Boston, 1850–59).

Chapter 3: Science, Matter, and Mind Cure

1. Quimby, *Complete Writings*, 3:175. Most of Quimby's thoughts were written down toward the end of his life, between 1859 and 1865, at the urging of his students and patients.

2. Tocqueville, *Democracy in America*, 430.

3. Catherine L. Albanese identified this lost character of Quimby's thought in "Physic and Metaphysic in Nineteenth-Century America: Medical Sectarians and Religious Healing," *Church History* 55 (December 1986): 497–501, and in *Nature Religion in America*, 107–15.

4. Albanese, *Nature Religion in America*, 109.

5. Phineas Parkhurst Quimby, *The Quimby Manuscripts*, ed. Horatio W. Dresser (New York: Thomas Y. Crowell, 1921), 8; George quoted in Quimby, *Complete Writings*, 1:20.

6. Maurice Daumas, *Scientific Instruments of the Seventeenth and Eighteenth Centuries*, trans. and ed. Mary Holbrook (New York: Praeger, 1972), 117. For details concerning the early American connection between clock making and scientific instruments, see Silvio A. Bedini, *Early American Scientific Instruments and Their Makers* (Washington, D.C.: Smithsonian Institution, 1964).

7. Franz Anton Mesmer, "Dissertation on the Discovery of Animal Magnetism," in *Mesmerism: A Translation of the Original Scientific and Medical Writings of F. A. Mesmer*, trans. and comp. George Bloch (Los Altos, Calif.: William Kaufmann, 1980); Robert Darnton, *Mesmerism and the End of the Enlightenment in France* (Cambridge, Mass.: Harvard University Press, 1968), vii.

8. Robert C. Fuller, *Mesmerism and the American Cure of Souls* (Philadelphia: University of Pennsylvania Press, 1982), 17–18.

9. Quoted in Quimby, *Complete Writings*, 1:20. There is some dispute about whether it was Charles Poyen or another mesmerist, Robert H. Collyer, with whom Quimby first had contact. Some light was shed on this question with the publication of all of Quimby's extant writings in 1988. Quimby's own writings seem to indicate that he had personal contact with Poyen only. However, a number of years after his initial contact with Poyen, Quimby dismissed Poyen's demonstrations as "humbug." Although it does not appear that Quimby had personal contact with Collyer, the writings clearly indicate that Quimby was familiar with his thought and had read some of his publications. Ibid., 1:103–4.

10. Ibid., 3:197.

11. Ibid., 3:197, 1:191, 2:301, 1:131.

12. J. Marion Sims, *The Story of My Life* (New York: Appleton, 1884), 150, quoted in William G. Rothstein, *American Physicians in the Nineteenth Century: From Sects to Science* (Baltimore: Johns Hopkins University Press, 1972), 62. See also ibid., 61, 249; and Ronald L. Numbers, "The Fall and Rise of the American Medical Profession," in *Sickness and Health in America: Readings in the History of Medicine and Public Health,* 2d ed., ed. Judith Walzer Leavitt and Ronald L. Numbers (Madison: University of Wisconsin Press, 1985), 185–96.

13. Stewart W. Holmes, "Phineas Parkhurst Quimby: Scientist of Transcendentalism," *New England Quarterly* 17 (September 1944): 360–61.

14. Braden, *Spirits in Rebellion*, 81.

15. Quimby, *Complete Writings*, 2:24.

16. Ibid., 3:337.

17. Ibid., 2:361–62, 1:361; Albanese, "Physic and Metaphysic in Nineteenth-Century America," 498.

18. Quimby, *Complete Writings*, 1:211, 2:68–69.

19. Braden, *Spirits in Rebellion*, 68, 71.

20. Horatio W. Dresser, *Health and the Inner Life: An Account of the Life and Teachings of P. P. Quimby* (New York: G. P. Putnam's Sons, 1906), as cited in Braden, *Spirits in Rebellion*, 69.

21. Holmes, "Phineas Parkhurst Quimby," 357.

22. From Dresser's biographical sketch of Quimby in Quimby, *Quimby Manuscripts*, 12.

23. Quimby, *Complete Writings*, 3:203.

24. Ibid., 1:343.

25. Mary Baker Eddy, *Science and Health with Key to the Scriptures* (Boston: Trustees under the will of Mary Baker G. Eddy, 1906), 144.

26. Quimby, *Complete Writings*, 2:297. For a discussion of monism, dualism, and pluralism in the relationship between science and metaphysical concerns, see Erwin N. Hiebert, "Modern Physics and Christian Faith," in *God and Nature*, ed. Lindberg and Numbers, 434–44.

27. Quimby, *Complete Writings*, 3:92. For Quimby on the new senses, see ibid., 1:185. Catherine L. Albanese made this point in "Physic and Metaphysic in Nineteenth-Century America," 497–501, and in *Nature Religion in America*, 107–15.

28. Quimby, *Complete Writings*, 1:354, 1:401, 2:297.

29. Ibid., 3:87, 3:174, 1:370.

30. Ibid., 1:367, 2:296, 3:179, 3:73.

31. From Dresser's "editor's summary" in Quimby, *Quimby Manuscripts*, 422.

32. For an introduction to the history of psychosomatic medicine, see Franz G. Alexander and Sheldon T. Selesnick, *The History of Psychiatry: An Evaluation of Psychiatric Thought and Practice from Prehistoric Times to the Present* (New York: Harper and Row, 1966), 388–401.

33. R. Moore, "Spiritualism and Science," 486–87; C. Allen, "Baconianism and the Bible in the Disciples of Christ," 66–67.

34. Quimby, *Quimby Manuscripts*, 385.

35. Quimby, *Complete Writings*, 1:159, 3:477.

36. Ibid., 2:276–77.

37. Robert Nisbet, *History of the Idea of Progress* (New York: Basic Books, 1980), 171.

38. Quimby, *Complete Writings*, 1:234.

39. Ibid., 3:226.

40. Ibid., 2:244.

41. Ibid., 3:119–20.

42. Ibid., 2:284–85.

43. Ibid., 1:225, 2:253, 1:320.

44. Ibid., 2:392.

45. Ibid., 3:262.

46. Ibid., 1:249.

47. Ibid., 2:172, 2:261, 2:336.

48. Ibid., 3:181, 1:61, 2:26.

49. Ibid., 3:325, 2:299.

50. Ibid., 1:159, 1:160, 2:336.

51. Ibid., 1:186, 1:245, 1:291–92, 2:79, 2:83, 3:293, 1:289.

52. Ibid., 2:125–26 (emphasis added).

53. Newton, *Opticks*, 400. Stephen Toulmin and June Goodfield maintain that this passage "remained an unquestioned presupposition of Newtonian science" for "nearly two hundred years." Stephen Toulmin and June Goodfield, *The Architecture of Matter* (New York: Harper and Row, 1962), 192–93.

54. Quimby, *Complete Writings*, 1:288, 1:160, 1:289.

55. Ibid., 1:103, 1:98, 1:107; Mesmer, "Dissertation on the Discovery of Animal Magnetism," 67.

56. Quimby, *Complete Writings*, 1:102–3.

57. Ibid., 1:108.

58. Ibid., 2:205. Horatio Dresser called the period of Quimby's "Lecture Notes" the "mesmeric period" and dates it between 1843 and 1847 (comment by Dresser in Quimby, *Quimby Manuscripts*, 53–55). Given the material in the notes and the dates of books Quimby references, Dresser is probably on the right track.

59. Quimby, *Complete Writings*, 2:71; 1:264.

60. G. N. Cantor and M. J. S. Hodge, "Introduction: Major Themes in the Development of Ether Theories from the Ancients to 1900," in *Conceptions of Ether*, ed. Cantor and Hodge, 34.

61. Quimby, *Complete Writings*, 3:127, 2:321.

62. Ibid., 3:94–95. See also ibid., 1:240–41, 3:93, 2:57, 2:56, and 3:90. For another look at Quimby's concept of odor, see Albanese, *Nature Religion in America*, 108–9.

63. O. Pratt, *Absurdities of Immaterialism*, 15; P. Pratt, *Key to the Science of Theology*, 38; B. Young, "When I Contemplate the Subject of Salvation," 82.

64. Quimby, *Complete Writings*, 3:31–32.

65. Ibid., 3:196, 3:181, 3:253.

66. Ibid., 2:142. On Quimby's claim to be a medium, see ibid., 2:411.

67. Ibid., 2:142.

68. Ibid., 2:142, 2:252, 2:336.

69. Dresser's editorial comment in Quimby, *Quimby Manuscripts*, 390.

70. For example, especially embarrassing to Dresser was the unequivocal statement by Quimby that "ideas are matter" (Quimby, *Complete Writings*, 2:364). In his edition, Dresser unabashedly inserted the word "spiritual" before "matter" into Quimby's text (Quimby, *Quimby Manuscripts*, 391). For more of Dresser's interpretive comments on Quimby and matter, see Quimby, *Quimby Manuscripts*, 179, 275.

71. Holmes, "Phineas Parkhurst Quimby"; Fuller, *Mesmerism and the America Cure of Souls;* Braden, *Spirits in Rebellion;* Lester M. Hirsch, "Phineas Parkhurst Quimby," *New-England Galaxy* 19 (Winter 1978): 27–31; Ferenc M. Szasz, "'New Thought' and the American West," *Journal of the West* 23 (January 1984): 83–90.

72. Albanese, *Nature Religion in America*, 114–15; G. Adolf Koch, *Republican Religion: The American Revolution and the Cult of Reason* (New York: Henry Holt, 1933), 16.

Conclusion

1. Orson S. Fowler, *The Christian Phrenologist: Or the Natural Theology and Moral Bearings of Phrenology; Its Aspect on and Harmony with Revelation; Including Answers to the Objections that Phrenology Leads to Fatalism and Materialism, and Is Compatible with a Change of Heart, &c.* (Cazenovia, N.Y.: n.p., 1843), 3.

2. Ibid.

3. Jon Butler, *Awash in a Sea of Faith*, 255.

4. Hatch, *Democratization of American Christianity*, 34.

Bibliography

Works by Orson Pratt

Absurdities of Immaterialism, or, A Reply to T. W. P. Taylder's Pamphlet, Entitled, "The Materialism of the Mormons or Latter-day Saints, Examined and Exposed." Liverpool: R. James, 1849.

"Concentration of the Mind, Remarks by Elder Orson Pratt, Delivered in the Tabernacle, Great Salt Lake City, February 12, 1860." In *Journal of Discourses, by Brigham Young, President of the Church of Jesus Christ Latter-day Saints, His Two Counselors, the Twelve Apostles, and Others*, 7:154–57. Liverpool: F. D. Richards, 1855–66.

"A Discourse by Elder Orson Pratt, Delivered in the Tabernacle, Salt Lake City, Sunday Afternoon, August 8th, 1880." In *Journal of Discourses, by Brigham Young, President of the Church of Jesus Christ of Latter-day Saints, His Two Counselors, the Twelve Apostles, and Others*, 21:232–40. Liverpool: F. D. Richards, 1855–66.

Divine Authenticity of the Book of Mormon. Liverpool: R. James, 1850.

Divine Authority, or the Question, Was Joseph Smith Sent of God? Liverpool: R. James, 1848.

"The Figure and Magnitude of Spirits." *Seer* 1 (March 1953): 33–36.

Great First Cause; or the Self-Moving Forces of the Universe. Liverpool: R. James, 1851.

"The Great Prophetic Pyramid—An Important Discovery by Prof. O. Pratt, Sen." *Latter-day Saints' Millennial Star* 41 (May 5, 1879): 280–83.

"History of Orson Pratt." *Deseret News Weekly* 8 (1858).

The Holy Spirit. Liverpool: Latter-day Saints Book and Millennial Star Depot, 1856.

"The Holy Spirit and the Godhead: A Discourse by Elder Orson Pratt, Delivered in the Open Air, on the Temple Block, Great Salt Lake City, February 18, 1855." In *Journal of Discourses, by Brigham Young, President of the Church of Jesus Christ of Latter-day Saints, His Two Counselors, the Twelve Apostles, and Others*, 2:334–97. Liverpool: F. D. Richards, 1855–66.

A Interesting Account of Several Remarkable Visions, and the Late Discovery of Ancient American Records Giving an Account of the Commencement of the Work of the Lord in This Generation. Edinburgh: Ballantyne and Hughes, 1840.

Key to the Universe, or a New Theory of Its Mechanism. Liverpool, 1879.

The Kingdom of God. Liverpool: R. James, 1848–49.

"Lectures on Astronomy." In *Wonders of the Universe, or a Compilation of the Astronomi-*

cal Writings of Orson Pratt, compiled by Nels B. Lundwall. Salt Lake City: Nels B. Lundwall, 1937.

"'Let Brother Pratt Do as He Will': Orson Pratt's 29 January 1860 Confessional Discourse—Unrevised." *Dialogue: A Journal of Mormon Thought* 13 (Summer 1980): 50–58.

New and Easy Method of Solution of the Cubic and Biquadratic Equations, Embracing Several New Formulas, Greatly Simplifying This Department of Mathematical Science. Designed as a Sequel to the Elements of Algebra, and for the Use of Schools and Academies. London: Longmans, Green, Reader, and Dyer, 1866.

The Orson Pratt Journals. Compiled by Elden J. Watson. Salt Lake City: Elden J. Watson, 1975.

"The Powers of Nature." *Seer* 2 (March 1854): 225–27.

"The Pre-existence of Man." *Seer* 1 (March 1953): 37–41.

Prophetic Almanac for 1845. New York: Prophet Office, 1844.

Reply to a Pamphlet Printed in Glasgow, with the "Approbation of Clergymen of Different Denominations," Entitled "Remarks on Mormonism." Liverpool: R. James, 1849.

"Resurrection of the Saints." *Seer* 2 (June 1854): 273–88.

Spiritual Gifts. Liverpool and London: Latter-day Saints Book and Millennial Star Depot, 1856.

WORKS BY ROBERT HARE

A Brief Exposition of the Injury Done to the Community and Especially to the Poor, by the Prohibition of Bills under Five Dollars, While Such Bills Are Permitted to Circulate in Adjoining States, in a Letter to William B. Reed, Esq., also, a Subsequent Letter, on the Failure of the Late Effort to Resume Specie Payments, to Which Is Annexed, a Scheme for a National Currency. Philadelphia: n.p., 1841.

A Brief View of the Policy and Resources of the United States: Comprising Some Strictures on "A Letter on the Genius and Dispositions of the French Government." Philadelphia: Bradford and Inskeep, 1810.

A Compendium of the Course of Chemical Instruction in the Medical Department of the University of Pennsylvania. 3d ed. Philadelphia: n.p., 1836.

Experimental Investigation of the Spirit Manifestations, Demonstrating the Existence of Spirits and Their Communion with Mortals. Doctrine of the Spirit World respecting Heaven, Hell, Morality, and God. Also, the Influence of Scripture on the Morals of Christians. New York: Partridge and Brittan, 1855.

"Letter in Opposition to the Conjecture That Heat May Be Motion and in Favor of the Existence of a Material Cause of Calorific Repulsion." *American Journal of Science* 4 (1822): 148.

Memoir of the Supply and Application of the Blow-Pipe. Containing an Account of the New Method of Supplying the Blowpipe Either with Common Air or Oxygen Gas: and Also of the Effects of the Intense Heat Produced by the Combustion of Hydrogen and Oxygen Gases. Philadelphia: H. Maxwell, Columbia House, 1802.

"Objections to the Theories Severally of Franklin, Dufay, and Ampere, with an Effort to Explain Electrical Phenomena, by Statical or Undulatory Polarization." 1848. In Robert Hare, *Experimental Investigation of Spirit Manifestations*, 439–60. New York: Partridge and Brittan, 1855.

[Disciple of the Washington School, pseud.]. *Oregon: The Cost and the Consequences.* Philadelphia: J. C. Clark, 1846.

[Eldred Grayson, pseud.]. *Overing, or, the Heir of Wycherly: A Historical Romance.* New York: Cornish, Lamport, 1852.

Proofs That Credit as Money in a Truly Free Country Is to a Great Extent Preferable to Coin. Philadelphia: J. C. Clark, 1834.

[Eldred Grayson, pseud.]. *Standish the Puritan: A Tale of the American Revolution.* New York: Harper, 1850.

Suggestions respecting the Reformation of the Banking System. Philadelphia: J. C. Clark, 1837.

WORKS BY PHINEAS PARKHURST QUIMBY

Phineas Parkhurst Quimby: The Complete Writings. Edited by Ervin Seale. 3 vols. Marina Del Rey, Calif.: DeVorss, 1988.

The Quimby Manuscripts. Edited by Horatio W. Dresser. New York: Thomas Y. Crowell, 1921.

OTHER PRIMARY SOURCES

Abercrombie, John. *Inquiries concerning the Intellectual Powers and the Investigation of Truth.* Edinburgh: Waugh and Innes, 1830.

Allen, Ethan. *Reason the Only Oracle of Man; or, a Compenduous System of Natural Religion.* Bennington, Vt.: Haswell and Russell, 1784.

"Astronomy." *Scientific American* 6 (October 12, 1850): 11.

Boscovich, Roger J. *A Theory of Natural Philosophy.* 1763. Reprint, Boston: MIT Press, 1966.

Breckinridge, Robert J. *The Knowledge of God, Objectively Considered, Being the First Part of Theology Considered as a Science of Positive Truth, Both Inductive and Deductive.* New York: Robert Carter and Brothers, 1858.

Britten, Emma Hardinge. *Modern American Spiritualism: A Twenty Years' Record of the Communion between Earth and the World of Spirits.* 1870. Reprint, Hyde Park, N.Y.: University Books, 1970.

Brown, Thomas. *Lectures on the Philosophy of the Human Mind by the Late Thomas Brown.* Edinburgh: W. and C. Tait, 1820.

Butler, Joseph. *The Analogy of Religion, Natural and Revealed, to the Constitution and Course of Nature.* New Haven, Conn.: A. H. Maltby, 1822.

Campbell, Alexander. *Delusions: An Analysis of the Book of Mormon; with an Examination of Its Internal and External Evidences, and a Refutation of Its Pretences to Divine Authority.* Boston: B. H. Greene, 1832.

Capron, E. W. *Modern Spiritualism: Its Facts and Fanaticisms, Its Consistencies and Contradictions.* Boston: Bela Marsh, 1855.

Capron, Eliab Wilkinson, and Henry D. Varron. *Singular Revelations: Explanations and History of the Mysterious Communion with Spirits, Comprehending the Rise and Progress of the Mysterious Noises in Western New York* Auburn, N.Y.: Capron and Barron, 1850.

Charnock, Stephen. *Discourses upon the Existence and Attributes of God.* New York: Robert Carter and Brothers, 1853.

Darwin, Erasmus. *Zoonomia, or, The Laws of Organic Life.* London: J. Johnson, 1794–96.

Davis, Andrew Jackson. *The Great Harmonia: Being a Philosophical Revelation of the Natural, Spiritual, and Celestial Universe.* 5 vols. New York and Boston, 1850–59.

———. *The Principles of Nature, Her Divine Revelations, and a Voice to Mankind.* New York: Lyon and Fishbough, 1847.

Dewey, Dellon Marcus. *History of the Strange Sounds or Rappings, Heard in Rochester and Western New York, and Usually Called the Mysterious Noises!* Rochester, N.Y.: D. M. Dewey, 1850.

The Doctrine and Covenants of the Church of Jesus Christ of Latter-day Saints. Salt Lake City: Church of Jesus Christ of Latter-day Saints, 1876.

Draper, John William. *The History of the Conflict between Religion and Science.* New York: D. Appleton, 1898.

Dwight, Timothy. *Theology, Explained and Defended, in a Series of Sermons.* Glasgow: Blackie and Sons, 1836.

Eddy, Mary Baker. *Science and Health with Key to the Scriptures.* Boston: Trustees under the will of Mary Baker G. Eddy, 1906.

Fowler, Orson S. *The Christian Phrenologist: Or the Natural Theology and Moral Bearings of Phrenology; Its Aspect on and Harmony with Revelation; Including Answers to the Objections that Phrenology Leads to Fatalism and Materialism, and Is Compatible with a Change of Heart, &c.* Cazenovia, N.Y.: n.p., 1843.

Good, John Mason. *The Book of Nature.* Boston: Wells and Lilly, 1826.

Hodge, Charles. *Systematic Theology.* New York: Scribner, 1872–73.

Kirkwood, Daniel. "On a New Analogy in the Periods of Rotation of the Primary Planets." *American Journal of Science and Arts,* 2d ser., 9 (May 1850): 395–99.

"Kirkwood's Analogy." In *Annual of Scientific Discovery,* 35–38. Boston: Gould, Kendall, and Lincoln, 1850.

Lardner, Dionysius. *Popular Lectures on Science and Art, Delivered in the Principle Cities and Towns of the United States.* New York: Greely and McElrath, 1846.

Mattison, A. H. *Spirit Rappings Unveiled!* New York: J. C. Derby, 1855.

Mesmer, Franz Anton. "Dissertation on the Discovery of Animal Magnetism." In *Mesmerism: A Translation of the Original Scientific and Medical Writings of F. A. Mesmer,* translated and compiled by George Bloch. Los Altos, Calif.: William Kaufmann, 1980.

Newton, Isaac. *Opticks: Or, a Treatise of the Reflexions, Refractions, Inflections and Colours of Light.* Foreword by Albert Einstein, introduction by Edmund Whittaker, preface by I. Bernard Cohen, analytical table of contents by Duane H. D. Roller. Based on the 4th edition, London, 1730. New York: Dover Publications, 1952.

———. *Principia Mathematica.* Translated by Andrew Motte. London: Printed for B. Motte, 1729.

Owen, Robert Dale. *The Debatable Land between This World and the Next.* New York: G. W. Carleton, 1872.

Paine, Thomas. *The Age of Reason.* 1793. Reprint, Secaucus, N.J.: Citadel, 1974.

The Pearl of Great Price. Liverpool: F. D. Richards, 1851.

Penrose, Charles W. "Discourse Delivered by Elder Charles W. Penrose, Delivered in the Tabernacle, Salt Lake City, Sunday Afternoon, November 16, 1884." In *Journal of Discourses, by Brigham Young, President of the Church of Jesus Christ of Latter-day Saints, His Two Counselors, the Twelve Apostles, and Others,* 26:18–29. Liverpool: F. D. Richards, 1855–66.

Pratt, Parley P. *An Answer to Mr. William Hewitt's Tract against the Latter-day Saints.* Manchester: W. R. Thomas, 1840.

———. *Autobiography of Parley P. Pratt.* Salt Lake City: Deseret Book, 1985.

———. *Key to the Science of Theology: Designed as an Introduction to the First Principles of Spiritual Philosophy; Religion; Law and Government; as Delivered by the Ancients, and as Restored in This Age, for the Final Development of Universal Peace, Truth and Knowledge.* Liverpool and London: F. D. Richards, 1855.

———. *The Millennium, and Other Poems: To Which Is Annexed, A Treatise on the Regeneration and Eternal Duration of Matter.* New York: W. Molineux, 1840.

———. *Mormonism Unveiled: Zion's Watchman Unmasked, and Its Editor, Mr. L. R. Sunderland, Exposed; Truth Vindicated; the Devil Mad, and Priestcraft in Danger!* New York: n.p., 1838.

———. *Plain Facts, Showing the Falsehood and Folly of the Rev. C. S. Bush, (a Church Minister of the Parish Peover,) Being a Reply to His Tract against the Latter-day Saints.* Manchester: W. R. Thomas, [1840].

———. *A Reply to Mr. Thomas Taylor's "Complete Failure," &c., and Mr. Richard Livesey's "Mormonism Exposed."* Manchester: W. R. Thomas, 1840.

———. "Spiritual Communication: A Sermon Delivered by Elder P. P. Pratt, Senr, before the Conference at Salt Lake City, April 7, 1853." In *The Essential Parley P. Pratt,* 172–83. Classics in Mormon Thought Series. Salt Lake City: Signature Books, 1990.

———. *Truth Defended, or a Reply to the "Preston Chronicle," and to Mr. J. B. Rollo's "Mormonism Exposed."* Manchester: P. P. Pratt, 1841.

Priestley, Joseph. *Disquisitions relating to Matter and Spirit.* London: J. Johnson, 1777; reprint, New York: Arno, 1975.

Roberts, Brigham H. *Seventy's Course in Theology.* 5 vols. Salt Lake City: Deseret News, 1907–12.

Robison, John. *A System of Mechanical Philosophy, with Notes by David Brewster.* Edinburgh: J. Murray, 1822.

Smith, Joseph. *History of the Church.* Edited by B. H. Roberts. Rev. ed. 7 vols. Salt Lake City: Deseret Book, 1954.

Smith, Joseph Fielding, Jr. *Doctrines of Salvation.* 3 vols. Salt Lake City: Bookcraft, 1954–56.

Smyth, C[harles] Piazzi. "On a New Analogy in the Periods of Rotation of the Primary Planets Discovered by Daniel Kirkwood of Pottsville, Pennsylvania." *Edinburgh New Philosophical Journal* 49 (July 1850): 169–70.

———. *Our Inheritance in the Great Pyramid.* 3d ed. London: Daldy, Isbister, 1877.

Strong, George Templeton. *The Diary of George Templeton Strong.* 4 vols. Edited by Allan Nevins and Milton Halsey Thomas. New York: Macmillan, 1952.

Swedenborg, Emanuel. *Heaven and Hell.* 2d ed. Translated by George F. Dole. New York: Swedenborg Foundation, 1979.

———. *Marital Love.* Translated by W. F. Wunsch. New York: Swedenborg Foundation, 1975.

Talmadge, James E. *Jesus the Christ: A Study of the Messiah and His Mission according to Holy Scriptures Both Ancient and Modern.* Salt Lake City: Deseret News, 1915.

———. *A Study of the Articles of Faith, Being a Consideration of the Principal Doctrines of the Church of Jesus Christ of Latter-day Saints.* Salt Lake City: Church of Jesus Christ of Latter-day Saints, 1979.

Taylder, T. W. P. *The Materialism of the Mormons, or Latter Day Saints, Examined and Exposed.* Woolwich: R. Jones, 1849.

Taylor, Isaac. *Physical Theory of Another Life.* New York: D. Appleton, 1836.

Tocqueville, Alexis de. *Democracy in America.* Edited by J. P. Mayer. Translated by George Lawrence. Garden City, N.Y.: Anchor Books, 1969.

Tullidge, Edward W. *Life of Brigham Young.* New York: n.p., 1876.

———. *The Life of Joseph the Prophet.* New York: Tullidge and Crandall, 1878.

Whewell, William. "Demonstration That All Matter Is Heavy." *Transactions of the Cambridge Philosophical Society* 7, no. 2 (1841): 197–207.

White, Andrew Dickson. *The Warfare of Science.* New York: D. Appleton, 1876.

Widtsoe, John A. *Rational Theology; as Taught by the Church of Jesus Christ of Latter-day Saints.* Salt Lake City: Deseret News, 1915.

Young, Brigham. "A Discourse by President Brigham Young Delivered in the Temple Court, Great Salt Lake City, March 23, 1856." In *Journal of Discourses, by Brigham Young, President of the Church of Jesus Christ of Latter-day Saints, His Two Counselors, the Twelve Apostles, and Others,* 3:272–79. Liverpool: F. D. Richards, 1855–66.

———. "Remarks by President Brigham Young, Delivered in Salt Lake City, May 14, 1871." In *Journal of Discourses, by Brigham Young, President of the Church of Jesus Christ of Latter-day Saints, His Two Counselors, the Twelve Apostles, and Others,* 14:115–18. Liverpool: F. D. Richards, 1855–66.

———. "The Resurrection: A Discourse by Brigham Young, President of the Church of Jesus Christ of Latter-day Saints, Delivered in the New Tabernacle, Salt Lake City at the General Conference, October 8, 1875." In *The Essential Brigham Young,* 218–21. Salt Lake City: Signature Books, 1992.

———. "True and False Riches: A Sermon Delivered on 14 August 1853." In *Journal of Discourses, by Brigham Young, President of the Church of Jesus Christ of Latter-day Saints, His Two Counselors, the Twelve Apostles, and Others,* 1:264–76. Liverpool: F. D. Richards, 1855–66.

———. "When I Contemplate the Subject of Salvation: A Sermon Delivered on 12 February 1854." In *The Essential Brigham Young,* 74–85. Salt Lake City: Signature Books, 1992.

Young, John. *The Christ of History: An Argument Grounded in the Facts of His Life on Earth.* New York: Robert Carver, 1856.

SECONDARY SOURCES

Albanese, Catherine L. *Corresponding Motion: Transcendental Religion and the New America.* Philadelphia: Temple University Press, 1977.

———. *Nature Religion in America: From the Algonkian Indians to the New Age.* Chicago: University of Chicago Press, 1990.

———. "On the Matter of Spirit: Andrew Jackson Davis and the Marriage of God and Nature." *Journal of the American Academy of Religion* 60 (Spring 1992): 1–17.

———. "Physic and Metaphysic in Nineteenth-Century America: Medical Sectarians and Religious Healing." *Church History* 55 (December 1986): 489–502.

Alexander, Franz G., and Sheldon T. Selesnick. *The History of Psychiatry: An Evaluation of Psychiatric Thought and Practice from Prehistoric Times to the Present.* New York: Harper and Row, 1966.

Allen, C. Leonard. "Baconianism and the Bible in the Disciples of Christ: James S. Lamar and *The Organon of Scripture.*" *Church History* 55 (March 1986): 65–80.

Andrus, Hyrum L. *God, Man and the Universe.* Salt Lake City: Bookcraft, 1968.

Backman, Milton V., Jr. *American Religions and the Rise of Mormonism.* Salt Lake City: Deseret Book, 1965.

Bedini, Silvio A. *Early American Scientific Instruments and Their Makers.* Washington, D.C.: Smithsonian Institution, 1964.

Bednarowski, Mary Farrell. "Nineteenth Century American Spiritualism: An Attempt at a Scientific Religion." Ph.D. diss., University of Minnesota, 1973.

———. "Spiritualism in Wisconsin in the Nineteenth Century." *Wisconsin Magazine of History* 59 (Autumn 1975): 2–19.

Bergera, Gary James. "The Orson Pratt–Brigham Young Controversies: Conflict within the Quorums, 1853 to 1868." *Dialogue: A Journal of Mormon Thought* 13 (Summer 1980): 7–49.

Block, Marguerite. *The New Church in the New World: A Study of Swedenborgianism in America.* New York: Holt, Rinehart and Winston, 1932.

Bode, Carl. *The American Lyceum: Town Meeting of the Mind.* New York: Oxford University Press, 1956.

Bozeman, Theodore Dwight. *Protestants in an Age of Science: The Baconian Ideal and Antebellum American Religious Thought.* Chapel Hill: University of North Carolina Press, 1977.

Braden, Charles S. *Spirits in Rebellion: The Rise and Development of New Thought.* Dallas: Southern Methodist University Press, 1963.

Branch, E. Douglas. *The Sentimental Years.* New York: D. Appleton-Century, 1934.

Braude, Ann. "News from the Spirit World: A Checklist of American Spiritualist Periodicals, 1847–1900." *Proceedings of the American Antiquarian Society* 99 (1989): 399–462.

———. *Radical Spirits: Spiritualism and Women's Rights in Nineteenth-Century America.* Boston: Beacon, 1989.

Brodie, Fawn. *No Man Knows My History.* New York: A. A. Knopf, 1945.

Brooke, John L. *The Refiner's Fire: The Making of Mormon Cosmology, 1644–1844.* Cambridge: Cambridge University Press, 1994.

Brown, Chando Michael. *Benjamin Silliman: A Life in the Young Republic.* Princeton, N.J.: Princeton University Press, 1989.

Bruce, Robert V. *The Launching of Modern American Science, 1846–1876.* Ithaca, N.Y.: Cornell University Press, 1987.

Bunker, Gary L., and Davis Bitton. "Mesmerism and Mormonism." *Brigham Young University Studies* 15 (Winter 1975): 146–70.

———. "Phrenology among the Mormons." *Dialogue: A Journal of Mormon Thought* 9 (Spring 1974): 42–61.

Butler, Jon. *Awash in a Sea of Faith: Christianizing the American People.* Cambridge, Mass.: Harvard University Press, 1990.

Cantor, G. N., and M. J. S. Hodge. "Introduction: Major Themes in the Development of Ether Theories from the Ancients to 1900." In *Conceptions of Ether: Studies in the*

History of Ether Theories, 1740–1900, edited by G. N. Cantor and M. J. S. Hodge, 1–60. Cambridge: Cambridge University Press, 1981.

Cantor, Geoffrey. *Michael Faraday, Sandemanian and Scientist: A Study of Science and Religion in the Nineteenth Century.* New York: St. Martin's, 1991.

Carroll, Bret E. *Spiritualism in Antebellum America.* Bloomington: Indiana University Press, 1997.

Chambliss, J. J. "James G. Carter on Baconian Induction." *History of Education Quarterly* 3 (December 1963): 198–209.

Christensen, William J. "Critical Review of Orson Pratt Senior's Published Scientific Books." M.A. thesis, University of Utah, 1929.

Conser, Walter H., Jr. *God and the Natural World: Religion and Science in Antebellum America.* Columbia: University of South Carolina Press, 1993.

Crawley, Peter L. "Parley P. Pratt: Father of Mormon Pamphleteering." *Dialogue: A Journal of Mormon Thought* 15 (Fall 1982): 13–26.

Crawley, Peter L., and Chad J. Flake. *A Mormon Fifty: An Exhibition in the Harold B. Lee Library in Conjunction with the Annual Conference of the Mormon History Association.* Provo, Utah: Friends of the Brigham Young University Library, 1984.

Cross, Whitney R. *The Burned-over District: The Social and Intellectual History of Enthusiastic Religion in Western New York, 1800–1850.* Ithaca, N.Y.: Cornell University Press, 1950.

Daniels, George H. *American Science in the Age of Jackson.* New York: Columbia University Press, 1968.

———. "The Process of Professionalization in American Science: The Emergent Period, 1820–1860." In *Science in America since 1820,* edited by Nathan Reingold, 63–78. New York: Science History Publications, 1976.

Darnton, Robert. *Mesmerism and the End of the Enlightenment in France.* Cambridge, Mass.: Harvard University Press, 1968.

Daumas, Maurice. *Scientific Instruments of the Seventeenth and Eighteenth Centuries.* Edited and translated by Mary Holbrook. New York: Praeger, 1972.

Delp, Robert W. "American Spiritualism and Social Reform, 1847–1900." *Northwest Ohio Quarterly* 44 (Fall 1972): 85–99.

———. "The Southern Press and the Rise of American Spiritualism, 1847–1860." *Journal of American Culture* 7 (Fall 1984): 88–95.

De Pillis, Mario S. "The Quest for Religious Authority and the Rise of Mormonism." *Dialogue: A Journal of Mormon Thought* 1 (Spring 1966): 68–88.

Dictionary of American Biography, 1931. S.v. "Hare, Robert."

Dictionary of Scientific Biography, 1970. S.v. "Hare, Robert."

Drake, Milton. *Almanacs of the United States, Part I.* New York: Scarecrow, 1962.

Dresser, Horatio W. *Health and the Inner Life: An Account of the Life and Teachings of P. P. Quimby.* New York: G. P. Putnam's Sons, 1906.

Edwards, Paul. "Panpsychism." In *Encyclopedia of Philosophy,* edited by Paul Edwards, 6:22–31. New York: Macmillan, 1967.

Encyclopedia of Occultism and Parapsychology, 2d ed. S. v. "Hare, Robert, M.D." and "Spiritualism."

England, Breck. *The Life and Thought of Orson Pratt.* Salt Lake City: University of Utah Press, 1985.

Fisher, George P. *Life of Benjamin Silliman, M.D., LL.D., Late Professor of Chemistry, Mineralogy, and Geology in Yale College.* New York: C. Scribner, 1866.

Fuller, Robert C. *Mesmerism and the American Cure of Souls.* Philadelphia: University of Pennsylvania Press, 1982.

Fulton, John F., and Elizabeth H. Thomson. *Benjamin Silliman, 1779–1864: Pathfinder in American Science.* New York: Schuman, 1947.

Gabay, Al. "Alfred Deakin and Swedenborg: An Australian Experience." In *Swedenborg and His Influence,* edited by Erland J. Brock. Bryn Athyn, Pa.: Academy of the New Church, 1988.

Gabriel, Ralph Henry. *Religion and Learning at Yale: The Church of Christ in the College and University, 1757–1957.* New Haven, Conn.: Yale University Press, 1958.

Goldfarb, Russell M., and Clare R. Goldfarb. *Spiritualism and Nineteenth-Century Letters.* London: Associated University Presses, 1978.

Gottschalk, Stephen. *The Emergence of Christian Science in American Religious Life.* Berkeley: University of California Press, 1973.

Greene, John C. *American Science in the Age of Jefferson.* Ames: Iowa State University Press, 1984.

———. "Benjamin Silliman." In *Benjamin Silliman and His Circle: Studies on the Influence of Benjamin Silliman on Science in America, Prepared in Honor of Elizabeth H. Thomson,* edited by Leonard G. Wilson, 11–27. New York: Science History Publications, 1979.

Hansen, Klaus J. *Mormonism and the American Experience.* Chicago: University of Chicago Press, 1981.

Hartshorne, Charles. "Panpsychism." In *A History of Philosophical Systems,* edited by Vergilius T. Ferm, 442–53. Freeport, N.Y.: Books for Libraries Press, 1970.

Hatch, Nathan O. *The Democratization of American Christianity.* New Haven, Conn.: Yale University Press, 1989.

Heilbron, J. L. *Weighing Imponderables and Other Quantitative Science around 1800.* Berkeley: University of California Press, 1993.

Heimann, P. M. "Ether and Imponderables." In *Conceptions of Ether: Studies in the History of Ether Theories, 1740–1900,* edited by G. N. Cantor and M. J. S. Hodge, 61–83. Cambridge: Cambridge University Press, 1981.

Hiebert, Erwin N. "Modern Physics and Christian Faith." In *God and Nature: Historical Essays on the Encounter between Christianity and Science,* edited by David C. Lindberg and Ronald L. Numbers, 424–47. Berkeley: University of California Press, 1986.

Hill, Marvin S. *Quest for Refuge: The Mormon Flight from American Pluralism.* Salt Lake City: Signature Books, 1989.

Hirsch, Lester M. "Phineas Parkhurst Quimby." *New-England Galaxy* 19 (Winter 1978): 27–31.

Hogan, Edward. "Orson Pratt as Mathematician." *Utah Historical Quarterly* 41 (Winter 1973): 59–68.

Holmes, Stewart W. "Phineas Parkhurst Quimby: Scientist of Transcendentalism." *New England Quarterly* 17 (September 1944): 356–80.

Hovenkamp, Herbert. *Science and Religion in America, 1800–1860.* Philadelphia: University of Pennsylvania Press, 1978.

Howe, Eber D. *Mormonism Unvailed: Or, A Faithful Account of That Singular Imposition and Delusion, from Its Rise to the Present Time, with a Sketch of Its Propagators.* Painesville, Ohio: E. D. Howe, 1834.

Hughes, Richard T. "Soaring with the Gods: Early Mormons and the Eclipse of Religious Pluralism." In *The Lively Experiment Continued,* edited by Jerald C. Brauer, 135–59. Macon, Ga.: Mercer University Press, 1987.

Hullinger, Robert N. *Joseph Smith's Response to Skepticism.* Salt Lake City: Signature Books, 1992.

Isaacs, Ernest. "The Fox Sisters and American Spiritualism." In *The Occult in America: New Historical Perspectives,* edited by Howard Kerr and Charles L. Crow, 79–110. Urbana: University of Illinois Press, 1983.

———. "A History of Nineteenth Century American Spiritualism as a Religious and Social Movement." Ph.D. diss., University of Wisconsin, 1975.

Jaffee, David. "The Village Enlightenment in New England, 1760–1820." *William and Mary Quarterly* 47 (July 1990): 327–46.

Kerr, Howard. *Mediums, and Spirit-Rappers, and Roaring Radicals: Spiritualism in American Literature, 1850–1900.* Urbana: University of Illinois Press, 1972.

Koch, G. Adolf. *Republican Religion: The American Revolution and the Cult of Reason.* New York: Henry Holt, 1933.

Laudan, Larry. "The Medium and Its Message: A Study of Some of the Philosophical Controversies about Ether." In *Conceptions of Ether: Studies in the History of Ether Theories, 1740–1900,* edited by G. N. Cantor and M. J. S. Hodge, 157–85. Cambridge: Cambridge University Press, 1981.

Lindberg, David C., and Ronald L. Numbers. "Beyond War and Peace: A Reappraisal of the Encounter between Christianity and Science." *Perspectives on Science and Christian Faith* 39 (September 1987): 140–49.

———, eds. *God and Nature: Historical Essays on the Encounter between Christianity and Science.* Berkeley: University of California Press, 1986.

Lyon, Thomas Edgar. "Orson Pratt—Early Mormon Leader." M.A. thesis, University of Chicago, 1932.

Marsden, George M. "Understanding Fundamentalist Views of Science." In *Science and Creationism,* edited by Ashley Montague, 95–116. New York: Oxford University Press, 1984.

May, Henry F. *The Enlightenment in America.* Oxford: Oxford University Press, 1976.

McCabe, Joseph. *Spiritualism: A Popular History from 1847.* London: T. F. Unwin, 1920.

McConkie, Bruce. *Mormon Doctrine.* 2d ed. Salt Lake City: Bookcraft, 1966.

McDannell, Colleen, and Bernhard Lang. *Heaven: A History.* New Haven, Conn.: Yale University Press, 1988.

McMurrin, Sterling. *The Philosophical Foundations of Mormon Theology.* Salt Lake City: University of Utah Press, 1959.

———. *The Theological Foundations of the Mormon Religion.* Salt Lake City: University of Utah Press, 1965.

Miles, Wyndham D. "Robert Hare." In *American Chemists and Chemical Engineers,* edited by Wyndham D. Miles, 195–96. Washington. D.C.: American Chemical Society, 1976.

———. "Robert Hare." In *Great Chemists,* edited by Eduard Farber, 420–33. New York: Interscience Publishers, 1961.

Moore, James R. *The Post-Darwinian Controversies: A Study of the Protestant Struggle to Come to Terms with Darwin in Great Britain and America, 1870–1900.* Cambridge: Cambridge University Press, 1979.

Moore, R. Laurence. *In Search of White Crows: Spiritualism, Parapsychology, and American Culture.* New York: Oxford University Press, 1977.

———. "Spiritualism and Science: Reflections on the First Decade of the Spirit Rappings." *American Quarterly* 24 (October 1972): 474–500.

Nelson, William O. "Anti-Mormon Publications." In *Encyclopedia of Mormonism*, edited by David H. Ludlow, 1:45–52. New York: Macmillan, 1992.

Nersessian, Nancy J. "Aether/Or: The Creation of Scientific Concepts." *Studies in the History and Philosophy of Science* 15, no. 3 (1984): 175–212.

Nisbet, Robert. *History of the Idea of Progress.* New York: Basic Books, 1980.

Nolan, Max. "Materialism and the Mormon Faith." *Dialogue: A Journal of Mormon Thought* 22 (Winter 1989): 62–75.

Noyes, John Humphrey. *History of American Socialisms.* 1870. Reprint, New York: Dover Publications, 1966.

Numbers, Ronald L. *Creation by Natural Law: Laplace's Nebular Hypothesis in American Thought.* Seattle: University of Washington Press, 1977.

———. "The Fall and Rise of the American Medical Profession." In *Sickness and Health in America: Readings in the History of Medicine and Public Health*, 2d ed., edited by Judith Walzer Leavitt and Ronald L. Numbers, 185–96. Madison: University of Wisconsin Press, 1985.

O'Sullivan, Michael Anthony. "A Harmony of Worlds: Spiritualism and the Quest for Community in Nineteenth-Century America." Ph.D. diss., University of Southern California, 1981.

Paul, Erich Robert. *Science, Religion, and Mormon Cosmology.* Chicago: University of Illinois Press, 1992.

Pratt, Milando. "Life and Labor of Orson Pratt." *Contributor* 12 (January 1891): 1–12.

Quinn, D. Michael. *Early Mormonism and the Magic World View.* Salt Lake City: Signature Books, 1987.

Rasmussen, Dennis. "Metaphysics." In *Encyclopedia of Mormonism*, edited by David H. Ludlow, 2:894–95. New York: Macmillan, 1992.

Riley, I. Woodbridge. *The Founder of Mormonism: A Psychological Study of Joseph Smith, Jr.* London: W. Heinemann, 1903.

Robbins, Peggy. "The Lincolns and Spiritualism." *Civil War Times Illustrated* 15, no. 5 (1976): 4–47.

Rothstein, William G. *American Physicians in the Nineteenth Century: From Sects to Science.* Baltimore: Johns Hopkins University Press, 1972.

Sagendorph, Robb. *America and Her Almanacs: Wit, Wisdom, and Weather, 1639–1970.* Boston: Little, Brown, 1970.

Scott, Donald M. "The Popular Lecture and the Creation of a Public in Mid-Nineteenth-Century America." *Journal of American History* 66 (March 1980): 791–809.

Shipps, Jan. *Mormonism: The Story of a New Religious Tradition.* Urbana: University of Illinois Press, 1985.

Shoemaker, Philip. "Seers and Seances: The Course of Spiritualism in Nineteenth-Century Wisconsin." *Journal of Religious Studies* 7 (Fall 1979): 39–57.

Skabelund, Donald. "Cosmology on the American Frontier: Orson Pratt's Key to the Universe." *Centaurus: International Magazine of the History of Mathematics, Science, and Technology* 11, no. 3 (1965): 190–204.

Smith, Edgar Fahs. *Chemistry in America: Chapters from the History of the Science in the United States.* New York: D. Appleton, 1914; reprint, New York: Arno, 1972.

———. *The Life of Robert Hare: An American Chemist, 1781–1858.* Philadelphia: J. B. Lippincott, 1917.

Sollors, Werner. "Dr. Benjamin Franklin's Celestial Telegraph, or Indian Blessings to Gaslit American Drawing Rooms." *American Quarterly* 35 (Winter 1983): 459–80.

Stenhouse, T. B. H. *Rocky Mountain Saints.* New York: D. Appleton, 1873.

Swanson, Vern G. "The Development of the Concept of a Holy Ghost in Mormon Theology." In *Line upon Line: Essays on Mormon Doctrine,* edited by Gary James Bergera, 89–101. Salt Lake City: Signature Books, 1989.

Szasz, Ferenc M. "'New Thought' and the American West." *Journal of the West* 23 (January 1984): 83–90.

Tanner, Jerald, and Sandra Tanner. *Changes in the Key to Theology.* Salt Lake City: Utah Lighthouse Ministry, 1965.

Toulmin, Stephen, and June Goodfield. *The Architecture of Matter.* New York: Harper and Row, 1962.

Tyler, Alice Felt. *Freedom's Ferment: Phases of American Social History from the Colonial Period to the Outbreak of the Civil War.* 1944. Reprint, New York: Harper and Row, 1962.

Tyler, Moses Coit. *A History of American Literature, 1607–1765.* Ithaca, N.Y.: Cornell University Press, 1949.

Whittaker, David J. "Orson Pratt: Prolific Pamphleteer." *Dialogue: A Journal of Mormon Thought* 15 (Fall 1982): 27–41.

Whittaker, Edmund. *A History of the Theories of Aether and Electricity.* 2 vols. London: Thomas Nelson and Sons, 1951; reprint, New York: Dover Publications, 1989.

Wrobel, Arthur, ed. *Pseudo-Science and Society in Nineteenth-Century America.* Lexington: University Press of Kentucky, 1987.

Zochert, Donald. "Science and the Common Man in Antebellum America." In *Science in America since 1820,* edited by Nathan Reingold, 7–32. New York: Science History Publications, 1976.

Index

Abercrombie, John, 157n.82
Absurdities of Immaterialism (O. Pratt), 41–47
Action at a distance, 48–49, 55–56, 109–10, 122, 140, 149
Adams, Samuel, 80
Aether. *See* Ether
Agassiz, Louis, 12
Age of Reason, 112
Albanese, Catherine L., 7, 78, 116, 122, 145
Albany, N.Y., 74
Alcott, Bronson, 145
Allen, C. Leonard, 8
Allen, Ethan, 61, 112, 145
American Academy of Arts and Sciences, 71
American Association for the Advancement of Science, 31, 74
American Journal of Science and Arts, 66
American Philosophical Society, 66, 70–71
Ampère, Andre-Marie, 106
Analyst (Des Moines, Iowa), 25
Andrus, Hyrum, 63
Animal magnetism, 57, 118, 139
Annales de chimie (Paris), 70
Anticlericalism, 6
Antisupernaturalism, 6
Apostles, Quorum of the Twelve (Mormon), 20, 23, 54, 59
Articles of Faith. *See* Mormon theology

Bacon, Francis, 9, 10, 12, 27, 81
Baconianism, 16, 26–28, 57, 63, 68, 69, 83–84, 91–92, 98, 107, 111, 118, 126, 128–30, 141, 148, 152n.18, 171n.110, 171n.120; defined, 7–10; and popular science, 13–14

Ballou, Adin, 92
Bancroft, George, 81
Banner of Light, 82
Bednarowski, Mary Farrell, 78
Belfast, Maine, 113, 116, 118, 146
Bennett, James Gordon, 59
Bergera, Gary, 63
Berzelius, Jöns Jacob, 72
Bohr, Neils, 160n.106
Book of Mormon, 18, 19, 40, 59–60, 155n.41
Book of Moses (Mormon), 51
Boscovich, Roger, 72
Bozeman, Theodore Dwight, 2–3, 8, 10, 12
Braden, Charles S., 8, 121, 123, 145
Branch, E. Douglas, 168n.48
Braude, Ann, 172n.127
Breckinridge, Robert, 102
Brittan, Samuel B., 73, 76, 82, 111
Britten, Emma Hardinge, 80
Brodie, Fawn M., 60
Brooke, John L., 158n.97
Brown, Thomas, 27, 157n.82
Bruce, Robert V., 65
Bryant, William Cullen, 81
Buchanan, Charles, 117
Burkmar, Lucius, 118–19
Burned-over district, 20, 61
Burr, Charles Chauncy, 79
Burr, Herman, 79
Butler, Jon, 2, 69
Butler, Joseph, 157n.82

Calvinism, 96, 105, 127, 133
Campbell, Alexander, 59, 61
Cannon, George Q., 52

Cantor, G. N., 140
Capron, E. W., 77, 81, 167n.45
Carroll, Bret E., 78
Celestial mechanics, 33, 35, 36
Certainty: quest for, 39, 102
Channeling, 2
Channing, William Ellery, 11, 81
Charnock, Stephen, 157n.82
Chemical Society of Philadelphia, 65, 70
Christensen, William J., 35
Christian Phrenologist (Fowler), 147
Christian Science, 3, 114, 124, 125, 130,
    152n.10
Clairvoyance, 118–19, 122, 139
Clarke, Edward, 165n.19
Collyer, Robert, 138, 173n.9
Common-sense philosophy, 9, 26, 41
Cooper, James Fenimore, 81
Correspondence, law of spiritual. *See* Law
    of spiritual correspondence
Coxe, John Redman, 71
Crawley, Peter, 23, 41
Creation ex nihilo, 50, 97
Creationism, 2
Cross, Whitney R., 20, 168n.48

Daguerreotype, 117, 122, 127
Dana, James Dwight, 12
Daniels, George H., 8–10, 27, 71, 72, 171n.120
Darnton, Robert, 118
Darwin, Erasmus, 32, 43–44
Davenport, Ira, 80
Davenport, William, 80
Davis, Andrew Jackson, 78, 82, 94, 98–99,
    111, 167n.46
Deism, 6, 60–62, 97, 101, 102, 134, 145–46,
    169n.79
Democracy, 116; influences of, on American
    culture, 7, 13–14, 102, 111
Demonstration That All Matter Is Heavy
    (Whewell), 106
De Pillis, Mario S., 60
Descartes, Rene, 140, 143
Design argument, 58
Dewey, Dellon, 77
Dictionary of American Biography, 71
*Dissertation on the Discovery of Animal
    Magnetism* (Mesmer), 138
Divine Authority (O. Pratt), 28, 39
Divine Science, 3, 114
Doctrine and Covenants, 36, 52

Dods, John Bovee, 117, 138
Draper, John W., 1–2
Dresser, Annetta, 114, 144–45
Dresser, Horatio, 114, 116, 123, 125, 128, 144–
    45, 175n.70
Dresser, Julius, 114, 144–45
Dualism, 45–46, 49, 109, 122, 149
Dwight, Timothy, 158n.84

Eddy, Mary Baker, 114, 125, 136, 145, 152n.10,
    152n.18
Edinburgh, Scotland, 26–27
Edmonds, John Worth, 81, 82, 111
Edwards, Paul, 158–59n.97
Einstein, Albert, 35, 49
Emerson, Ralph Waldo, 98, 124, 145
Empiricism, 10
England, Breck, 15, 21, 26, 46
Enlightenment: Scottish, 26. *See also* Vil-
    lage Enlightenment
Ether: and Hare's theory of matter, 106–10,
    149; and nineteenth-century science, 33,
    55; and O. Pratt's *Key to the Universe,* 33–
    36, 49; and O. Pratt's theology, 49, 55,
    58–59, 63; and Quimby's cosmology,
    138–42, 144
Evans, Warren Felt, 114
Everett, Edward, 9
*Experimental Investigation of the Spirit
    Manifestations* (Hare), 68, 73, 92, 108

Faraday, Michael, 48, 72, 85, 106
Fay, Charles-François du, 106
Field theory, 48–49
Fillmore, Charles, 152n.10
Fizeau, Hippolyte, 35
Flake, Chad J., 23
Fluid, mesmeric or magnetic. *See* Ether
Founder of Mormonism, The (Riley), 60
Fourier, Charles, 78
Fowler, Orson S., 147–48
Fox, Kate, 76–77, 81, 86, 167n.44
Fox, Margaret, 76–77, 81, 86, 167n.44
Franklin, Benjamin, 6, 69, 80–81, 105–6, 145,
    168n.53
Fuller, Robert C., 118, 145

Godhead: Mormon views of, 51–55, 63
God of the gaps, 51, 140
Good, John Mason, 157n.82
Goodfield, June, 174n.53

Gordon, Henry, 80
Gottschalk, Stephen, 152n.18
Gravitation, 32, 33, 35–36, 57, 140, 141
Grayson, Eldred (pen name of Robert Hare), 73
Great First Cause (O. Pratt), 47–49, 55, 57–58
Greeley, Horace, 77, 81
Grimes, James Stanley, 79

Hancock, John, 80
Hansen, Klaus J., 60
Hare, Harriett Clark, 76
Hare, Robert: and action at a distance, 109–10; on "great first cause," 108; on matter, mind, and spirit, 68, 105, 141, 144; on matter and "will," 108–9; on the nature of matter, 105–10; as novelist, 73; as professor of chemistry, 69–73; on science and religion, 68; and scientific worship, 101; on the soul, 108; and spiritualism, 73–76, 82, 83–92; as village Enlightenment figure, 4, 5, 7, 8, 148–49
Hare, Robert, Sr., 69–70, 93, 99, 100
Hare's American Porter, 70
Harmonial philosophy, 78, 82
Harvard College, 71
Hascall, A. P., 167n.45
Hatch, Nathan O., 6, 149
Heaven, 98–99
Henry, Joseph, 12, 74, 76
Herald of Progress, 82
Hermetic, 30, 60, 156n.46
Herschel, John, 27, 31
Hill, Marvin S., 60
History of the Strange Sounds or Rappings (Dewey), 77
Hodge, Charles, 3, 155n.40
Hodge, M. J. S., 140
Hoek, Martin, 35
Holbrook, Josiah, 11
Holcombe, Amasa, 85, 169n.67
Holmes, Stewart W., 121, 122, 124, 129, 145
Holy Ghost. *See* Holy Spirit
Holy Spirit (Holy Ghost): Joseph Smith on, 52, 53; in Mormon thought, 51–53; O. Pratt on, 54–59, 63, 160n.120. *See also* God the the gaps
Holy Spirit (O. Pratt), 47
Home, D. D., 80
Home Journal, 80

Hovenkamp, Herbert, 2–3
Howe, Eber D., 59
Hydesville, N.Y., 76, 78
Hylozoism, 158–59n.97

Inductive method. *See* Baconiansim
Interesting Account of Several Remarkable Visions (O. Pratt), 26, 28
Isaacs, Ernest, 78–79, 168n.48

Jaffee, David, 5, 62
James, David, 157n.82
Jefferson, Thomas, 6, 145
Jesus, 82, 96, 123, 125, 169n.79

Kant, Immanuel, 3
Kepler, Johannes, 4, 29, 32
Key to the Science of Theology (P. Pratt), 161n.133
Key to the Universe (O. Pratt), 33–37, 49
Kingdom of God (O. Pratt), 41, 43
Kirkwood, Daniel, 30–32
Kirkwood's Analogy, 31
Koch, G. Adolf, 146

Lang, Bernhard, 99
Lanning, J. F., 93
Laplace, Pierre Simon de, 31–33
Lardner, Dionysius, 158n.82
Launching of Modern American Science (Bruce), 65
Law of planetary rotation (O. Pratt), 29–32, 36, 37
Law of spiritual correspondence, 98–100, 135
Lebanon, N.H., 116
"Lectures on Faith," 52
Lehi (the prophet), 18
Leverrier, Urbain, 31
Lincoln, Abraham, 81, 111
Lincoln, Mary Todd, 81
Lind, Jenny, 81
Lindberg, David C., 1–2

Magic: folk, 30, 155n.45
Magic world view, 30, 60, 158n.97
Marsden, George M., 2
Marx, Karl, 95
Materialism, 69, 111–12, 149; in Mormon thought, 16, 25, 31–32, 36, 40–46, 158n.94, 159n.98

Mathematics Monthly (Cambridge, Mass.), 25
Matter: ponderable and imponderable, 72, 106–8, 171n.120
Maxwell, James Clerke, 48
May, Henry F., 6
McCabe, Joseph, 73
McConkie, Bruce R., 63
McDannell, Colleen, 99
McMurrin, Sterling, 159n.98
Medicine: state of, 120
Mediums: spiritualist, 77, 86–89, 143
Mental healing, 114, 116, 118, 119, 129
Mesmer, Franz Anton, 118, 138
Mesmerism, 2, 8, 9, 12, 56–57, 78–79, 118–19, 122, 129, 138–39, 161n.133
Metaphysical movement. *See* Mind-cure movement
Millennial Star, 22
Mind-body problem. *See* Dualism
Mind-body relationship, 114
Mind-cure movement, 114, 121, 124, 127
Moore, James R., 1
Moore, R. Laurence, 78–79
Mormon Doctrine (McConkie), 63
Mormonism: origins of, 59–62. *See also* Mormon theology
Mormonism and the American Experience (Hansen), 60
Mormonism Unvailed (Howe), 60
Mormon theology, 12, 21, 22, 124
Moroni, 18, 155n.41

Naturalism, 31–32
Natural law, 6, 28, 36, 97–98, 105, 111, 144
Nature, 148–49
Nebular hypothesis, 31–33
New Age, 2
New and Easy Method of Solution of the Cubic and Biquadratic Equations (O. Pratt), 37
New England Spiritualist Association, 80
New Thought, 8, 114, 116, 124, 128
Newton, Isaac, 4, 10, 27, 81, 101, 104, 117, 140; on gravitation, 32, 36, 55, 57; and Joseph Smith, 47; on the nature of matter, 44–45, 72, 137; O. Pratt's adjustments to, 47–49
New York: upstate, 18, 20
New York City, 76, 77, 80
New York Weekly Tribune, 77

Nisbet, Robert, 131
Nolan, Max, 159n.98
No Man Knows My History (Brodie), 60
North American Review, 80
Numbers, Ronald L., 1–2

Occult, 30, 60, 78, 156n.46
Odor, 141–42
Oersted, Hans, 48
Of Matter, Mind, and Spirit (Hare), 108
Opinions: negative aspect of, 7, 10, 40, 61, 83, 102, 111, 126, 132
Opticks (Newton), 47, 137
Orson Pratt's Works (O. Pratt), 23
Our Inheritance in the Great Pyramid (Smyth), 37
Overing (Hare), 73
Oxyhydrogen blowpipe, 70–72

Paine, Thomas, 61, 81, 112, 145
Paley, William, 58
Palmer, Elihu, 62, 101–2, 112, 145, 170n.107
Panpsychism, 158–59n.97
Parker, Theodore, 81
Partridge, Charles, 73, 76, 77, 80
Paul, Erich Robert, 48
Penrose, Charles W., 63, 162n.133
Philadelphia, 65–66, 69–71, 80
Philosophical Magazine (London), 70
Philosophy. *See* Common-sense philosophy; Harmonial philosophy
Phrenology, 2, 9, 12, 129, 147–48
Physical Theory of Another Life (Taylor), 98
Plural marriage, 23
Popular religion, 6–7, 147–49
Portland, Maine, 119
Poyen, Charles, 118, 138, 173n.9
Pratt, Charity, 19
Pratt, Jared, 19
Pratt, Orson, 15–64, 68–69, 91, 93, 97–98, 110, 141, 144; amateur scientific work of, 25–39; and astronomy, 21; conversion of, 18–19; early life and education of, 19–20; in Edinburgh, Scotland, 20; on essence of substances, 45–46; influence of, on Mormon thought, 16, 22–23; on miracles, 162n.141; as Mormon apostle, 20–25; on the nature of matter, 33, 49–51; as professor of mathematics, 21; on science and religion, 38–39, 40, 63–64; on self-moving particles, 47–51, 57–59; on

solidity, 45–46, 55; as village Enlightenment figure, 4, 5, 7, 8, 14, 16, 23, 59, 62, 64, 148–49

Pratt, Parley P., 19, 20, 22, 28, 41–42, 54, 57, 142, 159n.97, 160n.117, 161n.133

Pratt, Sarah, 25

Priestley, Joseph, 32, 43–44, 66, 107

Principles of Nature, The (Davis), 78

Progress: concept of, 6, 12, 23, 95–98, 124; Quimby on, 131–33, 145

Prophetic Almanac (O. Pratt), 21–22

Psychosomatic medicine, 128

Pyramids, 37–38

Quimby, George, 116, 119

Quimby, Phineas Parkhurst, 68–69, 91, 93, 97–98, 110; account of his life, 116–19; Charles S. Braden on, 8; as clockmaker, 116–17; on concept of science, 116, 124–31, 144; on concept of wisdom, 116, 129, 133–38; on First Cause, 134, 143, 145; healing of, 113–14, 118–19; as imprecise communicator, 125, 130; and Joseph Smith, 131; as lyceum performer, 12, 119; on mainstream medicine, 120–21; on materialism, 114–16, 144–45; mental healing theory and method of, 120–22; on mind and matter, 121–22, 135; on natural man, 132–34, 143; on progress, 131–33, 145; and scientific language, 8; as "Scientist of Transcendentalism," 124, 129; on solidity, 136–39; as village Enlightenment figure, 4, 5, 7, 116, 146, 148–49

Quinn, D. Michael, 30

Quorum of the Twelve Apostles. *See* Apostles, Quorum of the Twelve (Mormon)

Rapping, 76–77, 80, 85–86

Redfield, William C., 72, 165n.23

Reformed Egyptian, 155n.41

Reid, Thomas, 9

Relativity: special theory of, 35

Religion, popular. *See* Popular religion

Religious Science, 114, 128

Restoration: Mormon, 37, 59

Rigdon, Sidney, 28, 41, 59

Roberts, B. H., 52, 63

Robison, James, 158n.82

Rochester, N.Y., 77

Rutherford, Ernest, 160n.106

Science: authoritativeness of, in antebellum culture, 3–4, 7, 102, 124, 129, 147; popularity of, in antebellum culture, 11–14; professionalization of, 11, 14

Science and religion, 2–3, 22, 40, 147–49; and warfare thesis, 1–2, 5, 8, 22, 129, 147, 151n.4, 152n.11

Science of Health and Happiness (Quimby), 114, 126, 133

Science of Mind, 114, 128

Science of the Soul, 3

Scientology, 2

Scottish philosophy. *See* Common-sense philosophy

Séances, 77–78, 81, 89, 92, 100, 101, 110, 143

Seer, 23, 24, 47

Seer stones, 18, 30

Senses: priority of, 10, 12, 56–57, 80, 84, 102–3, 107, 126, 141, 149

Shakers, 78

Shakespeare, William, 81

Shipps, Jan, 60

Silliman, Benjamin, 11, 65–68, 71, 165n.19

Singular Revelations (Capron), 77

Skabelund, Donald, 25, 29, 33, 35

Smith, Edgar Fahs, 69, 70, 74, 165n.19, 165n.23

Smith, Joseph, Jr., 16, 18–21, 28, 36–40, 47, 51, 59–63, 155n.41, 159n.97; first vision of, 21, 30

Smith, Joseph Fielding, 52–53, 63

Smithsonian Institution, 65, 76

Smyth, Charles Piazzi, 37–38

Snow, Erastus, 15

Spaulding, Solomon, 60

Spirit circles. *See* Séances

Spirit Messenger, 82

Spiritoscope, 86–90, 100

Spirit spheres: and celestial marriage, 99, 170n.94; and economics, 95; and God and religion, 96–97; and government and law, 94–95; and hell and Hades, 96; and language, 99; and law of affinity, 100; and law of progression, 95–97, 111; life in, 94–100; material nature of, 101, 103; origin of, 94; senses in, 103–4; and supernatural heavens, 96; and unity of physical and moral law, 104–5

Spiritualism, 56–57, 68, 116, 124, 143–44; decline of, 110–11; doctrines of, 92; history of, in America, 76–82; and investigation,

78–79, 86–90; and law of harmony, 111; and materialism, 72; periodicals on, 82, 92; philosophical, 78; and reform movements, 82, 111; and science, 82; and women, 82
Spiritual matter: Hare on, 101; O. Pratt on, 43–45, 50–51; Quimby on, 122, 141–45
Spiritual Philosopher, 82
Spiritual Telegraph, 74, 76, 82
Spirit World, 80, 82
Standish the Puritan (Hare), 73
Stenhouse, T. B. H., 16
Stewart, Dugald, 9, 27
Stowe, Harriet Beecher, 81
Strong, George Templeton, 80
Struve, F. G. W., 31
Sunderland, LeRoy, 117
Swedenborg, Emanuel, 78, 81, 94, 98–99, 135, 170n.94

Table turning (tipping), 80, 84–88
Tallmadge, Nathaniel P., 81, 82, 168n.51
Talmadge, James E., 52
Taylder, T. W. P., 41–44
Taylor, Isaac, 98–99
Theocracy, Mormon, 21, 41
Thompson, J. J., 160n.106
Thoreau, Henry David, 145
Tilloch, Alexander, 70
Tipping. *See* Table turning
Tocqueville, Alexis de, 114, 170n.104
Toulmin, Stephen, 174n.53
Townshend, Chauncey, 138
Tracts by Orson Pratt, 23
Trance communication, 80
Transcendentalists, 8, 98, 145
Transcendental Meditation, 2
Treatise on the Regeneration and Eternal Duration of Matter (P. Pratt), 41
Tullidge, Edward, 16, 22, 40

Unification Church, 2
Unitarians, 8
Unity, 114
Univercoelum, 82
University of Buffalo Medical School, 79
University of Pennsylvania, 65–66, 69–71
Urim and Thummim. *See* Seer stones

Village Enlightenment, 16, 39, 69, 93, 95, 98, 99, 103, 112, 148–49; definition of, 5–6; and the elite Enlightenment, 6–7, 16, 102; place of reason in, 101–2, 144–45

Warfare thesis, 1–2, 5, 8, 22, 129, 147, 151n.4, 152n.11
Washington, D.C., 23, 74, 76
Washington, George, 81
Whewell, William, 72, 106
White, Andrew Dickson, 1–2
Whittaker, David J., 16, 20, 23
Whittaker, Edmund, 33
Widtsoe, John A., 52
Willing, Margaret, 69
Willis, Nathaniel Parker, 80
Woodhouse, James, 65–66, 70–71
Woodruff, Wilford, 16

Yale College, 65–66, 71
Young, Brigham, 15, 28, 51, 142, 158n.95, 159n.97, 160n.110, 161n.131; doctrinal conflict with O. Pratt, 23, 54–55, 63
Young, John, 68
Young, Thomas, 48

Zochert, Donald, 11, 12

CRAIG JAMES HAZEN is an associate professor of comparative religion at Biola University in La Mirada, California. He received his Ph.D. in religious studies from the University of California, Santa Barbara. His work on the interaction of religion and science has earned awards from the Pacific divisions of the American Academy of Religion and of the American Association for the Advancement of Science. He is the editor of the journal *Philosophia Christi* and lives in southern California with his wife, Karen, and four children.

Typeset in 10.5/13 Minion
with Rotis display
Designed by Paula Newcomb
Composed by Jim Proefrock
at the University of Illinois Press
Manufactured by Cushing-Malloy, Inc.

University of Illinois Press
1325 South Oak Street
Champaign, IL 61820-6903
www.press.uillinois.edu